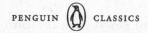

PENGUIN CLASSICS

JOHANN WOLFGANG VON GOETHE:
SELECTED POETRY

'Goethe is the most sensual, as well as the most sublime, of German poets. Faithful and felicitous, these verse translations by David Luke are an excellent introduction to his genius' Daniel Johnson, *Daily Telegraph*

'The quality and persistent originality of his scope as a poet is unrivalled ... Luke's rhythm's carry one along' Linda Holt, *The Times*

'Exquisite' *Literary Review*

'Goethe is the most human of poets, passionate, kindly, urbane ... *Selected Poetry* from David Luke sets a crown upon the lifetime's effort of our most committed Goethe translator' D. M. Black, *The Times Literary Supplement*

'[A] truly universal and unendingly fascinating writer ... Luke gives us much to delight and much to ponder' Francis Lamport, *Oxford Magazine*

'Superb ... Luke is wonderfully attentive to Goethe's rhythms' Martin Swales, *The Times Higher Education Supplement*

T0368865

JOHANN WOLFGANG VON GOETHE was born in Frankfurt-am-Main in 1749. He studied at Leipzig, where he showed an interest in the occult, and in Strasbourg, where Herder introduced him to Shakespeare's works and to folk poetry. He produced some essays and lyrical verse, and at twenty-four wrote *Götz von Berlichingen*, a play which brought him national fame and established him in the current *Sturm und Drang* movement. *Werther*, a tragic romance, was an even greater success.

Goethe began work on *Faust*, and *Egmont*, another tragedy, before being invited to join the government of Weimar. His interest in the classical world led him to leave suddenly for Italy in 1786, and the *Italian Journey* recounts his travels there. *Iphigenie auf Tauris* and *Torquato Tasso*, classical dramas, were begun at this time.

Returning to Weimar, Goethe started the second part of *Faust*, encouraged by Schiller. During this late period he finished the series of *Wilhelm Meister* books and wrote many other works, including *The Oriental Divan* and *Elective Affinities*. He also directed the State Theatre and worked on numerous scientific theories in evolutionary botany, anatomy and colour.

Goethe was married in 1806. He finished *Faust* before he died in 1832.

DAVID LUKE is an Emeritus Fellow of Christ Church, Oxford. Among the German authors he has written about and translated are Goethe, Kleist, the brothers Grimm and Thomas Mann.

JOHANN WOLFGANG VON GOETHE

Selected Poetry

Translated with an Introduction and notes by
DAVID LUKE

PENGUIN BOOKS

PENGUIN BOOKS

Published by the Penguin Group
Penguin Books Ltd, 80 Strand, London WC2R ORL, England
Penguin Group (USA) Inc., 375 Hudson Street, New York, New York 10014, USA
Penguin Group (Canada), 10 Alcorn Avenue, Toronto, Ontario, Canada M4V 3B2
(a division of Pearson Penguin Canada Inc.)
Penguin Ireland, 25 St Stephen's Green, Dublin 2, Ireland
(a division of Penguin Books Ltd)
Penguin Group (Australia), 250 Camberwell Road, Camberwell, Victoria 3124, Australia
(a division of Pearson Australia Group Pty Ltd)
Penguin Books India Pvt Ltd, 11 Community Centre, Panchsheel Park, New Delhi – 110 017, India
Penguin Group (NZ), cnr Airborne and Rosedale Roads, Albany,
Auckland 1310, New Zealand (a division of Pearson New Zealand Ltd)
Penguin Books (South Africa) (Pty) Ltd, 24 Sturdee Avenue, Rosebank 2196, South Africa

Penguin Books Ltd, Registered Offices: 80 Strand, London WC2R ORL, England

www.penguin.com

First published by Libris 1999
Reprinted in Penguin Classics 2005

033

Translation, introduction and notes copyright © David Luke, 1999
All rights reserved

The moral right of the editor has been asserted

Printed and bound in Great Britain by Clays Ltd, Elcograf S.p.A.

ISBN-13: 978–0–14–042456–0

www.greenpenguin.co.uk

Contents

* Square brackets indicate editorial titles not used by Goethe.

III. The later Goethe (1810–1832)

From the West-Eastern Divan, *1814–1818*

Bibliographical note and acknowledgements

The present anthology is in some ways similar to my earlier bilingual
Goethe edition (*Selected Verse*, Penguin, 1964), which though containing
more material offered only prose translations. The German texts are again,
for the most part, those of the 'Gedenkausgabe' (general editor Ernst
Beutler), which began publication in 1949 to mark the bicentenary of
Goethe's birth (*Gedenkausgabe der Werke, Briefe und Gespräche*, Artemis
Verlag, Zürich and Stuttgart). This 'memorial edition' is a modern,
accurate and complete *Leseausgabe* for the general reader, with scholarly
introductory essays by Emil Staiger but unencumbered by annotations.
The poems (ed. Emil Staiger, 1950–53) are in vols i and ii of this edition, the
Divan and *Hermann und Dorothea* in vol. iii, *Faust* in vol. v and *Iphigenie* in
vol. vi. In the present anthology, the German texts of the *Römische Elegien*,
the *Venezianische Epigramme* and *Das Tagebuch* are taken from the bi-
lingual edition of Goethe's erotic poems by myself and Hans Rudolf Vaget
(*Erotic Poems*, Oxford University Press World's Classics, 1997). The trans-
lations from *Faust* are extracted from my World's Classics editions of Part
One (1987) and Part Two (1994) also published by Oxford University
Press, to whom acknowledgment is made. The commentary material
(Introduction and Notes) in these editions is occasionally referred to, using
the abbreviations *Erotic Poems*, *Faust*OUP1 and *Faust*OUP2. My translat-
ions of *Iphigenie* and *Hermann und Dorothea* were published in vol. viii
of the Suhrkamp edition of *Goethe's Collected Works*, ed. C. Hamlin and
F. Ryder (New York, 1987, reprinted later in paperback by Princeton
University Press);* that of the poem on Schiller's skull (no. 89) was first
published in *German Life and Letters*, vol. xv (1961/2). For purposes of the
Introduction and Notes I have again mainly relied on Staiger's succinctly
annotated edition of the poems (*Gedichte*, 3 vols, Manesse Verlag, Zürich,
1949) and Max Rychner's similar edition of the *Divan* (Manesse Verlag,
1952). A few other German sources have been consulted, including Stai-
ger's main study of Goethe's life and work (*Goethe*, 3 vols, Atlantis Verlag,
Freiburg and Zürich, 1952–59). Passages from Goethe's conversations

* Line numbers of extracts from these longer works are given in the contents pages
above.

with Eckermann and others, and from his letters and autobiography, are quoted in translations of my own. *Faust* OUP 1, *Faust* OUP 2 and *Erotic Poems* contain fuller bibliographies of editions and translations of Goethe's works and of biographical or critical material in English. Recent additions to the latter are Nicholas Boyle's fascinatingly detailed critical biography (*Goethe: the Poet and the Age*, i: *The Poetry of Desire (1749–1790)*, Clarendon Press, 1991) and John R. Williams's illuminating study *The Life of Goethe: A Critical Biography* (Blackwell, 1998). I particularly wish to emphasize my indebtedness to Boyle, whose second volume is soon to be published; though regrettably only the first (which covers the first half of Goethe's life) was available to me during the preparation of the present edition. This first volume is here referred to simply as 'Boyle'.

Introduction

Although Goethe, at the age of twenty-five, became internationally famous as the author of a novel, and although his dramatic works, or one of them at least, also achieved European greatness, it is scarcely disputed, either in or outside Germany, that he was above all else a poet; that it was above all, and perhaps only, in the genre of poetry (lyric, narrative, dramatic, epigrammatic) that he was truly at his best, most truly a virtuoso and a master. His achievement in other fields, both literary and non-literary, was varied and impressive by any standards. But it remains to be asked what Goethe's international status would now be if by some impossible mischance he had written none of his poetry. He would not even be above all the author of *Faust*, since much of his greatest poetry is contained in *Faust*. The famed universality of his genius would be a 'universality' with something indispensable missing. As Nicholas Boyle remarks, he had a natural affinity with the rhythms of the German language (Boyle, p. viii), and his poetry is of the essence of German. Unfortunately for translators, and for readers of Goethe unfamiliar with German, the converse is also true: the poetry of the German language is of the essence of Goethe. There is not much to be done about this situation. The present anthology is a personal response to it: an attempt to imitate or mediate in English verse something like a hundred favourite poems or (since some extracts from longer works are included) a hundred favourite pieces of Goethe's poetry, simply considered as poetry. The choice of material attempts to be representative within the limits of personal predilection (thus, I have omitted a few poems which in the traditional Goethe canon are no doubt rightly considered important, but which I no doubt wrongly find portentous).

There are different poets within Goethe, and they can be variously differentiated. Of the three traditional, broad divisions – the young Goethe, the classical Goethe and the late Goethe – each has taken its fashionable turn in posterity's reception of the six decades of his work and development. They will do well enough if equally emphasized and suitably subdivided. If we call the first 'the younger Goethe', it conveniently splits at the year 1775, the important turning-point in his life when he left his

native Frankfurt and accepted the patronage of the Duke of Weimar, abandoning his 'Storm and Stress' role and transforming himself into the ascetic, courtly devotee of Charlotte von Stein. The maturer, central, 'classical' Goethe begins in 1786, when he suddenly abandoned Frau von Stein and was transmuted into the initiate of Priapus and the Roman Faustina. This could be described as the first, erotic phase of his great classical period, the time of the *Roman Elegies*. From about 1795, its second and principal phase (to which he seems to be referring when he speaks to Boisserée on 3 August 1815 of 'my best period', 'die beste Zeit'), is dominated by his intellectual and creative comradeship-in-arms with Friedrich Schiller (1759–1805), when together they became the authoritative co-regents of German literary culture, establishing, or seeking to establish, its laws once and for all; this is also the time of the completion of *Faust* Part One. The death of Schiller in 1805, an event much more traumatic for Goethe than the Napoleonic wars or the abolition of the Holy Roman Empire of the German Nation in 1806, is followed by a transitional period, awkward to classify, during which the noble Olympian mask is cast off, until eventually Goethe the lyric poet, the real or essential Goethe, gets a new lease of life as the post-classical, 'west-eastern' Hāfiz-Hatem. I have included a selection from the *West-Eastern Divan* to illustrate this: officially it is a separate work, often not represented in collections of the poems, but in fact no anthology of Goethe's poetry is complete unless it contains some examples from the *Divan* as well. They nearly all belong to 1814 and 1815, after which the orientalizing phase was also over – dropped, as he says to Eckermann, 'like a cast snakeskin' (14 January 1827). But it leads naturally into the impressive and mysterious poems of the last ten to fifteen years of his life, the true 'late Goethe', culminating in the extraordinary music of the second Part of *Faust*. I have of course also included extracts from *Faust*, but in an anthology intended to illustrate Goethe's development it makes no sense to place them all together, as if *Faust* (written intermittently over sixty years) were a unified work, when in fact its conception kept changing as Goethe himself did. The biographical facts again invite a three-part arrangement: a separate sample, first, of the unfinished and unpublished 'Urfaust' which was the masterpiece of his youth, then (in its proper chronological position) a separate representation of the material added by the 'classical' Goethe by way of completing 'Part One', and finally a selection from the posthumously published Part Two. This is old-fashioned

'Biographismus', for which I make no theoretical apology. The closeness of Goethe's work to his life was remarked on by Goethe himself and has been discussed ever since, a discussion which has now become so subtle that the mere facts of biography and history, the date and development and variation of a text, even the author himself and his intentions and comments, have largely disappeared into a limbo of alleged critical irrelevance. The work is undeniably more important than the life, but grows out of it, and a minimal introductory sketch of the life cannot here be omitted. Where more detailed biographical or critical points arise, the reader is referred to the Notes which follow the bilingual selection. The latter, I suppose, should ideally (and again setting current fashion aside) be read in the linear sequence in which it appears.

It has usually been pointed out that the young or younger Goethe was born (on 28 August 1749 in the Imperial free city of Frankfurt) into a privileged social position which gave him a degree of freedom unique among German writers of that time. His parents were rich upper bourgeoisie, his father, Caspar Goethe, was enlightened and supportive, his mother loving and sympathetic. A sister, Cornelia, was and remained very close to him; four younger siblings died in childhood. He could afford to be the rebellious young genius, the apostle of nature, developing in his own way, unconstrained by (for instance) the religious views of any employer or patron. The current ferment of religious doubt and theological reinterpretation in late-Enlightenment Germany suited him well. The evangelical pietism of his mother's circle influenced him at first, and perhaps in a subliminal way all his life, but he was also free to strike aggressively anti-Christian attitudes, such as that of Prometheus (in his poem of 1774 – see no. 4 below) whose God is a sleepy old Zeus only fit to be defied by tormented humanity. This powerful ode (which Hugo Wolf's music a century later was to enhance still further) sums up the twenty-five-year-old Goethe's personal version of the 'Storm and Stress (Sturm und Drang)', as the current literary youth-movement was called: a movement which he led, himself largely invented and quickly abandoned. Four years earlier, at Strasbourg where he was officially studying law, he had already found his own lyric voice and discovered his purpose as a writer. He owed this clarification to his encounter at Strasbourg with the critic and cultural historian Johann Gottfried Herder (1744–1803), an eccentric but highly original and influential thinker who became the first of the two most

important literary mentors in Goethe's career. Their friendship was momentous: we may even say that modern German literature was born out of it and began in that year, 1770, as in Philip Larkin's hyperbolic sense sexual intercourse began in 1963. Herder's aim was to promote the creation of a national German literature based on a living national language, and he was on the look-out for young writers of what was then beginning to be called 'genius' who might serve this project. Goethe for his part was in need of an intellectual context, an interpretation of what his instincts were telling him to become. The apt pupil acquired an apt tutor. Herder's theory of literature was predicated on his recently published theory of language as such, as the defining creative activity of the human species, developing in man without any supernatural cause or assistance. The writing of original German poetry was to be something not isolated and merely personal, but the sharing of a great national–cultural enterprise. At the same time Goethe was discovering his own, entirely compatible view of the nature of poetry, that is of his own poetry which he was beginning to write. It would be a kind of symbolic autobiography, born from occasion to occasion in an unending self-interpretative process. As his medium of self-understanding it would be a secular *via salutis*, a replacement for Christianity perhaps. Herder's theory and Goethe's were in harmony with each other: both were secular, monistic, leaving no room for supernatural intervention. The fact that Herder was a cleric (he later occupied a high ecclesiastical post in the Duchy of Weimar after following Goethe there) seemed to make little difference to all this. Man, the creative speech-animal, had invented himself without higher aid. Similarly, God had not marked out *homo sapiens* as a unique, higher species by refraining from giving him an intermaxillary bone, as the theologians had supposed: years later, in one of his excursions into the sciences, Goethe was to be the first, as he thought, to discover that the bone had been there all the time, and that the unity of nature was thereby vindicated.

Under Herder's decisive influence, the young Goethe learnt a reinterpretative approach both to religion and to literature, and explored new literary territories. He greatly extended his knowledge and understanding of Shakespeare, studied translations of old Norse epic poetry, tried to read Homer in Greek, wrote a lyrical essay on Strasbourg's Gothic minster, and even travelled around the Alsatian countryside, where the French influence was less pervasive than in the city, collecting old folksongs and

ballads from ancient peasant women who still remembered them. At the village of Sesenheim, deep in rural Alsace, he also made the acquaintance of Pastor Brion and his family. Of his much-discussed dealings with the younger daughter Friederike it may briefly be said that he wrote poems and irresponsibly charming letters to her, that he visited the family on several further occasions including a month's stay in the early summer of 1771, that Friederike fell in love with him and could reasonably entertain hopes that he might marry her; that in August 1771 he left Strasbourg for good, and from Frankfurt wrote her a letter which effectively broke off the relationship. Friederike fell seriously ill at this time and afterwards never married. Eight years later Goethe, now a famous writer and a member of the Duke of Weimar's Privy Council, briefly revisited Sesenheim where the family received him kindly and forgivingly; this reconciliation makes it unlikely that he had (as legend asserts) seduced Friederike and even fathered a child on her. Nevertheless, little more can be said by way of apologia for his behaviour than that when he received, in October 1771, her heartbroken reply to his parting letter of August, he did at least allow himself to be plunged into remorse. His self-reproach was aggravated by the coincidence of a criminal trial which during that winter was the talk of Frankfurt: that of Susanna Margareta Brandt, a simple uneducated girl who had killed her illegitimate child, was imprisoned almost next door to the Goethe family house and publicly beheaded in January 1772. Shocked by what might have been the consequences to Friederike of his trifling with her feelings and abandoning her, Goethe took refuge in the redemptive process of literary creation, of symbolically autobiographical art. By far the most important of the works traceable in this sense to the not very creditable Sesenheim affair is a fragmentary poetic drama: the long unpublished and unfinished early version of *Faust*, containing as its dominant theme the story of a simple girl not unlike Friederike, who suffers the fate of Susanna Brandt.

This fragmentary *Faust* drama, usually called the 'original *Faust* (Urfaust)', is the central hidden masterpiece of the Storm and Stress, of Goethe the young dramatist and of Goethe the young poet. It was largely written in 1774, in the same year as 'Prometheus' and in the same year as the famous and notorious novel *The Sufferings of Young Werther*. The primary material was the traditional tale, handed down from Marlowe's tragedy (*c.* 1592) and its later popularizations, of a legendary and ill-famed

sixteenth-century figure, 'Doctor Faustus' the theological rebel and magician who sells himself to the Devil for forbidden knowledge and experience. With a stroke of genius Goethe transformed this theme by combining it with the at first sight unrelated story of Margarete (Gretchen) and her fateful love-affair with Faust. There was no precedent in the Faustus legend for this major additional episode, which was one of Goethe's two wholly original developments of the material. The other was his fascinating invention of a second and superior demonic (but not necessarily evil) figure, the Earth Spirit (see no. 6 below), who so far as we can judge from the incomplete text was intended to have ultimate authority over Faust and over Mephistopheles, the cynical tempter-devil who is given immediate charge of him. One of the tantalizing lacunae in *Faust* is that this demonological situation is never clarified, either in the 'Urfaust' or in the later versions. There is a compelling coherence, however, in the sequence of scenes (roughly the second half of the whole drama) that deals with the seduction and ruin of Gretchen.

Goethe's presentation of her story (the 'Gretchen tragedy') most strikingly and poetically reveals the importance to him, in this phase of his career, of the folksong or ballad culture which Herder had taught him to explore with such enthusiasm. The young Goethe's Alsatian field-work was only a part of this search; Herder's brilliant translations of foreign ballads helped him to cast his net wider, and he is on record as reciting to his friends in passionate tones the terrifying Scottish tale of 'Edward' whose sword drips with his father's blood. The interest was not merely folkloristic. Many years later, Goethe observed to Eckermann (25 February 1824) that 'there are great and mysterious effects inherent in the various poetical forms'. The context was a discussion of the *Roman Elegies* and his late poem *The Diary*, but this remark about the 'mysterious' effects of verse-forms could have been made with equal truth in the 1770s. The characteristic anonymous folk-ballad, if we are to define it, is a simple narrative poem, typically in four-line stanzas between which there is not always a clear logical continuity: the narrative is elliptical, laconic, leaping from high point to high point and leaving enough to the hearer's imagination to create an element of mystery. As a poet and dramatist, Goethe must have recognized the vivid and powerful effects that could be obtained in this way. The Gretchen sequence has been described as a dramatic application of this folk-ballad technique: a headlong rush of scenes, omitting

inessentials, but all leading to a simple and devastating climax. In addition, Gretchen herself is like a figure in a ballad or folktale; she is *märchenhaft*, and her situation as a girl abandoned by her lover and driven to infanticide is old and internationally widespread in folksong and folklore. The general effect is further reinforced by interspersal into the action of ballad-like songs such as Gretchen's tale of 'The King of Thulè', her famous soliloquy at the spinning-wheel which is virtually in folk-ballad style, and the mad little snatch of a song that she sings in her prison (respectively nos. 7, 8 and 10 below). Above all, this ballad-style Gretchen-drama, like 'Edward' and many other examples of the ballad-style poem, is tragic and sinister; and this was chiefly because Goethe had decided to integrate it with the drama of Faust and Mephistopheles. That dark context turns what might have been a mere touching domestic melodrama of innocence betrayed into something much more original and subtle. In the presence of Mephistopheles, in the light of his constant worldly and cynical commentary, the element of eighteenth-century sentimentalism, so pervasive in *Werther*, dissolves into irony. There is intense dramatic (situational) irony, too, in Gretchen's ignorance of the true state of affairs, the fact that she never knows her lover's real name, that as a simple Catholic believer she is troubled because he never goes to church, that she feels an unaccountable, instinctive aversion to his constant companion ('that man you have with you'), that she realizes only at the last moment who Mephistopheles is, and at the cost of her life turns from Faust in horror and refuses his offered rescue.

The 'Urfaust' would probably, if it had been published in the 1770s, have changed the history of German literature. But Goethe postponed the continuation and completion of *Faust* for many years, and destroyed the original manuscript, the contents of which were only discovered when a contemporary copy came to light by chance at the end of the nineteenth century. Although much of this first, unrevised version was written in prose, we are concerned with it here as also containing supreme examples of the kind of poetry Goethe was writing in his twenties, at this time of his first maturity. The expressive force of its verse dialogue and of its songs was something he would never surpass, though he was still writing lyric poetry of a high order nearly sixty years later. A notable feature at this 'Urfaust' or 'Storm and Stress' stage was his use of the neologistic compounds to which German so easily lends itself: 'Wissensqualm' in Faust's opening speech

(no. 5) is parallelled by 'Lebensfluten', 'Blütendampf', 'Nebeltal', 'Blüten-träume' (nos. 6, 1, 3, 4), etc., which all amount to original re-creations of the language and which remained characteristic of Goethe. Later he returned occasionally to the folk-ballad style, notably (to mention only the most famous examples) in no. 17 ('The Fisherman', 1778) and no. 18 ('The Elf King', 1782), but he had already demonstrated his complete mastery of it in Gretchen's 'The King of Thulè'. Significantly, the 'far north land' of Thulè seems to be a Germanic, Nordic kingdom. Although the phenomenon of folksong and folklore is of course international, Herder mistakenly thought of it as primarily and essentially German, and saw it as relevant to his ambition of creating a national literature in opposition to the prevailing Enlightenment culture, which modelled itself, in literature as in politics, on France. The sixteenth century as such, the great age of Luther, Hans Sachs, Paracelsus and Faust himself in so far as he historically existed, also belonged for Herder and the young Goethe to the national myth; it would be recalled again a century later, when Richard Wagner celebrated the 'sacred German art' of the Mastersingers of Nuremberg.

In 1775 Goethe was faced with two related decisions which would affect his whole life: one was whether to get married, the other was whether to leave Frankfurt, probably for ever, and settle elsewhere at the court of a princely patron. Karl August of Saxe-Weimar-Eisenach (1757–1828), whose coming of age in September 1775 made him absolute ruler of his small Thuringian duchy, had in the preceding year or two been on his travels, carrying out the usual educational tour of a young prince, and Frankfurt was on his itinerary. When he and Goethe met they took an instant liking to each other. Karl August's invitation to Goethe to visit Weimar for an indefinite stay is the context for the poet's brief but intense emotional attachment to Anna Elisabeth ('Lili') Schönemann, the daughter of a well-to-do Frankfurt family. Lili was the only woman to whom he was ever formally engaged, with whom he could very probably have made a successful marriage as between equals. To Eckermann (5 March 1830) he remarked at the end of his life that he had loved her more than any other woman and come nearest to his happiness with her than with any other. There were no insuperable obstacles to the marriage, no serious financial or social problems; he probably could, despite all the pressures on him to stay on in Frankfurt, have decided to settle in Weimar and taken Lili with him. His reasons for leaving, as he did, both Frankfurt and Lili, were internal

and are still not wholly clear. But the behaviour pattern of attachment followed by flight had already established itself in his life. The breach with Friederike had the character of a flight; the fictional Werther had fled, though in vain, from his beloved Lotte in a story closely based on its author's 'real life' affair with Lotte Kästner, the wife of a friend. Lili, unlike Lotte, was available, but once again his motives for leaving her must certainly have included, as Boyle observes, a profound need to remain 'un-accountable, unpredictable, uncommitted', even if this would mean some degree of isolation and frustration – an instinctive conviction that to live in unsatisfied desire was more conducive to his poetic creativity than to conform to a settled happiness (Boyle, 199f.). And ultimately, this creativity was more important to him than any human attachment. On the deep-er psychological level there is room for the usual speculations: a shrinking from Lili's availability, the fact that she was not his beloved sister Cornelia – who as he records in his autobiography was herself unhappily married, for reasons almost certainly connected with Wolfgang, and who advised or begged him not to marry Lili. (Adherents of the latest fashion in biography may wish to note that in Goethe's case there is a good deal more evidence of a latent incestuous fixation on his sister than of any latent homosexuality, a conjecture that has recently surfaced rather late in the day.) In the event, he arrived in Weimar in November 1775 not committed to Karl August's patronage either, or to staying in the duchy for any length of time (and few there supposed he would). But the options did not remain open. Cornelia, to her brother's great grief, died in June 1777, and Lili married a rich Frankfurt banker in 1778.

And in the event, too, Weimar became Goethe's permanent home for the rest of his life. Again there were complex reasons for this decision, or rather for this growing conviction simply that Weimar was the right place for him to be, but an outstanding factor must have been his excellent per-sonal relations with the young Duke. The distinctly educative, pedagogical character of this friendship continued for the first four or five years, and if Karl August succeeded in becoming an enlightened and benevolent despot, as he did, it was largely due to Goethe's influence. This fact was appreciated by the Duke, by his mother the Dowager Duchess Anna Amalia, and not least by Goethe himself, who thus acquired something of a mission, a sense of personal destiny. Karl August also effectively protected his new favourite against the social prejudice he had at first encountered in

Weimar. The mere 'Doctor Goethe' had brought his Frankfurt origins with him: like his acclaimed fictional *alter ego* Werther, he was not aristocratic, but upper middle class at most, and had quickly been made to feel that he had not arrived as an equal at a ducal court. He was literally made to sit at a different table. Karl August's Prime Minister threatened to resign rather than accept this upstart's appointment to the Privy Council. All this changed as Goethe's responsibilities grew and diversified. For years he was above all else a civil servant and administrator, particularly concerned with various schemes designed to put the finances of the duchy on a sounder basis. The Duke found him increasingly indispensable, and rewarded him with a high salary, an expensively restored 'garden house' on the river Ilm just outside Weimar, and later an elegant residence on the Frauenplan in the centre of town. In 1782 he also set the social problem to rights by petitioning the Emperor Joseph II to grant Goethe the particle 'von' and thus technically raise him to the nobility. Goethe's role was much more than that of court poet or higher entertainer: he became here a man of power and influence. And this was also an environment congenial to his long-term literary aims: not merely in the sense that he and Anna Amalia between them had attracted other men of literary talent to Weimar and made it famous as a 'court of the Muses', but also because he could here observe at close quarters, with some degree of personal involvement, the operation on a small scale of absolute political power in a tiny but independent state, one of the many that composed and constituted what was nominally the German Empire. His imperial ennoblement was symbolic: the representative of a middle-class and politically powerless city–republic, the sometime leader of the Frankfurt Storm and Stress, had established himself in a centre of courtly, *ancien régime* culture, and it was to be by a synthesis of these two worlds that his unique literary creativity would survive and mature. It would enlarge its scope, accommodate conflicting elements, reflect not only old popular traditions but courtly values as well, not only the Germany of Frankfurt but the much larger Germany of the autocratic principalities, and thus come nearer to being a truly national art.

Increasingly, of course, as time passed, Goethe understood that it was beyond his power to create a national culture by educating one among many princes and helping to govern one among many miniature states. This gradual realization was to lead to his almost total withdrawal, by the end of his first ten years in the duchy, from involvement in its

administrative affairs. Other interests were asserting themselves: notably, from about 1780 onwards, a passionate curiosity about the natural sciences (above all geology, anatomy and botany) which was to remain with him all his life. There was also another personal attachment, which had indeed begun very shortly after his arrival in Weimar in 1775, but which continued compulsively during the whole of his first eleven years there. This was his protracted and yet, as it seems, entirely 'platonic' relationship – again an educative one, though this time the pupil was Goethe and the influence by no means beneficial – with Charlotte, the wife of the Duke's Chief Equerry, Oberstallmeister Baron von Stein. He wooed her as a lover for many years, safe in the knowledge that she would never accept him in this role. The parameters of the friendship were purity, intellectuality, propriety and renunciation, an obsessive marriage of souls. Although certainly a neurotic personality and not even particularly beautiful, Charlotte von Stein exercised an extraordinary power over Goethe, less by what she was than by what she meant to him, namely an ideal of courtly life, a spiritualized Weimar perceived by him as the antithesis of Frankfurt and its bourgeois ethos of Storm and Stress. Charlotte for her part saw it as her function to educate the newcomer in the social refinements, to teach this still only half-tamed poet, for instance, to address her as 'Sie' and not 'du' as he persistently did. It is most unlikely that she ever allowed him the intimacies he may have demanded. Weimar was a small and confined society, where gossip and ribald comment and the general minding of other people's business were the order of the day; and yet not the least particle of evidence has survived to suggest that an adulterous liaison either took place or was even jokingly alleged by anyone. Baron von Stein was not the man to accept the role of *mari complaisant*, and yet his relations with Goethe were always entirely friendly. The puzzle is that this bizarre sexual stalemate should have lasted so long. An enormous mass of touchingly affectionate correspondence from Goethe to Charlotte has been preserved; her own letters to him were demanded back and destroyed when the relationship eventually broke down in 1789, in the aftermath of his journey to Italy. The main literary legacy of the affair was probably the symbolic verse drama *Iphigenia in Tauris* with its brother–sister theme, though some credit for this must perhaps also be given to the lost Cornelia; but two remarkable and enigmatic lyric poems, 'To the Moon' (no. 16) and 'Why was deep insight given to us' (no. 13) (the relevant Notes discuss these in

more detail) may serve to epitomize the Charlotte epoch just as 'On the Lake' (no. 11) may be said to commemorate the episode of Lili.

Such lyrical moments were rare, however, in what by the mid-1780s had become a decade of comparative poetic sterility. Goethe told Eckermann on 3 May 1827 'that in the first ten years of my life as minister and courtier in Weimar I did next to nothing; I was driven to Italy by despair'. The despair was about loss of creativity: 'did next to nothing' meant 'wrote next to no poetry'. His duties in the Weimar administration were time-consuming because performed with great conscientiousness; by 1785 he had been able to disengage himself from most of them. This was not the problem. In 1786 he decided to put together a first edition of his collected works, whether already published or unpublished and whether finished or not: but he despaired to see how many, including *Faust*, had remained fragments. He had forced himself to write an early version of the first part of his second novel, *Wilhelm Meister*. There were two acts extant of *Torquato Tasso*, a verse drama, in much the same style as *Iphigenia*, about the psychopathology of a court poet. Even *Iphigenia*, the most important product of this earlier Weimar period but first written in prose, did not reach its final form until 1787. In the scientific fields into which he was now also venturing, there had been the beginnings of a geological treatise (the fragment on granite) and a paper on comparative anatomy (the intermaxillary bone). In all these years, apart from a few immortal examples, he had not been primarily Goethe the lyric poet. He was 'driven to Italy' by a hope of renewal. An extended visit to Rome in particular was a deep-rooted, long cherished wish, in which his father, on the basis of his own memories, had always encouraged him. Caspar Goethe had at first opposed the Weimar connection, urging his son in 1775 to go to Italy instead, and Goethe had nearly done so. His longing was now not simply for a change of scene and a different culture. As Boyle points out, this was to be 'the supreme educational journey', profoundly appropriate for a German intellectual: 'Rome was not just an important stage in the itinerary of the grand tour, (it was) the capital of the Empire of the Caesars, from whom the liege-lord of all Frankfurt citizens, the Holy Roman Emperor, claimed lineal constitutional descent. . . It was, in a ghostly sense, Germany's non-existent national metropolis' (Boyle, 391f.). Goethe did not suddenly decide on Italy for a much-needed holiday, or for an antiquarian glimpse of the classical world: the 'classical soil' which he invokes in the *Roman*

Elegies (VII – no. 28) is not simply the vestige of Roman civilization, it is the classical soil of himself, of his own creativity, a key element in a living synthesis.

It is also evident that Goethe's Italian journey was strongly motivated by his instinctive need to escape from the spell of Charlotte von Stein. The pattern of self-extrication and sudden flight asserted itself again, and not for the last time. In 1786, determined to travel both alone and incognito, he told no one in Weimar of his plans; Frau von Stein was only given a vague indication that he would be away for a while; to Karl August he wrote requesting indefinite leave, assuring him that all administrative matters would be looked after during his absence, but not detailing his destination or itinerary. He used a visit to the Bohemian spa of Carlsbad, where he had already sampled the waters and the society during the previous summer, as a cover for his longer, clandestine journey. From Carlsbad, at the beginning of September 1786, he set out and travelled directly southwards without returning to Weimar, but continuing through Bavaria, via the Brenner Pass, Lake Garda, Verona, Vicenza and Venice (where he saw the sea for the first time in his life) and then pressing on to Rome, the true goal of his pilgrimage, where he arrived at the end of October. He took modest lodgings and spent in the first instance about four months in Rome, associating with the German colony of writers and painters, studying art, drawing and writing. Having contracted with his publisher for an edition of his works in eight small volumes, he now found that the agreed deadlines were a stimulus. The final iambic version of *Iphigenia* was finished in Italy, progress was made on *Tasso*, and above all the Storm and Stress *Faust*, the 'Urfaust', was significantly revised and augmented, though in the end Goethe still decided to publish it incomplete ('*Faust*: a fragment', 1790). In the early months of 1787 he visited Naples and Sicily. It is significant that his appetite for ancient culture was not strong enough to impel him to travel on to Greece, although he was more than once offered the opportunity of doing so. He returned to Rome in June and remained there for the rest of his stay in Italy. The Duke, Charlotte and other Weimar friends had by now been informed of his whereabouts and expected movements. After some negotiation with Karl August his leave was extended until Easter 1788, though Weimar society was beginning to doubt whether the wayward minister would ever return at all. But the central educative event of Goethe's whole Italian expedition was still to come. In January 1788 he met

a young widow whose name may or may not have been Faustina Antonini – 'Faustina', at least, was what with a certain literary appropriateness he would call her in the *Roman Elegies*. Strange as it may today seem to many, this was not only Goethe's first documented sexual encounter, although he was now in his thirty-ninth year, but also his first fully satisfying physical relationship with a woman. Financial inducements and an eventual pay-off will certainly have been involved, nevertheless the transforming effect on Goethe was profound. In his letters he wrote repeatedly of having undergone a 'rebirth', though without mentioning what must be presumed to have been its principal cause.

Goethe finally returned to Weimar in June 1788, and from his sexual initiation or liberation in Rome two important consequences now followed. Firstly, in July, he chanced to make the acquaintance of the then twenty-three-year-old Christiane Vulpius, with whom he was to live for the next twenty-eight years until her death in 1816. The liaison amounted to a marriage, though it was not officially formalized as such until 1806. 'Faustina' had been Christiane's emboldening predecessor; it was as if Goethe were trying to reconstitute in Weimar a personal Rome, a private pre-Christian world, in scandalous defiance of Weimar's courtly conventions. In Frankfurt, on the other hand, his mother (now a widow) was delighted when she heard the news that he had at last found a woman to make him happy, and quickly set up a warm correspondence with her son's 'little bed-companion'. Goethe and Christiane were not social or intellectual equals. 'It is strange,' he remarks, 'the little creature can't understand any poetry at all.' But they remained devoted to each other, as their correspondence attests, and had several children, though only the first, a son, survived infancy. The other consequence of the Roman palingenesis was the writing of the remarkable and to Goethe's contemporaries equally scandalous cycle of poems first called 'Erotica Romana', which later became known as the *Roman Elegies*, and in which Goethe may be said to have reinvented German and indeed European erotic poetry. Their inspiration was of course cultural as well as personal: they are Goethe's homage to Rome as such, more particularly the ancient Rome of the classical Latin poets, especially Propertius whom he read soon after his return to Weimar. They are written in a close imitation of ancient 'elegiac' verse, substituting accentual for quantitative metre, and using the classical sequence of hexameter–pentameter couplets (distichs). Goethe discovered

in this verse-form a perfect, slightly distancing stylization for the erotic content of the *Elegies*, their candid and touching love-story in which his new happiness in Weimar is fictionally but subtly backdated and relocated to Rome, and both Faustina and Christiane are recreated as a single beloved. He began to write them in October 1788 and had finished them by 1790, though they were not published until 1795. The reasons for this are discussed below in the Notes, along with further commentary on the selection of elegies here included.

At this time of the resumption or renewal of his life in Weimar, Goethe also discovered that irreparable damage had been done to his relationship with Charlotte von Stein, whom he had bitterly offended by his secretive departure for Italy without taking her into his confidence. She had also been dissatisfied with his subsequent letters, in which she read no more than an account of what a delightful time he was having despite being hundreds of miles from her for the best part of two years. From the reports of his journey which he gave to all and sundry after his return, she apparently had the same impression, and treated him with marked coldness. It goes without saying that when she discovered his new arrangements with 'the Vulpius girl', which he could not keep secret for long, her resentment knew no bounds, although as Goethe pointed out with an air of injured innocence, his relations with 'the poor creature' were something of which she had very little right to complain. In the same letter (1 June 1789) he suggested that she was damaging her mental health by continuing to drink too much coffee, a detestable substance against which he had always advised her. There was no reconciliation between them for many years. In the same summer, as he broke with Charlotte, Goethe learnt from Christiane that she was pregnant and would bear his child in December, a development which caused some upheaval in his domestic arrangements. He still did not wish to marry her with full ceremony, but was too fond of her now even to consider simply paying her off like Faustina, or arranging to maintain her as his mistress at a separate address, perhaps even retaining the option of finding himself a socially more suitable wife in due course. He settled for a characteristic compromise between the courtly and the bourgeois solution by moving to a larger house which could accommodate Christiane, their children, the half-sister and aunt whom she brought with her, and Goethe himself under the same roof but in a discreetly separate 'bachelor' apartment. Goethe's son was born on 25 December and in

a hurried informal ceremony christened Julius August Walther Vulpius; the Duke stood godfather, but the father was not named.

Satisfyingly, however, the first collected edition of Goethe's works was by this time complete, and by not far into 1790 it had all been published. The only unfinished work left in it was, deliberately, *Faust*, now presented in volume vii in such a way as not to preclude or preempt a future continuation. The eighth and last volume consisted mainly of the collected shorter poems, with a number of slight revisions, usually improvements, to the famous lyrics of his youth such as 'Welcome and Parting' (no. 2) and 'On the Lake' (no. 11). The kind of short poems he was writing now, however, which could broadly be categorized as 'erotica', found no place in this official edition. The 'Erotica Romana / Roman Elegies' would have to wait another few years before appearing; so would his new collection of elegiac epigrams, about a third of which he himself withheld as unsuitable for publication. These were written during his second, brief and rather disappointing visit to Italy between March and May 1790. Goethe undertook this journey as a personal service to Karl August's mother, who was now travelling in Italy and whom he would meet in Venice to escort her back to Weimar. But he went unwillingly, having now discovered that sexual happiness was more profoundly important than any environment, however susceptible to idealization as a classic place of pilgrimage. He even asserted in a letter to the Duke that this second Italian trip had destroyed his love for Italy. What it certainly did was to separate him from Christiane and the three-month-old August, to whom he longed to return as he waited impatiently in Venice for the delayed arrival of the Dowager Duchess. Given these circumstances, the rather sour mood of many of the 'Venetian Epigrams', as they came to be known, is understandable. The targets of their satirical attack were various. One was the French Revolution, which had broken out only months before, and which Goethe would always regard as an appalling peak of human insanity. A number of the Epigrams, especially among those that remained unpublished, are erotically explicit (no. 35 is an example), and some also for the first time openly vent Goethe's spleen against Christianity and its everlasting phobic–puritanical campaign, as he saw it, against the sexual life which he himself had only discovered so recently and with such joy (no. 38).

Goethe was rescued from intellectual isolation in these years by his new friendship with Schiller, who in 1789 became professor of history in the

university town of Jena, not far from Weimar. There had at first been a certain antagonism between them: Goethe had little sympathy for Schiller's early melodramas in the Storm and Stress manner, whereas Schiller felt for Goethe a mixture of admiration, envy and rivalry, and found his personality cold and rebarbative. Schiller had recently, however, undergone a far-reaching change, almost an intellectual equivalent to the transformation brought about in Goethe by his Italian journey: in Schiller's case, rather strangely, it was the result of his recent intensive study of Kant's moral and aesthetic philosophy. In the summer of 1794, meeting again in Jena after attending a scientific lecture and falling into conversation, Goethe and Schiller discovered that they held profoundly similar views on topics of central importance to both of them. By independent and different routes they had reached a harmony and complementarity of outlook. The exchange of letters between them that now began and continued for more than ten years must rank as one of the most important of extant correspondences between writers of genius. In the decade of his alliance and collaboration with Goethe, Schiller wrote his greatest dramatic masterpieces (*Wallenstein*, *Maria Stuart*), and Goethe, under the stimulus of Schiller's interest and encouragement, again turned his mind to *Faust*. It was at this time (1797) that he decided to divide it into two parts, Part One and Part Two 'of the tragedy'. Part One would have, or so he hoped, a certain completeness in itself, while making it clear that something was to follow and would be added at some future date. The whole work would be designated a 'tragedy', but would be preceded by a 'prologue in heaven' in the manner of a mystery-play, a prologue to both the Parts considered as a whole, putting the whole story in a higher perspective. The ending of Part One, as published, would be starkly tragic, but without excluding some mysterious final resolution. The Gretchen tragedy, taken over from the 'Urfaust' with only minor revisions, concludes the drama with undiminished force: the execution of the crazed infanticide, her lover's vain attempt to rescue her, Mephistopheles dragging him away. But there remains an interesting and rather strange discrepancy of tone between this 'Ur'-substance of Part One and the new scenes added in the composition-phase that began in 1797: all the latter are essentially non-tragic and optimistic, hinting at a positive destiny for Faust who is now a kind of symbolic Everyman. This even includes his new negotiations with Mephistopheles, in which the traditional life-and-death, heaven-and-hell bargain with the

Devil is converted into a wager and thus loses some of its seriousness; God, also rather non-seriously, is now a third player in this game. Part One, which for all its great dramatic power and beauty has something about it of a provisional compromise, was essentially finished in about 1801 but for various practical reasons not published till 1808.

It is doubtful whether Goethe would have continued *Faust* at all but for Schiller's enthusiastic intellectual support. Their increasingly close association was also marked by intensive theoretical discussions of the aesthetics of literature, the exact nature of the sublime, of the tragic, of the idyllic. Goethe's tragically and dramatically nuanced hexameter idyll *Hermann and Dorothea* (1796–7) was a further important poetic response to Schiller's subtle exploration of these theoretical issues. Like Herder at an earlier stage, Schiller provided Goethe with a philosophic context for his creativity. It is much to his credit that although erotic poetry was less germane to his more austere temperament, he not only published the *Roman Elegies* in 1795 in his newly founded journal *Die Horen*, but included a strong critical defence of them in his great treatise *On Naive and Sentimental* [Reflective] *Poetry* (1795–6), which contained among other things a theory of the modern idyll. The more decent of the *Venetian Epigrams* also appeared in 1796 under Schiller's auspices. In 1799, resigning from his Jena professorship to be nearer Goethe, Schiller settled in Weimar. The association between them was so inspiring that Goethe could again feel, as in Italy, that he was living through a new springtime of his life, with everything budding and burgeoning all round him: 'you have given me a second youth,' he wrote to Schiller in January 1798, 'and made me a poet again, which I had as good as ceased to be.' The two of them were virtual co-directors of the Weimar court theatre for several years, during which Schiller's greatest plays were written and produced. More than ever, at this time, the tiny principality became a centre of national culture, visited by such luminaries as Wilhelm von Humboldt, the educational reformer who founded the University of Berlin, his brother the explorer and scientist Alexander von Humboldt, the literary brothers Friedrich and August Wilhelm von Schlegel, the philosophers Hegel, Schelling and Fichte, and the poets Tieck and Novalis who represented what official nomenclature calls the early Romantic Movement. But this was now the high noon of 'Weimar Classicism', rather strangely placed between Storm and Stress and Romanticism *sensu strictiori*; it was a phenomenon unique in Europe

and central to the literary history of Germany. With the partnership that chiefly constituted it, it came to an end in 1805. Schiller had long been a chronic invalid, and in the early months of that year both he and Goethe were almost too ill to communicate with each other. At the beginning of May, with a last effort, Goethe went to call on Schiller and found him just leaving for the theatre, but felt too unwell to accompany him, and at Schiller's front door they parted for the last time. Even those closest to Goethe scarcely dared bring him the news of his friend's death a few days later. 'I thought I was losing my own life,' he wrote in June, 'and now I lose a friend, and with him half my existence.'

Napoleon's victorious wars in Germany at this time, and his occupation and reorganization of the German territories, certainly concerned Goethe less than the death of Schiller. Twenty years later, when Eckermann reminded him that he had been widely criticized by his younger contemporaries for failing even to lift his pen against the French invaders, he replied that the only thing that really mattered to him was culture and its stand against barbarism, and why should he polemicize against one of the most cultivated nations on earth, for which he felt no hatred and to which he owed so much of his own education? After the massive defeat of Prussian forces at the battle of Jena in October 1806, marauding French troops raided his house in Weimar, and he probably owed his life to the courageous behaviour of Christiane, who is said to have declared, with bold proleptic exaggeration, that this was the home of a friend of Napoleon. A few days after this, in gratitude and for her protection, Goethe finally married his faithful companion. But two years later he did indeed make the acquaintance of Napoleon whom, like many cultivated Germans of the time, he greatly admired. L'auteur de 'Werther' was received in audience during the Congress of Erfurt in 1808. According to his later memoir of this treasured encounter, the Emperor greatly impressed him by his intelligent comments on his work, and even quite seriously invited him to leave Weimar for good and settle in Paris. Goethe's political, or rather quite non-political attitude during the Napoleonic years did, however, estrange him from many of his fellow-countrymen. In particular he attracted much adverse comment by refusing to let his son August volunteer for military service in 1814, and persuading Karl August to appoint him to a sinecure which would keep him in Weimar. Needless to say, this seriously damaged the young man's standing with his contemporaries, who when they

returned from defeating the French mocked him as a coward, even taunting him with his illegitimate birth. When August challenged one of his tormentors to a duel, his father intervened and used his influence to prevent that as well. It was at about this time, not surprisingly, that August's drinking and womanizing became a serious problem. Goethe's troubles had been further compounded by the generally cool reaction of Weimar society to his official marriage with Christiane, who incurred even greater obloquy as his wife, Geheimrätin von Goethe, than as merely his mistress, 'die Mamsell Vulpius'. All this, added to the loss of Schiller, drove him in his late fifties and early sixties into even deeper personal isolation. He withdrew into himself and his writing, working on various scientific and literary projects. *Faust* Part One had been largely completed before the time of Schiller's death, and thus does not strictly belong to this phase. But work on *Wilhelm Meister* was resumed, and most importantly (at least in his own estimation) Goethe devoted a massive treatise on optics, *Zur Farbenlehre* (*The Theory of Colour*, 1810), to his attempt to disprove Newton's theory of colour, an attempt which has never been endorsed by scientific opinion. He also decided to write at least a partial autobiography, covering the period up to 1775 when he left Frankfurt for Weimar. Its title, *Dichtung und Wahrheit* (*Fiction and Truth* rather than *Poetry and Truth*), acknowledges that a middle-aged man's description of his earlier life is inevitably somewhat stylized (Goethe's selective account of subsequent events appeared as the *Italian Journey* in 1816–7 and later). But this intensive preoccupation for about four years with the experiences of his youth, and a careful rereading and rearranging of all his own poetry in preparation for the 1815 edition of his works in twenty volumes, must both have helped to stimulate the lyrical creativity that fully re-emerged in 1814.

It had not, of course, been entirely latent during the Napoleonic period, even if we disregard *Faust*. In 1807–8, for instance, he produced his only sonnet sequence, marking the reappearance in his emotional landscape of the figure of a young girl, yet again to be poetically courted, loved and renounced. She has been identified by some as Minna Herzlieb, the adopted daughter of a Jena bookseller, and by others as Silvie von Ziegesar, whose father Goethe met at Carlsbad and visited on his country estate. Minna (or Silvie) may also have had something to do with the genesis of the strange and controversial novel *Die Wahlverwandtschaften* (*Elective Affinities*, 1809), which posterity has picked out as a major literary

work from this phase. It was a study of marital behaviour among the landed aristocracy, and had first been conceived as a long-short story or 'Novelle'; the irrelevant *longueurs* with which Goethe filled it out make it a matter of regret that he did not adhere to the earlier plan. Particularly remarkable and original, however, is his treatment of the sexual theme in its central episode. A middle-aged husband empowers himself by imaginary adultery to beget a child on his wife: in his fantasy, his partner is the young girl with whom he is in love. The wife's corresponding dream is that she is in the arms of a young officer. A child is born of this union which, as if by magic or divine judgment, exactly resembles not its biological parents but both the young girl and the officer. The story, not surprisingly, ends in tragedy. But by a curious thematic connection, we are led from *Elective Affinities* to an outstanding, but largely unknown, poetic masterpiece written in 1810, about a year after the novel, and taking its candid sexual realism much further: the erotic narrative poem in twenty-four stanzas curiously called *Das Tagebuch* (*The Diary* – no. 57). Goethe never even attempted to publish this poem, which remained suppressed, apart from pirated and bowdlerized editions, until well into the present century. Its fictional protagonist, again a married man apparently of middle years, is returning from a business trip to his wife, for whom he lovingly keeps a diary of his travels. He attempts to seduce a young girl at a wayside inn, but at the crucial moment is defeated by impotence. Astonished at this unprecedented failure, he remembers with some explicitness his innumerable previous successes, only to realize that they were made possible by his genuine passion for the woman to whom he is more truly committed. As he understands this, his potency is restored, but he renounces the casual encounter; his wife has so to speak reclaimed *in absentia* her prior entitlement to the services of the wise and capricious organ which turns out to be on the side of virtue after all. This simple yet highly sophisticated moral tale is told with a formal virtuosity and an exquisite blend of seriousness and conciliatory humour which set *The Diary* apart from the tragic pathos of *Elective Affinities* and make it one of Goethe's most important and fascinating poems, despite being for historical reasons one of the least read.

In the years after writing *The Diary*, the story of a middle-aged man reinvigorated by vivid memories of his youth, Goethe rediscovered his own youth, not only by his work on *Fiction and Truth* and the earlier

poems, but even more by a literal journey into his past, which was made possible by the ending of the Napoleonic wars. In 1814 he was able for the first time in decades to revisit the scenes of his earlier life in Frankfurt and the Main and Rhine area generally. It was with this *voyage sentimental* that the great creative renewal began. There were two further decisive factors: the first was Goethe's rediscovery of an enthusiasm for oriental and especially Persian poetry, which Herder had kindled in him long ago. In a recently published German translation, he now reread the work of the great fourteenth-century Persian master Shams ud-din Muhammad, known as Hāfiz, who in politically troubled times had celebrated the joys of life in a '*divan*' (assembly, collection) of lyric poems which Goethe now felt inspired to imitate. The result was the *Westöstlicher Divan* (*West-Eastern Divan*), Goethe's tribute to a poet who chiefly appealed to him as a hedonist and enemy of dogmatic orthodoxy, and whom he saw, with some simplification, as a kind of Persian Horace or Voltaire. The second crucial experience of 1814 was his meeting in Wiesbaden with Marianne von Willemer, the 'Suleika' of the *Divan*, and their mutual love. The parallel between this journey to the Main and Rhine and Neckar in 1814–5 and his journey to Italy in 1786–8 was clear to him. Both were liberations, they represented discoveries or rediscoveries both literary and personal. Borrowing the official name of the event from which the Islamic calendar is dated, the momentous journey or 'flight' (Arabic 'hijra') of the Prophet from Mecca to Medina in AD 622, Goethe applied it to his present journey (letter to Knebel, 8 February 1815) as well as giving the title 'Hegira' to one of the first and most remarkable poems in the *Divan* (no. 58). In his *Italian Journey* he uses the same word, 'hegira', for his departure from Carlsbad in September 1786, when he set out for Rome. As in Rome then, so in Frankfurt now, Goethe not only found an earlier historical culture to identify with, however approximately, but he was also, however temporarily, experiencing personal happiness. Marianne von Willemer, *née* Jung, was the attractive and gifted Austrian protégée of Johann Jakob von Willemer, a rich Frankfurt banker, who had at first made her his adopted daughter and later his third wife. She was thirty when Goethe first met her in 1814. The Willemers had a country house, the 'Gerbermühle' on the Main near Frankfurt, and Goethe visited them here at about the time of their marriage, in September, and again in October 1814. It was at this time, and especially during his further visit to the Gerbermühle in the summer of

1815, that he wrote a rapidly increasing number of poems 'in the manner' of Hāfiz and in passionate homage to Marianne.

He did not in fact imitate Hāfiz with any degree of strictness; a few more or less close translations from him appear among free paraphrases, stanzas composed of passages from different poems and even by different poets, or poems without any particularly oriental colouring that would not seem out of place elsewhere in Goethe's work. Nor did he to a serious extent adopt Hāfiz's characteristic verse-form, the Arabic 'ghasel', a stanza of paired lines with a reiterated rhyme-word at the end of each pair. Hāfiz's German translator Hammer-Purgstall had sometimes tried to turn this metre into Graeco-Latin elegiacs, but Goethe had for years been freeing himself from classical metres and eschewed such experiments. He had tried out the fashionable Italian sonnet form in 1807, and used the even stricter *ottava rima* stanza in *The Diary*; now he was intent on developing a new style that would be post-classical and quasi-oriental. The *Divan*, like its model, was planned in twelve sections or 'books' with subtitles such as 'The Book of the Singer', 'The Book of Hāfiz', 'The Book of Love', 'The Book of Paradise', etc. The longest and most complete section is 'The Book of Suleika'. Marianne, who in the poems is 'Suleika' to Goethe's 'Hatem', was herself poetically talented, and became deeply involved in the *Divan* project. In the intensive correspondence that developed between her and Goethe, they would send each other coded messages by numerical allusion to Hāfiz's poems. Long after Goethe's death, but while Marianne was still living, the scholar Hermann Grimm discovered that several of the *Divan* poems were in fact by her, adopted with slight alterations by Goethe and barely distinguishable from his own work. The theme of creative imitation inspired by love is movingly developed in one of the later poems (no. 73), and again in *Faust* Part Two.

Fourteen years later, looking back on all this and on his life generally, Goethe makes it clear in an important conversation with Eckermann (11 March 1828) that he recognizes in himself the recurrent phenomenon of creative renewal and rejuvenation. Using a sexually coloured metaphor, he calls it the phenomenon of 'repeated puberty (*wiederholte Pubertät*)'. 'In exceptionally gifted men,' he observes, 'fresh periods of unusual productivity may still be seen to occur even when they are old. They seem from time to time to undergo a temporary rejuvenation, which is what I should like to call repeated puberty.' He plainly implies that in the course of life

such 'repetitions of puberty' may happen several times. In his own case, as we have seen, the first of them was the 'rebirth' in Rome, and the great creative period with Schiller may be said to have been the second. In the conversation of 11 March 1828, without mentioning either of these (though he was at this time again working on his account of the Italian journey), he speaks particularly of the third recurrence, the 'happy period after the War of Liberation when the poems of the *Divan* had me in their power, (and when) I was productive enough to be able to write two or three of them in a day'. And yet, for whatever reason, the inspiration of Hāfiz and Marianne was transient. In another conversation (14 January 1827) he tells Eckermann quite brutally that 'the orientalism (in these poems) and the passion in them are no longer alive in me; they have dropped off by the wayside like a cast snakeskin'.

Goethe's wife Christiane, to his extreme grief, died in June 1816 of a long and painful illness. It is not clear in what way her death was related to his sudden flight from Marianne. There is no evidence that the west-eastern romance had been more than purely literary, and Willemer himself seems to have welcomed this emotional attachment between his young wife and the famous poet; later he even proposed that Goethe should leave Weimar and return to Frankfurt to live with them on a permanent basis. They had met once more in Heidelberg for a few days in September 1815, neither knowing that this was to be their last meeting. Not quite a year later, six weeks after Christiane's death, Goethe set off again towards Frankfurt, but two hours after leaving Weimar the axle of his carriage broke on the unrepaired road, and although he was not injured he interpreted this mishap as a warning omen. He cancelled the intended journey and then without explanation, despite desperate pleas from both Marianne and her husband, stopped writing to her altogether. Once again it was a flight of the other kind – not a rejuvenating return to simplicity, to his origins, but a painful sudden withdrawal from the reju-venating experience. He eventually resumed his correspondence with her in 1819, the year of the publication of the *Divan*, but strictly avoided any further meeting. Did he shrink from too great an emotional involvement, or did he simply no longer wish to see her because both she and the whole *Divan* experience was something he had left behind him? His remark to Eckermann in 1827 seems to suggest this. It is also notable, however, that in 1831, about a year before the end of his life, Goethe decided to return

Marianne's letters, but then could not bring himself to part with them. On 10 February 1832 he wrote to her again, mentioning that he was making good use of his remaining time by tidying up his innumerable papers, and that he had found among them 'certain letters which remind me of the happiest days of my life. . . They now lie before me in a packet addressed to you'. The letters were finally dispatched on 29 February 1832, accompanied by a request that the packet should be left unopened 'until the uncertain hour has come'. Goethe died about three weeks later, and the package was found to contain a short poem (no. 92 below), written a year earlier, which appeared in 1833 among his posthumous works with the editorial title 'A Legacy'. Marianne lived on until 1860.

Six months after Christiane's death, Goethe acquired a daughter-in-law when his son August married Ottilie von Pogwitz, the daughter of an aristocratic Prussian officer and a lady of the Weimar court. Three grandchildren followed, though the marriage was not a success. But Ottilie enjoyed the role of hostess, and in the ensuing years there was some revival of social life at the house on the Frauenplan. Parties of guests were entertained to dinner with fair frequency, and as time passed the ageing Goethe became more and more of an institution, a cultural monument to be visited whether or not one knew anything about his writings. Large numbers of casual callers, of greater or lesser distinction, came from various parts of Europe; many were English lords doing their grand tour, for whom Ottilie was said to have had a particular predilection. Goethe's continuing interest in a large variety of people, notwithstanding his advancing years, was nourished by his apparently inexhaustible intellectual curiosity. As John Williams notes (pp. 46ff.), his guests included musicians such as Mendelssohn and Paganini, philosophers such as Hegel and Schopenhauer, politicians such as Freiherr vom Stein and members of the Prussian, Bavarian and Russian royal and imperial families, as well as many foreign and some German writers (one was Heine, whom Goethe treated with ironic reserve, another the Austrian dramatist Grillparzer, whom he invited to spend the evening tête-à-tête with him but who was so intimidated by this prospect that he failed to keep the appointment). His many personal encounters were supplemented and continued by his prodigious correspondence, partners in which included Walter Scott, Thomas Carlyle and notably Byron, one of the few contemporary poets by whose personality and talent Goethe was fascinated, an admiration expressed symbolically in

Act 3 of the Second Part of *Faust*. Both his letters and his talk show that Goethe's interest also extended to various practical matters such as trade and communications, the beginnings of the Industrial Revolution, the development of steam technology in shipping and railways, the projected future construction of the Panama, Suez and Rhine-Danube canals. Inevitably, many visitors and friends kept records of their conversations with him. The most famous and systematic of these was compiled by the already mentioned Johann Peter Eckermann, and covers the years from 1823 to the poet's death in 1832. Eckermann was a humble and adoring drudge, of whose devotion and poverty Goethe rather shamelessly took advantage, needing as he did an unofficial secretary and general editorial factotum. At the same time, Goethe's own diaries (which he had kept with absolute regularity since 1806) show that he came more and more to respect his young protégé, who was not without literary and critical talent. He eventually appointed him one of his literary executors, asked his advice on his own work, and even remarked that he would probably not be completing the Second Part of *Faust* if it were not for the stimulus of Eckermann's intelligent interest. Eckermann's *Conversations with Goethe during the last years of his life* appeared in 1836, and has become a more widely read book than many of Goethe's own. Its hero is certainly stylized and monumentalized into the Olympian figure that is still Goethe's stereotype, but it remains a vital biographical source and a work of art in itself. A balancing impression is given by the more down to earth and humanly candid notations of Friedrich von Müller, a lawyer who entered the Weimar government service and rose to the rank of Chancellor. His ironic cast of mind was similar to that of Goethe, who treated him as a social and intellectual equal, and with whose not infrequent moods of despondency and boredom Müller was well in tune. His material, not published until nearly forty years later, covers the whole period from 1808 to 1832.

In his middle age, Goethe formed the habit of going regularly, sometimes for up to two months, to the fashionable Bohemian watering-places (Carlsbad, Marienbad, Franzensbad and Teplitz, today respectively called Karlovy Vary, Mariánské Lázné, Františkovy Lázné and Teplice). Such resorts were patronized by the young and beautiful Empress Maria Ludovica of Austria and the high Austrian nobility generally, including the patrons of Beethoven; in 1812 Goethe also met Beethoven himself, a composer whose work he instinctively disliked, though in 1830, when the young

virtuoso Felix Mendelssohn visited him and insisted on playing the first movement of the Fifth Symphony to him on the piano, some of his prejudice was charmed away. In 1821 he made an acquaintance in Marienbad which was to lead to a personal crisis and inspire one of his greatest love-poems. Ulrike von Levetzow, fresh from school on a visit to her mother and grandmother, was seventeen at the time. Goethe sought out her company in three successive summers, and she received the attentions of 'such a kind, charming old gentleman' with guileless innocence. According to her reported account, they went on walks together, he made her a present of the 1821 edition of *Wilhelm Meister's Travels* (*Wilhelm Meisters Wanderjahre*), the sequel to *Wilhelm Meister's Apprenticeship*, and then told her, with suitable omissions, the rest of the story 'for hours on end'. By August 1823 the seventy-four-year-old Goethe had become so infatuated that he persuaded Karl August, who was also in Marienbad at the time, to propose marriage to Ulrike on his behalf. The Grand Duke (as he had now been since 1815) conveyed this message with some embarrassment to the girl's mother, who avoided a direct reply, but moved with her daughters to Carlsbad. At first Goethe followed them there, but early in September, inevitably, he finally renounced what was to be the last of his loves, and returned to Weimar. On this journey, and in the days that followed, he wrote the poem that came to be known as the 'Marienbad Elegy'. He attached exceptional importance to it, made a fair copy in Latin script on special paper and bound it in a red leather folder, declaring that it would never be published and showing it only to his closest friends. One of these was the composer Zelter, the only friend with whom in the latter part of his life he was on 'du' terms (even Schiller had not been an exception, which says something for Goethe's essential isolation and reserve; after the Storm and Stress period he had reverted one-sidedly to ceremonial forms of address with Karl August, and even Christiane always called him 'Sie', at least in company). When Goethe fell seriously ill in November 1823, Zelter was asked to sit by his bed reading the 'Marienbad Elegy' aloud to him over and over again. After the experience which this poem represents, Goethe never again returned to Marienbad or the other resorts. It was as if his last attempt, his last fantasy of recreating his youth by marrying a teenager who thought of him as no more than a kind grandfather, had failed and must never be repeated. Ulrike, for her part, lived on to the age of ninety-five, dying in 1899, but (according to an almost certainly

apocryphal anecdote) not before she had received a courtesy call from the young novelist Thomas Mann, who later conceived the idea of using the story of Goethe's undignified infatuation with her as the basis for a story of his own. (Later still, he decided that the point of *Death in Venice* would be better made if the object of the fifty-year-old writer's fatal passion were to be a fourteen-year-old boy.)

In the end the 'Elegy' was published after all, combined with two other poems which, though written at different times, Goethe judged to be closely enough related in theme and mood to make an integrated sequence, the 'Trilogy of Passion' (no. 87), with the Elegy as its centre-piece. One was 'To Werther (An Werther)' a poem commissioned as a preface or prologue for a fiftieth anniversary reprint of his notorious novel of 1774. Goethe wrote this fifty-line piece in March 1824 for an agreed fee of fifty ducats, and it was eventually backdated to serve as a prologue to the Elegy. The third component of the Trilogy, a poem about the healing power of music which he was to call 'Reconcilement', was written in the summer of 1823, probably before the Elegy, as a tribute to Maria Szymanowska, a Polish pianist attached to the Imperial Russian court, whom Goethe met in Marienbad. Her playing moved and consoled him, and he heard it again after his parting from Ulrike, when Mme Szymanowska visited Weimar in October. The three poems, however, did not appear in their present sequence and under the new titles until 1827, in the final collection of Goethe's poems and other works.

This forty-volume definitive edition, the so-called 'Ausgabe letzter Hand' (1827–30), was the main publishing event of Goethe's last years, and these were also dominated by his need to finish what he now regarded as his 'Hauptgeschäft', his main task: the completion of *Faust* Part Two. Even so, he did not work on it continuously. He was also engaged in additions to his autobiography (a further section, for instance, of the *Italian Journey* was written in 1828) and in the seemingly endless and inconsequential continuation of *Wilhelm Meister's Travels*, which occupied him again between 1821 and 1828. *Faust* Part Two did not, in the event, appear until after his death, in the first of twenty volumes of posthumous work which Eckermann co-edited between 1832 and 1842. Fragments and sketches for it (the opening speech of Helen, for instance, and probably some version of the scenes leading up to the death of Faust) had already existed around 1800, and an important unpublished prose scenario was

written in 1816, but the main work was not seriously undertaken until 1825, and thus had to be compressed into the last five or six years of Goethe's life. Again it was intermittent, as if Goethe knew instinctively that he must take advantage of his creative moods as and when they came to him, even if it meant writing the end of a work first and the middle last. Nevertheless the composition, between the ages of seventy-six and eighty-one, of a dramatic poem of such length and complexity is an astonishing feat on any showing. It was as if he had been granted one further period of repeated puberty, a fourth and last rejuvenation.

It is of course not surprising that in *Faust* itself, Goethe's central and in some ways most profoundly autobiographical work, the theme of rejuvenation should be as prominent as it is in both Parts. In Part One, it is what literally happens to Faust in the 'Witch's Kitchen' scene, which (again not surprisingly) is one that Goethe actually wrote in Rome in 1788. Faust's magical transformation at this point from a disillusioned ageing scholar to a randy young man in hot pursuit of Helen or whatever substitute for her can be found, is not so much a dramatic necessity in the story of Faust as such, as a poetic reflection of a personal concern of Goethe's at the time of writing this part of it. (The same applies to Faust's hymn of thanksgiving to the Earth Spirit in the scene 'A Forest Cavern', also written in Rome, which plainly has more to do with Goethe's personal satisfaction at his progress in the natural sciences than with the dramatic necessities of the Faust story, in the context of which it makes no sense.) Particularly striking is his use of the rejuvenation motif in Part Two. The new drama begins with the hero lying asleep 'in a beautiful landscape', in the bosom of nature: elemental spirits are lulling him into forgetfulness of the horrifying events of Part One, for which he is responsible but of which, in readiness to start a new life, he now has total amnesia. He is not so much rejuvenated as reborn. Time has been turned back, there is no need for remorse or repentance, sin and guilt simply do not arise. Faust can continue his untroubled symbolic adventures until the last scene of Act 5, when angels carry him to a region of further transformations. The spirit 'once called Gretchen' greets him in ecstasy as he reappears to her in glorious youth, casting 'his outworn husk aside' and exchanging it for 'ethereal raiment'. This is a clear echo of the 'cast snakeskin' which Goethe left behind with Hāfiz and Marianne. Faust has not so much been resurrected in the Christian manner as granted recurrent puberty, with the Eternal Feminine drawing him on (extract no.

100) in a journey of continuing metamorphosis. The symbolic hero celestially endorses the principle of change, the ability to move on from previous selves, the process of 'dying into becoming' which the profoundest poem in the *Divan* (no. 77) so cryptically enjoins as the only path to earthly enlightenment. It is evident that the capacity for self-renewal, or at least fairly radical self-modification or self-revision, was one of Goethe's most important and precious gifts. 'Do you suppose,' he asks Kanzler von Müller on 24 August 1830, 'that I have lived to the age of eighty just to go on thinking the same things as I used to? On the contrary, I try every day to think something different, something new, in order to avoid becoming a bore. One must continually change and renew and rejuvenate oneself, or one will turn stale (*verstocken*).' So far as his poetry and other literary work is concerned, it must be acknowledged that his avoidance of self-repetition in so vast an *oeuvre* is one of its most striking features. What of the human implications of this Protean gift? In the traditional view, Goethe's repeated self-metamorphoses, his discarding of roles (and sometimes of the people who went with these roles) are simply the proof of his vitality and resilience, amounting to no more than the normal changes which, as he remarks, come about in the course of a long life. To less sympathetic critics, intent on puncturing the stereotype, it has suggested an existential flaw, almost a higher Don Juanism, sometimes ruthless, perhaps literally heartless: a deep disharmony and disunity, the search for a real self which is never found.

If there was a real and harmonious Goethean self, perhaps we should look for it, or its projection, in his vision of 'Gott-Natur', his compelling myth of the divine cosmic harmony which so filled his imagination and gave, especially, so characteristic a colouring to his scientific studies: the unity, the 'Urgestalt' or primal form in nature and all things. His evocations of this in poetry and prose give the impression that he has after all somehow discovered an identity and deep centre. The Faust who wakes in the high mountains at the beginning of Part Two (no. 94) to watch the rising sun gradually spreading its light over the peaks, and forming a rainbow ('changing yet ever still') in the spray of the waterfall, has seen this vision, which is a vision of paradise (line 4694); he will see it again in the paradise of Arcadia (no. 96), the kingdom of pure nature where 'all separate worlds unite at last'. We should also bear in mind, however, the essentially fantastic, even ironic character of Part Two as a whole, not only

in its central, anti-traditional theme of Faust's eventual and inevitable salvation, but also in Goethe's treatment of the traditional Helen story. When he published the first part of Act 3, the 'Helena' Act, in 1827 in advance of the rest, he gave it the title 'Helena: a classical-romantic phantasmagoria' – a phrase that sheds an ironic light on classicism, on romanticism, and on the 'phantasmagoria' itself. It was an indispensable feature of the old legend (and most famously in Marlowe's version) that Faustus, with Mephistopheles' help, should bring Helen of Troy back from the dead to be his 'paramour'. Goethe decided, however, not to treat this obligatory episode simply as a magical love-story (partly no doubt because the theme of Faust having to have his women procured for him by the Devil had already been well enough worked in Part One) but to raise it to the status of a grandly conceived allegory, a poetic tribute to the ancient classical world to which he owed so much, the symbolic union of two cultures over a timespan of three thousand years from the Trojan War to modern romantic poetry. Clearly this would be dream-like, not taking place in ordinary time at all; and considerable play is made, for example, with the ontological status of Helen herself. Is she the real, flesh-and-blood Helen, or some kind of phantasm representing her? Is she alive or dead? The cynical realist Mephistopheles takes pleasure in taunting her on this point, and Goethe backs it up with ancient parallels, ancient variants of the Greek myth: the story that by command of her father Zeus she was transferred for the duration of the Trojan War to the comparative safety of Egypt, leaving only a simulacrum of herself at Troy, and the story that after her death the hero Achilles, himself also dead, was permitted by the gods to meet her and beget on her, as Faust will do, a son called Euphorion. All this makes room for a certain delicate veneer of irony in Goethe's presentation, even in such lofty passages as the heroine's introductory speech at the beginning of Act 3 (no. 95). She is a figure in a story, stepping out of a legend, herself and yet not herself. Faust too, in this whole episode, seems rather less than real. As for the briefly appearing Euphorion, whom Goethe identified as an allegory of Byron or of modern poetry in general, his volatility is such that he loses contact with the earth and perishes almost at once. But the attendant nymph-chorus reverts magnificently (no. 97) to union with nature, with the earth to which they belong. The true magic and seriousness lie, here as elsewhere, in nature and the earth, and here as elsewhere in the words of the poetry.

Goethe finished *Faust* Part Two in July 1831, and sealed up the manuscript for publication after his death. He seems to have kept himself going by sheer strength of will, determined to complete this and other outstanding tasks. His unhappy, alcoholic son had predeceased him in 1830. In a last therapeutic attempt, August von Goethe had been sent to Rome, well provided with money and letters of introduction, but a sudden illness had carried him off on 28 October. He was buried, like Shelley and Keats, in the little Protestant cemetery near the Pyramid of Celsius, a resting-place mentioned in the *Roman Elegies* as one which his father would have wished for himself. The aged poet received the news with composure, but suffered a near-fatal haemorrhage a few weeks later. He recovered and returned to his work. In August 1831, to avoid the celebrations for his eighty-second birthday, he made one last short journey, to the little mountain hut near Ilmenau, and reread the poem he had written there on the wall fifty years earlier (no. 15). The end came at midday on 22 March 1832. The accounts of the details by Eckermann and other witnesses are largely idealized. According to his doctor, Karl Vogel, Goethe did not fade peacefully away but died in great pain and agitation, hardly able to breathe and with every appearance of mortal terror. Drifting in and out of sleep, he was heard to murmur: 'Look at that lovely woman's head – with black curls – in splendid colours – on a dark background!' And noticing a piece of paper on the floor: 'How can you leave Schiller's letters lying about like that!' We may assume that the often quoted final cry for 'more light' was the half-heard fragment of a request, as his eyes failed, for the shutters to be opened wider. When he was no longer able to speak he is said to have still moved his hand as if writing, finally forming a capital W which according to some stood for his own name, Wolfgang, or according to others for 'Welt (world)', as part of some last reflection on literature and humanity. He was buried with great ceremony, alongside Schiller and Karl August, in the Grand Ducal vault in Weimar.

I

THE YOUNGER GOETHE

1770–1786

MAILIED

Wie herrlich leuchtet
Mir die Natur!
Wie glänzt die Sonne!
Wie lacht die Flur!

Es dringen Blüten
Aus jedem Zweig
Und tausend Stimmen
Aus dem Gesträuch

Und Freud und Wonne
Aus jeder Brust.
O Erd, o Sonne!
O Glück, o Lust!

O Lieb, o Liebe!
So golden schön,
Wie Morgenwolken
Auf jenen Höhn!

Du segnest herrlich
Das frische Feld,
Im Blütendampfe
Die volle Welt.

O Mädchen, Mädchen,
Wie lieb ich dich!
Wie blickt dein Auge!
Wie liebst du mich!

MAY SONG

How bright, how splendid
Is everything!
How the sun shines down,
How the meadows sing!

Buds burst from every
Twig, and from all
The bushes a thousand
Voices call,

And all hearts pour forth
Their joy and delight.
Oh the earth, oh nature,
Oh dear sunlight!

Oh love, more lovely
Than break of day
On those golden hills
Where the clouds play!

In a mist of blossoms
Your fields renew
Their fullness, your world
Is blessed with dew.

Oh dearest girl,
Oh I love you so!
And you love me too,
As your bright eyes show!

So liebt die Lerche
Gesang und Luft,
Und Morgenblumen
Den Himmelsduft,

Wie ich dich liebe
Mit warmem Blut,
Die du mir Jugend
Und Freud und Mut

Zu neuen Liedern
Und Tänzen gibst.
Sei ewig glücklich,
Wie du mich liebst!

2

WILLKOMMEN UND ABSCHIED

Es schlug mein Herz, geschwind zu Pferde!
Es war getan fast eh gedacht.
Der Abend wiegte schon die Erde,
Und an den Bergen hing die Nacht;
Schon stand im Nebelkleid die Eiche,
Ein aufgetürmter Riese, da,
Wo Finsternis aus dem Gesträuche
Mit hundert schwarzen Augen sah.

Der Mond von einem Wolkenhügel
Sah kläglich aus dem Duft hervor,
Die Winde schwangen leise Flügel,
Umsausten schauerlich mein Ohr;

As the lark loves singing
And soaring high,
As the morning flowers
Love the breathing sky,

So I love you
With my heart's warm blood,
For you give me youth
And joy, and a mood

For new songs and dances.
Oh may you be
Ever happy, as ever
Your love for me!

2

WELCOME AND PARTING

A heartbeat, and my horse was ready!
Scarcely a thought, and it was done.
Earth lay in evening's arms already,
Night veiled the hills as I rode on;
The mist-clad oak already towered
Above me like a giant, where
From the deep thicket's gloom they glowered,
The hundred eyes of night's dark stare.

Through clouds to misty cloud-banks drifting
The sad moon showed its sleepy head;
The winds rushed by, their soft wings lifting,
Fanning my ears with sighs of dread;

Die Nacht schuf tausend Ungeheuer,
Doch frisch und fröhlich war mein Mut:
In meinen Adern welches Feuer!
In meinem Herzen welche Glut!

Dich sah ich, und die milde Freude
Floß von dem süßen Blick auf mich;
Ganz war mein Herz an deiner Seite
Und jeder Atemzug für dich.
Ein rosenfarbnes Frühlingswetter
Umgab das liebliche Gesicht,
Und Zärtlichkeit für mich – ihr Götter!
Ich hofft es, ich verdient es nicht!

Doch ach, schon mit der Morgensonne
Verengt der Abschied mir das Herz:
In deinen Küssen welche Wonne!
In deinem Auge welcher Schmerz!
Ich ging, du standst und sahst zur Erden,
Und sahst mir nach mit nassem Blick:
Und doch, welch Glück, geliebt zu werden!
Und lieben, Götter, welch ein Glück!

3

GANYMED

Wie im Morgenglanze
Du rings mich anglühst,
Frühling, Geliebter!
Mit tausendfacher Liebeswonne
Sich an mein Herz drängt

A thousand monsters night was spawning
And yet my spirits still were bold:
What ardour in my veins was burning,
What fire leapt up a thousandfold!

I saw you, felt your soul's outpouring
In the sweet kindness of your gaze;
My heart was yours and all adoring,
Each pulse for you, each breath your praise.
A rose-red glow of spring surrounded
Your dear face; in it I could see
Oh God, how undeserved, unbounded
That hope! your tender love for me.

But oh, we part, for day is breaking!
The rapture of your kiss must end
Already; how my heart is aching,
Seeing what grief your eyes portend!
Downcast, tears welling in distress,
You stood, I stood, you watched me go
And yet, oh God, what happiness
In being loved, in loving so!

3

GANYMEDE

How in the brightness of morning,
All round me, you glow upon me,
Oh spring, oh my lover!
With the rapture of a thousand loves
It thrusts at my heart,

Deiner ewigen Wärme
Heilig Gefühl,
Unendliche Schöne!

Daß ich dich fassen möcht
In diesen Arm!

Ach, an deinem Busen
Lieg ich, schmachte,
Und deine Blumen, dein Gras
Drängen sich an mein Herz.
Du kühlst den brennenden
Durst meines Busens,
Lieblicher Morgenwind!
Ruft drein die Nachtigall
Liebend nach mir aus dem Nebeltal.

Ich komm, ich komme!
Wohin? Ach, wohin?

Hinauf! Hinauf strebts.
Es schweben die Wolken
Abwärts, die Wolken
Neigen sich der sehnenden Liebe.
Mir! Mir!
In euerm Schoße
Aufwärts!
Umfangend umfangen!
Aufwarts an deinen Busen,
Alliebender Vater!

This sacred sense
Of your eternal ardour,
Oh infinite beauty!

Oh let me hold you
Here in my arms!

Ah, at your breast
I lie, I languish,
And your flowers, your grass,
They thrust at my heart.
You cool the burning
Thirst within me,
Sweet morning wind!
The nightingale calls to me,
Calls out in love from the misty valley.

I come, I come!
Oh where am I going?

Upwards, drawn upwards.
The clouds float down,
The clouds descend
To my love and my longing.
To me! To me!
Upwards, carried in their womb,
Embraced and embracing!
Borne aloft to your heart,
Oh father, lover of all!

4

PROMETHEUS

Bedecke deinen Himmel, Zeus,
Mit Wolkendunst
Und übe, dem Knaben gleich,
Der Disteln köpft,
An Eichen dich und Bergeshöhn;
Mußt mir meine Erde
Doch lassen stehn
Und meine Hütte, die du nicht gebaut,
Und meinen Herd,
Um dessen Glut
Du mich beneidest.

Ich kenne nichts Ärmeres
Unter der Sonn als euch, Götter!
Ihr nähret kümmerlich
Von Opfersteuern
Und Gebetshauch
Eure Majestät
Und darbtet, wären
Nicht Kinder und Bettler
Hoffnungsvolle Toren.

Da ich ein Kind war,
Nicht wußte, wo aus noch ein,
Kehrt ich mein verirrtes Auge
Zur Sonne, als wenn drüber wär
Ein Ohr, zu hören meine Klage,
Ein Herz wie meins,
Sich des Bedrängten zu erbarmen.

PROMETHEUS

Cover your heavens, Zeus,
With the fog of clouds,
And try your arm,
As a boy beheads thistles,
Against oak-trees and mountain heights:
You still must leave me
My round earth standing,
And my hut which you did not build,
And my hearth, the glowing
Home fire which fills you
With such envy.

I know of no poorer thing
Under the sun, than you gods!
Wretchedly you feed
Your own majesty
On sacrificial offerings
And the breath of prayers,
And you would starve
If children and beggars
Were not fools full of hope.

When I was a child
Not knowing my way about,
I would lift up my deluded eyes
To the sun, as though beyond it
There were an ear to hear my complaint,
A heart like my own
That would pity my anguish.

Wer half mir
Wider der Titanen Übermut?
Wer rettete vom Tode mich,
Von Sklaverei?
Hast du nicht alles selbst vollendet,
Heilig glühend Herz?
Und glühtest jung und gut,
Betrogen, Rettungsdank
Dem Schlafenden da droben?

Ich dich ehren? Wofür?
Hast du die Schmerzen gelindert
Je des Beladenen?
Hast du die Tränen gestillet
Je des Geängsteten?
Hat nicht mich zum Manne geschmiedet
Die allmächtige Zeit
Und das ewige Schicksal,
Meine Herrn und deine?

Wähntest du etwa,
Ich sollte das Leben hassen,
In Wüsten fliehen,
Weil nicht alle
Blütenträume reiften?

Hier sitz ich, forme Menschen
Nach meinem Bilde,
Ein Geschlecht, das mir gleich sei,
Zu leiden, zu weinen,
Zu genießen und zu freuen sich,
Und dein nicht zu achten,
Wie ich!

Who was my ally
Against the Titans and their insolence?
Who saved me from death,
Saved me from slavery?
Did you not accomplish all this yourself,
Oh heart of sacred fire?
And in your young well-meaning error
Did you not glow with gratitude for your deliverance
To that Sleeper up there?

I should respect you? For what?
Have you ever soothed
The pain that burdened me?
Have you ever dried
My terrified tears?
Was I not forged into manhood
By almighty Time
And everlasting Destiny,
My masters and yours?

Perhaps you thought
I should find life hateful
And flee into deserts
Because not all my dreams
Blossomed to ripeness?

Here I sit, making men
In my own image,
A race that shall be like me,
A race that shall suffer and weep
And know joy and delight too,
And heed you no more
Than I do!

FAUST Habe nun, ach! Philosophie,
Juristerei und Medizin
Und leider auch Theologie
Durchaus studiert, mit heißem Bemühn.
Da steh ich nun, ich armer Tor,
Und bin so klug als wie zuvor!
Heiße Magister, heiße Doktor gar,
Und ziehe schon an die zehen Jahr
Herauf, herab und quer und krumm
Meine Schüler an der Nase herum –
Und sehe, daß wir nichts wissen können!
Das will mir schier das Herz verbrennen.
Zwar bin ich gescheiter als alle die Laffen,
Doktoren, Magister, Schreiber und Pfaffen;
Mich plagen keine Skrupel noch Zweifel,
Fürchte mich weder vor Hölle noch Teufel –
Dafür ist mir auch alle Freud entrissen,
Bilde mir nicht ein, was Rechts zu wissen,
Bilde mir nicht ein, ich könnte was lehren,
Die Menschen zu bessern und zu bekehren.
Auch hab ich weder Gut noch Geld,
Noch Ehr und Herrlichkeit der Welt:
Es möchte kein Hund so länger leben!
Drum hab ich mich der Magie ergeben,
Ob mir durch Geistes Kraft und Mund
Nicht manch Geheimnis würde kund,
Daß ich nicht mehr mit sauerm Schweiß
Zu sagen brauche, was ich nicht weiß,
Daß ich erkenne, was die Welt
Im Innersten zusammenhält,

FAUST Well, that's Philosophy I've read,
And Law and Medicine, and I fear
Theology too, from A to Z;
Hard studies all, that have cost me dear.
And so I sit, poor silly man,
No wiser now than when I began.
They call me Professor and Doctor, forsooth,
For misleading many an innocent youth
These last ten years now, I suppose,
Pulling them to and fro by the nose;
And I see all our search for knowledge is vain,
And this burns my heart with bitter pain.
I've more sense, to be sure, than the learned fools,
The masters and pastors, the scribes from the schools;
No scruples to plague me, no irksome doubt,
No hell-fire or devil to worry about –
Yet I take no pleasure in anything now;
For I know I know nothing, I wonder how
I can still keep up the pretence of teaching
Or bettering mankind with my empty preaching.
Can I even boast any worldly success?
What fame or riches do I possess?
No dog would put up with such an existence!
And so I am seeking magic's assistance,
Calling on spirits and their might
To show me many a secret sight,
To relieve me of the wretched task
Of telling things I ought rather to ask,
To grant me a vision of Nature's forces
That bind the world, all its seeds and sources

from the URFAUST, *c.* 1774

Schau alle Wirkenskraft und Samen
Und tu nicht mehr in Worten kramen.

O sähst du, voller Mondenschein,
Zum letztenmal auf meine Pein,
Den ich so manche Mitternacht
An diesem Pult herangewacht:
Dann über Büchern und Papier,
Trübselger Freund, erschienst du mir!
Ach! könnt ich doch auf Bergeshöhn
In deinem lieben Lichte gehn,
Um Bergeshöhle mit Geistern schweben,
Auf Wiesen in deinem Dämmer weben,
Von allem Wissensqualm entladen,
In deinem Tau gesund mich baden!

6

DER ERDGEIST

In Lebensfluten, im Tatensturm
Wall ich auf und ab,
Wehe hin und her!
Geburt und Grab,
Ein ewiges Meer,
Ein wechselnd Weben,
Ein glühend Leben:
So schaff ich am sausenden Webstuhl der Zeit
Und wirke der Gottheit lebendiges Kleid.

And innermost life – all this I shall see,
And stop peddling in words that mean nothing to me.

Oh sad full moon, my friend, why must
You see me suffer? Look your last!
Here at this desk so many a night
I've watched and waited for your light
To visit me again and shine
Over this paper world of mine.
Oh, take me to the hilltops, there
To wander in the sweet moonlit air,
By mountain caves, through fields to roam,
Hovering with spirits in your gloam,
Cleansed of book-learning's fog and stew
And healed by bathing in your dew!

6

THE EARTH SPIRIT

In life like a flood, in deeds like a storm
I surge to and fro,
Up and down I flow!
Birth and the grave
An eternal wave,
Turning, returning,
A life ever burning:
At Time's whirring loom I work and I play,
God's living garment I weave and display.

7

GRETCHEN *singt*

Es war ein König in Thule,
Gar treu bis an das Grab,
Dem sterbend seine Buhle
Einen goldnen Becher gab.

Es ging ihm nichts darüber,
Er leert ihn jeden Schmaus;
Die Augen gingen ihm über,
So oft er trank daraus.

Und als er kam zu sterben,
Zählt er seine Städt im Reich,
Gönnt alles seinem Erben,
Den Becher nicht zugleich.

Er saß beim Königsmahle,
Die Ritter um ihn her,
Auf hohem Vätersaale,
Dort auf dem Schloß am Meer.

Dort stand der alte Zecher,
Trank letzte Lebensglut,
Und warf den heiligen Becher
Hinunter in die Flut.

Er sah ihn stürzen, trinken,
Und sinken tief ins Meer,
Die Augen täten ihm sinken.
Trank nie einen Tropfen mehr.

GRETCHEN *singing*

>There once was a king of Thulè,
>Of the far north land of old:
>His dying lady he loved so truly
>She gave him a cup of gold.
>
>There was no thing so dear to the king,
>And every time he wept
>As he drained that cup at each banqueting,
>So truly his faith he kept.
>
>And at last, they say, on his dying day
>His kingdom was willed and told,
>And his son and heir got all his share –
>But the king kept the cup of gold.
>
>They feasted long with wine and song,
>And there with his knights sat he,
>In the ancestral hall, in his castle tall
>On the cliffs high over the sea.
>
>The old man still drank as his life's flame sank,
>Then over the waves he stood,
>And the sacred cup he raised it up,
>Threw it down to the raging flood.
>
>He watched it fall to the distant shore
>And sink in the waters deep;
>And never a drop that king drank more,
>For he'd closed his eyes to sleep.

from the URFAUST, *c.* 1774

GRETCHEN *am Spinnrade*

Meine Ruh ist hin
Mein Herz ist schwer;
Ich finde sie nimmer
Und nimmermehr.

Wo ich ihn nicht hab,
Ist mir das Grab,
Die ganze Welt
Ist mir vergällt.

Mein armer Kopf
Ist mir verrückt,
Mein armer Sinn
Ist mir zerstückt.

Meine Ruh ist hin
Mein Herz ist schwer;
Ich finde sie nimmer
Und nimmermehr.

Nach ihm nur schau ich
Zum Fenster hinaus,
Nach ihm nur geh ich
Aus dem Haus.

Sein hoher Gang,
Sein edle Gestalt,
Seines Mundes Lächeln,
Seiner Augen Gewalt,

GRETCHEN *at her spinning-wheel*

My heart's so heavy
My heart's so sore,
How can ever my heart
Be at peace any more?

How dead the whole world is,
How dark the day,
How bitter my life is
Now he's away!

My poor head's troubled,
Oh what shall I do?
My poor mind's broken
And torn in two.

My heart's so heavy
My heart's so sore,
How can ever my heart
Be at peace any more?

When I look from my window
It's him I must see;
I walk out wondering
Where can he be?

Oh his step so proud
And his head so high
And the smile on his lips
And the spell of his eye,

Und seiner Rede
Zauberfluß,
Sein Händedruck,
Und ach, sein Kuß!

Meine Ruh ist hin,
Mein Herz ist schwer;
Ich finde sie nimmer
Und nimmermehr.

Mein Busen drängt
Sich nach ihm hin:
Ach, dürft ich fassen
Und halten ihn

Und küssen ihn,
So wie ich wollt,
An seinen Küssen
Vergehen sollt!

9

FAUST Was ist die Himmelsfreud in ihren Armen?
Laß mich an ihrer Brust erwarmen:
Fühl ich nicht immer ihre Not?
Bin ich der Flüchtling nicht? der Unbehauste?
Der Unmensch ohne Zweck und Ruh,
Der wie ein Wassersturz von Fels- zu Felsen brauste,
Begierig wütend, nach dem Abgrund zu?
Und seitwärts sie, mit kindlich-dumpfen Sinnen,
Im Hüttchen auf dem kleinen Alpenfeld,
Und all ihr häusliches Beginnen
Umfangen in der kleinen Welt!

And his voice, like a stream
Of magic it is,
And his hand pressing mine
And his kiss, his kiss!

My heart's so heavy,
My heart's so sore,
How can ever my heart
Be at peace any more?

My body's on fire
With wanting him so;
Oh when shall I hold him
And never let go

And kiss him at last
As I long to do,
And swoon on his kisses
And die there too!

9

FAUST What are the joys of heaven in her embrace?
So close to her, her dear love warming me,
Yet still I feel her misery!
Who am I? The unhoused, the fugitive,
The aimless, restless reprobate,
Plunging like some wild waterfall from cliff to cliff
Down to the abyss, in greedy furious spate!
And as I passed – she, childlike, innocent,
A hut, a meadow on the mountain-slope,
A home like that, such sweet content,
Her little world, her little scope!

from the URFAUST, *c.* 1774

Und ich, der Gottverhaßte,
Hatte nicht genug,
Daß ich die Felsen faßte
Und sie zu Trümmern schlug:
Sie, ihren Frieden mußt ich untergraben!
Du, Hölle, mußtest dieses Opfer haben!
Hilf, Teufel, mir die Zeit der Angst verkürzen!
Was muß geschehn, mags gleich geschehn!
Mag ihr Geschick auf mich zusammenstürzen
Und sie mit mir zugrunde gehn!

10

GRETCHENS STIMME

Meine Mutter, die Hur,
Die mich umgebracht hat!
Mein Vater, der Schelm,
Der mich gessen hat!
Mein Schwesterlein klein
Hub auf die Bein
An einem kühlen Ort –
Da ward ich ein schönes Waldvögelein,
Fliege fort, fliege fort!

And I, whom God had cursed,
Rocks could not satisfy
My rage to rive and burst
And wreck as I rushed by!
I had to ruin her, to undermine
Her peace; she was our victim, hell's and mine!
Help me, you devil, to cut short this waiting,
This fear! Let it be soon, if it must be!
May her fate crush me, my own fate out-fating,
And I be doomed with her, and she with me!

10

GRETCHEN'S VOICE

Who killed me dead?
My mother, the whore!
Who ate my flesh?
My father, for sure!
Little sister gathered
The bones he scattered;
In a cool, cool place they lie.
And then I became a birdie so fine,
And away I fly – away I fly.

from the URFAUST, *c.* 1774

AUF DEM SEE

Und frische Nahrung, neues Blut
Saug ich aus freier Welt;
Wie ist Natur so hold und gut,
Die mich am Busen hält!
Die Welle wieget unsern Kahn
Im Rudertakt hinauf,
Und Berge, wolkig himmelan,
Begegnen unserm Lauf.

Aug, mein Aug, was sinkst du nieder?
Goldne Träume, kommt ihr wieder?
Weg, du Traum! so gold du bist;
Hier auch Lieb und Leben ist.

Auf der Welle blinken
Tausend schwebende Sterne,
Weiche Nebel trinken
Rings die türmende Ferne;
Morgenwind umflügelt
Die beschattete Bucht,
Und im See bespiegelt
Sich die reifende Frucht.

ON THE LAKE

And so I suck from the wide world
Fresh nourishment, new blood;
How close to Nature I am held,
Her breast how kind and good!
Our rocking boat, our beating oars
Keep time, waves lift it high,
And mountains meet our onward course,
Cloud-clad into the sky.

Eyes, why downcast now? What shining
Dreams return, what past repining?
Golden dream, I break your spell!
Here is love and life as well.

On the lake they glitter,
Many a tremulous star,
Soft mist drinks the distance
As it towers afar,
Round the shady inlet
Winged winds of morning blow,
And to the water's mirror
Ripening fruit hangs low.

RASTLOSE LIEBE

Dem Schnee, dem Regen,
Dem Wind entgegen,
Im Dampf der Klüfte,
Durch Nebeldüfte,
Immer zu! Immer zu!
Ohne Rast und Ruh!

Lieber durch Leiden
Möcht ich mich schlagen,
Als so viel Freuden
Des Lebens ertragen.

Alle das Neigen
Von Herzen zu Herzen,
Ach, wie so eigen
Schaffet das Schmerzen!

Wie soll ich fliehen?
Wälderwärts ziehen?
Alles vergebens!
Krone des Lebens,
Glück ohne Ruh,
Liebe, bist du!

RESTLESS LOVE

Through the rain and snow,
Through the storm I go,
Along mountain ways
Through the mist and haze,
Without pause, without peace,
And never I cease.

Oh rather I'd fight
Through sorrow and strife
Than bear such a weight
Of the bliss of life!

Oh hearts that to one
And another are drawn,
How keen is the pain,
How the soul is torn!

Where shall my refuge be?
Can the woods shelter me?
How vain, all vain it is!
All life by love, by this
Joy without rest,
Is crowned and blessed.

1776

[AN CHARLOTTE VON STEIN]

Warum gabst du uns die tiefen Blicke,
Unsre Zukunft ahnungsvoll zu schaun,
Unsrer Liebe, unserm Erdenglücke
Wähnend selig nimmer hinzutraun?
Warum gabst uns, Schicksal, die Gefühle,
Uns einander in das Herz zu sehn,
Um durch all die seltenen Gewühle
Unser wahr Verhältnis auszuspähn?

Ach, so viele tausend Menschen kennen,
Dumpf sich treibend, kaum ihr eigen Herz,
Schweben zwecklos hin und her und rennen
Hoffnungslos in unversehnem Schmerz;
Jauchzen wieder, wenn der schnellen Freude
Unerwart'te Morgenröte tagt;
Nur uns armen Liebevollen beiden
Ist das wechselseitge Glück versagt,
Uns zu lieben, ohn uns zu verstehen,
In dem andern sehn, was er nie war,
Immer frisch auf Traumglück auszugehen
Und zu schwanken auch in Traumgefahr.

Glücklich, den ein leerer Traum beschäftigt,
Glücklich, dem die Ahndung eitel wär!
Jede Gegenwart und jeder Blick bekräftigt
Traum und Ahndung leider uns noch mehr.
Sag, was will das Schicksal uns bereiten?
Sag, wie band es uns so rein genau?

13

[TO CHARLOTTE VON STEIN]

Why was deep insight given to us, why this
Surmising, inkling of our future state,
Not a blind trusting to our love, a bliss
Of sweet illusion? Why instead did fate
So school our intuitions that we each
May spy into the other's heart and through
All its strange tumult? Must clear vision reach
So far into our mystery, the true
Bond that unites us?

 Thousands drift through life
Unthinking, aimless, floating to and fro,
Stumbling in haste through sudden pain and strife,
Their own hearts full of what they scarcely know,
And then exulting at the unlooked-for dawn
Of some delight, some pleasure's swift sunrise.
But we, poor loving souls, to us alone
Sad destiny that mutual joy denies:
The love that need not understand, the dream
Each dreams about the other, happiness
That never was, perils that merely seem,
Yet still are fresh pursued, still feared no less.

Happy are such vain dreamers! Happy those
Untroubled by foreboding thought! Alas
For us, whose every look, every encounter shows
Our vision true, our dreaming come to pass!
What is decreed for us? Oh were we not,
An age ago, in a lost previous life,

Ach, du warst in abgelebten Zeiten
Meine Schwester oder meine Frau.

Kanntest jeden Zug in meinem Wesen,
Spähtest wie die reinste Nerve klingt,
Konntest mich mit Einem Blicke lesen,
Den so schwer ein sterblich Aug durchdringt;
Tropftest Mäßigung dem heißen Blute,
Richtetest den wilden irren Lauf,
Und in deinen Engelsarmen ruhte
Die zerstörte Brust sich wieder auf;
Hieltest zauberleicht ihn angebunden
Und vergaukeltest ihm manchen Tag.
Welche Seligkeit glich jenen Wonnestunden,
Da er dankbar dir zu Füßen lag,
Fühlt' sein Herz an deinem Herzen schwellen,
Fühlte sich in deinem Auge gut,
Alle seine Sinnen sich erhellen
Und beruhigen sein brausend Blut!

Und von allem dem schwebt ein Erinnern
Nur noch um das ungewisse Herz,
Fühlt die alte Wahrheit ewig gleich im Innern,
Und der neue Zustand wird ihm Schmerz.
Und wir scheinen uns nur halb beseelet,
Dämmernd ist um uns der hellste Tag.
Glücklich, daß das Schicksal, das uns quälet
Uns doch nicht verändern mag!

Joined by some magical, some fateful knot:
Were you not then my sister or my wife?

Did you not know each motion of my soul,
The music of the subtlest nerve, with more
Than mortal sight, at one glance read the whole
Of my complexity? You could restore
Restraint to my rash nature, give my wild
And wandering course direction; holding me
In your dear arms, you soothed, revived and healed
My restless, ravaged heart. What sorcery
So lightly bound me to you! Every day
Passed in enchanted dreams; what blessed state
Could be compared to those sweet hours! I lay
There at your feet in gratitude; how great
The swelling of my heart, close to your own!
In your eyes I was good, as well I knew;
My every sense, how clear they all had grown!
And my young feverish blood, all was at peace with you.

What now is left? Only a memory
Hovering about my haunted breast again,
Where the old truth dwells ever constantly
And our new situation brings such pain.
We are but half alive, it seems; bright day
Surrounds us with mysterious twilight still.
Yet happy in our fate, for though it may
Torment us, change our love it never will.

14

WANDRERS NACHTLIED I

Der du von dem Himmel bist,
Alle Freud und Schmerzen stillest,
Den, der doppelt elend ist
Doppelt mit Erquickung füllest,
Ach, ich bin des Treibens müde!
Was soll all die Qual und Lust?
Süßer Friede,
Komm, ach komm in meine Brust!

15

WANDRERS NACHTLIED II

Über allen Gipfeln
Ist Ruh,
In allen Wipfeln
Spürest du
Kaum einen Hauch;
Die Vögelein schweigen im Walde.
Warte nur, balde
Ruhest du auch.

14

A WANDERER'S NIGHT SONG I

Messenger of heaven, the grief
Of our anguished souls restoring,
Twofold balm of sweet relief
On twice-wounded hearts downpouring,
Wearily I wander, feeling
Pain and joy, and find no rest:
Peace, oh healing
Blessed peace, come fill my breast!

15

A WANDERER'S NIGHT SONG II

Now stillness covers
All the hill-tops;
In all the tree-tops
Hardly a breath stirs.
The birds in the forest
Have finished their song.
Wait: you too shall rest
Before long.

1776/1780

16a

AN DEN MOND

(Erste Fassung)

Füllest wieder's liebe Tal
Still im Nebelglanz,
Lösest endlich auch einmal
Meine Seele ganz;

Breitest über mein Gefild
Lindernd deinen Blick,
Wie der Liebsten Auge mild
Über mein Geschick.

Das du so beweglich kennst,
Dieses Herz im Brand,
Haltet ihr wie ein Gespenst
An den Fluß gebannt,

Wenn in öder Winternacht
Er vom Tode schwillt
Und bei Frühlingslebens Pracht
An den Knospen quillt.

Selig, wer sich vor der Welt
Ohne Haß verschließt,
Einen Mann am Busen hält
Und mit dem genießt,

Was, den Menschen unbewußt
Oder wohl veracht,
Durch das Labyrinth der Brust
Wandelt in der Nacht.

TO THE MOON

(First version)

Now with your dear light again
All the valley's filled;
In your shining mist the pain
Of my soul is stilled.

Gazing as my love would gaze,
Kindly, soothingly,
So like hers your eye surveys
All my destiny.

You who know my heart's unrest
And how hot it glows,
Hold me spellbound like a ghost
Where this river flows,

Where its freezing wintry flood
Swells with death and doom,
Or spring flowers in splendid bud
On its sweet banks bloom.

Blest is she who with a heart
Free from bitterness
Shuns the world and lives apart
In a man's embrace,

There to learn, if learn we may,
What unknown delight
Through the soul's deep labyrinth-way
Wanders in the night.

16b

AN DEN MOND

(Letzte Fassung)

Füllest wieder Busch und Tal
Still mit Nebelglanz,
Lösest endlich auch einmal
Meine Seele ganz;

Breitest über mein Gefild
Lindernd deinen Blick,
Wie des Freundes Auge mild
Über mein Geschick.

Jeden Nachklang fühlt mein Herz
Froh- und trüber Zeit,
Wandle zwischen Freud und Schmerz
In der Einsamkeit.

Fließe, fließe, lieber Fluß!
Nimmer werd ich froh,
So verrauschte Scherz und Kuß,
Und die Treue so.

Ich besaß es doch einmal,
Was so köstlich ist!
Daß man doch zu seiner Qual
Nimmer es vergißt!

Rausche, Fluß, das Tal entlang,
Ohne Rast und Ruh,
Rausche, flüstre meinem Sang
Melodien zu,

16b

TO THE MOON

(Final version)

Now with your dear light again
Wood and dale are filled;
In your shining mist the pain
Of my soul is stilled.

Gazing as a friend would gaze,
Kindly, soothingly,
So your gentle eye surveys
My dark destiny.

Gladness, sadness, times gone by
Mingling mood with mood,
Echo through my heart as I
Walk in solitude.

River, run, dear river, flow!
When shall happiness
Come again, where did they go,
Love and love's caress?

Precious joy I had and lost
Lives in memory yet:
How it hurts, the vanished past
Never to forget!

Restless river, never stilled,
Murmur all along
This my valley, whisper wild
Music to my song:

Wenn du in der Winternacht
Wütend überschwillst,
Oder um die Frühlingspracht
Junger Knospen quillst.

Selig, wer sich vor der Welt
Ohne Haß verschließt,
Einen Freund am Busen hält
Und mit dem genießt,

Was, von Menschen nicht gewußt
Oder nicht bedacht,
Durch das Labyrinth der Brust
Wandelt in der Nacht.

17

DER FISCHER

Das Wasser rauscht', das Wasser schwoll,
Ein Fischer saß daran,
Sah nach dem Angel ruhevoll,
Kühl bis ans Herz hinan.
Und wie er sitzt und wie er lauscht,
Teilt sich die Flut empor;
Aus dem bewegten Wasser rauscht
Ein feuchtes Weib hervor.

Sie sang zu ihm, sie sprach zu ihm:
Was lockst du meine Brut
Mit Menschenwitz und Menschenlist
Hinauf in Todesglut?
Ach wüßtest du, wie's Fischlein ist

When your dark and wintry flood
Swirls to overflow
Or spring flowers in splendid bud
On your sweet banks grow.

Blest is one who with a heart
Free of bitterness
Shuns the world and lives apart
In a friend's embrace,

There to learn, if learn we can,
What unknown delight
Through the labyrinth-soul of man
Wanders in the night.

17

THE FISHERMAN

The water lapped, the water swirled,
An angler on the shore
Sat fishing, and his heart was cold,
Calm to its very core.
And as he sits there listening
The waters part and rise:
A woman wet and glistening
Swims up before his eyes.

She sang to him, she spoke to him:
Shame on your human skills,
Luring my little ones to die
In heat that chokes and kills!
How snug the little fishes are

So wohlig auf dem Grund,
Du stiegst herunter, wie du bist,
Und würdest erst gesund.

Labt sich die liebe Sonne nicht,
Der Mond sich nicht im Meer?
Kehrt wellenatmend ihr Gesicht
Nicht doppelt schöner her?
Lockt dich der tiefe Himmel nicht,
Das feuchtverklärte Blau?
Lockt dich dein eigen Angesicht
Nicht her in ewgen Tau?

Das Wasser rauscht', das Wasser schwoll,
Netzt' ihm den nackten Fuß;
Sein Herz wuchs ihm so sehnsuchtsvoll
Wie bei der Liebsten Gruß.
Sie sprach zu ihm, sie sang zu ihm;
Da wars um ihn geschehn:
Halb zog sie ihn, halb sank er hin,
Und ward nicht mehr gesehn.

18

ERLKÖNIG

Wer reitet so spät durch Nacht und Wind?
Es ist der Vater mit seinem Kind;
Er hat den Knaben wohl in dem Arm,
Er faßt ihn sicher, er hält ihn warm.

Mein Sohn, was birgst du so bang dein Gesicht? –
Siehst, Vater, du den Erlkönig nicht?

There in the depths below!
Come down to them, come live with them,
And true content you'll know!

Does the dear sun not bathe, the moon
Not dive into the sea,
And breathing from its waves return
Twice lovelier to see?
Does it not call you, the deep sky,
The moist-transfigured blue,
Your own face beckoning down, down
Into eternal dew?

The water lapped, the water swirled,
It wetted his bare feet;
His heart it heard his true love's word
Murmuring there so sweet.
She spoke to him, she sang to him,
Ah what could save him then?
Half dragged, half plunging, so he sank,
Never to rise again.

18

THE ELF KING

Who is riding so late on a night so wild?
A father is riding and carrying his child.
He holds the boy tight as he rides through the storm,
He grips him safely, he keeps him warm.

What's wrong, boy, why do you hide your face? –
Oh father, the Elf King's in that dark place!

Den Erlenkönig mit Kron und Schweif? –
Mein Sohn, es ist ein Nebelstreif. –

'Du liebes Kind, komm, geh mit mir!
Gar schöne Spiele spiel ich mit dir;
Manch bunte Blumen sind an dem Strand,
Meine Mutter hat manch gülden Gewand.'

Mein Vater, mein Vater, und hörest du nicht,
Was Erlenkönig mir leise verspricht? –
Sei ruhig, bleibe ruhig, mein Kind;
In dürren Blättern säuselt der Wind. –

'Willst, feiner Knabe, du mit mir gehn?
Meine Töchter sollen dich warten schön;
Meine Töchter führen den nächtlichen Reihn,
Und wiegen und tanzen und singen dich ein.'

Mein Vater, mein Vater, und siehst du nicht dort
Erlkönigs Töchter am düstern Ort? –
Mein Sohn, mein Sohn, ich seh es genau:
Es scheinen die alten Weiden so grau. –

'Ich liebe dich, mich reizt deine schöne Gestalt;
Und bist du nicht willig, so brauch ich Gewalt.'
Mein Vater, mein Vater, jetzt faßt er mich an!
Erlkönig hat mir ein Leids getan! –

Dem Vater grausets, er reitet geschwind,
Er hält in Armen das ächzende Kind,
Erreicht den Hof mit Mühe und Not;
In seinen Armen das Kind war tot.

Oh don't you see him, his robe and his crown? –
My son, it's the mists as the night comes down. –

'My dear child, come, come away with me!
Our games together, what games they'll be!
On the shore there are flowers, fine colours untold;
My mother will clothe you in cloth of gold.'

Oh father, oh father, oh can you not hear
What the Elf King is whispering into my ear? –
Hush, hush now, my son, all's well now, what's wrong?
It's the wind in the dry leaves singing its song. –

'Sweet boy, will you come, will you come my way?
My daughters shall wait on you night and day,
When it's dark, my daughters will dance in a ring,
You'll sleep when they rock you, you'll sleep when they sing.'

Oh father, oh father, oh do you not see
The Elf King's daughters looking at me? –
I see them, my son, I see all that's there:
It's the old willow-trees and their long grey hair. –

'I love you, your beauty has wakened my lust;
Little boy, I'll take you by force if I must.'
Oh father, oh father, don't let me go!
The Elf King has caught me, he hurts me so! –

The father shudders, he rides on fast,
With the poor moaning child he gets home at last,
He reaches his home with trouble and dread,
With the boy in his arms; but the boy is dead.

[DAS LIED DER PARZEN]

Es fürchte die Götter
Das Menschengeschlecht!
Sie halten die Herrschaft
In ewigen Händen,
Und können sie brauchen,
Wie's ihnen gefällt.

Der fürchte sie doppelt
Den je sie erheben!
Auf Klippen und Wolken
Sind Stühle bereitet
Um goldene Tische.

Erhebet ein Zwist sich,
So stürzen die Gäste,
Geschmäht und geschändet
In nächtliche Tiefen
Und harren vergebens,
Im Finstern gebunden,
Gerechten Gerichtes.

Sie aber, sie bleiben
In ewigen Festen
An goldenen Tischen.
Sie schreiten vom Berge
Zu Bergen hinüber:
Aus Schlünden der Tiefe
Dampft ihnen der Atem
Erstickter Titanen,

[THE SONG OF THE FATES]

Let the gods be feared
By the race of men!
For they are the masters,
In their hands they hold
Everlasting power
To use as they please.

Let him fear them doubly
Whom ever they honour!
On clouds and on cliff-tops
The chairs are in readiness
Round golden tables.

If strife arises
The guests are hurled headlong,
Reviled and dishonoured,
Deep down into darkness,
And bound in the shadows
They vainly lie waiting
For judgment and justice.

But still, everlastingly,
At golden tables,
The gods are feasting.
To them, as they stride
From mountain to mountain,
The breath of the stifled
Titans steams upwards
From bottomless caverns,

Gleich Opfergerüchen,
Ein leichtes Gewölke.

Es wenden die Herrscher
Ihr segnendes Auge
Von ganzen Geschlechtern
Und meiden, im Enkel
Die ehmals geliebten,
Still redenden Züge
Des Ahnherrn zu sehn.

So sangen die Parzen;
Es horcht der Verbannte
In nächtlichen Höhlen,
Der Alte, die Lieder,
Denkt Kinder und Enkel
Und schüttelt das Haupt.

20

GRENZEN DER MENSCHHEIT

Wenn der uralte
Heilige Vater
Mit gelassener Hand
Aus rollenden Wolken
Segnende Blitze
Über die Erde sät,
Küss ich den letzten
Saum seines Kleides,
Kindliche Schauer
Treu in der Brust.

Floats upwards like incense,
The lightest of vapours.

Those lords of the heavens
Avert from whole races
Their eyes that have blessed them,
And in the descendant
Are blind to the mute plea
Of once-loved features,
His forefather's face.

Thus the Three Fates sang;
The ancestor hears them,
The old man, exiled
In gloomy caverns,
And thinks of his children
And shakes his head.

20

HUMAN LIMITATIONS

When the ancient of days,
The holy father of all things,
With his hand's calm gesture,
From the rolling clouds
Scatters on the earth
A blessing of lightnings:
I kiss the uttermost
Hem of his garment,
And my faithful heart fills
With childlike awe.

Denn mit Göttern
Soll sich nicht messen
Irgend ein Mensch.
Hebt er sich aufwärts
Und berührt
Mit dem Scheitel die Sterne,
Nirgends haften dann
Die unsichern Sohlen,
Und mit ihm spielen
Wolken und Winde.

Steht er mit festen,
Markigen Knochen
Auf der wohlgegründeten
Dauernden Erde,
Reicht er nicht auf,
Nur mit der Eiche
Oder der Rebe
Sich zu vergleichen.

Was unterscheidet
Götter von Menschen?
Daß viele Wellen
Vor jenen wandeln,
Ein ewiger Strom:
Uns hebt die Welle,
Verschlingt die Welle,
Und wir versinken.

Ein kleiner Ring
Begrenzt unser Leben,
Und viele Geschlechter
Reihen sich dauernd
An ihres Daseins
Unendliche Kette.

For let no man ever
Measure his strength
Against that of the gods.
If he reaches up
And raises his head
To touch the stars,
Then his unsure feet
Will have no foothold,
And he will be the plaything
Of clouds and winds.

If he stands fast
With firm bone and marrow
On the well-established
Lasting earth,
Then what is his stature
That even to the oak-tree
Or to the vine
He should compare it?

Between gods and mankind
This is the difference:
That before them many
A wave moves onwards,
An unending stream:
But us the wave tosses,
Us the wave swallows,
And we sink and perish.

In a little ring
Our life is rounded:
And many generations
Succeed each other
On the eternal chain
Of their existence.

DAS GÖTTLICHE

Edel sei der Mensch
Hilfreich und gut!
Denn das allein
Unterscheidet ihn
Von allen Wesen,
Die wir kennen.

Heil den unbekannten
Höhern Wesen,
Die wir ahnen!
Ihnen gleiche der Mensch;
Sein Beispiel lehr uns
Jene glauben.

Denn unfühlend
Ist die Natur:
Es leuchtet die Sonne
Über Bös' und Gute,
Und dem Verbrecher
Glänzen wie dem Besten
Der Mond und die Sterne.

Wind und Ströme,
Donner und Hagel
Rauschen ihren Weg
Und ergreifen
Vorüber eilend
Einen um den andern.

DIVINITY

Let man be noble,
Generous and good:
For that alone
Distinguishes him
From all the living
Beings we know.

Hail to the unknown
Higher beings
Of our intuition!
Let man resemble them;
Let his example
Teach us to believe in them.

For the realm of nature
Is unfeeling:
The sun sheds its light
Over evil and good
And the moon and the stars
Shine on the criminal
As on the best of us.

The wind and the rivers
The hail and the thunder
Storm on their way
And snatch one victim
After another
As they rush past.

Auch so das Glück
Tappt unter die Menge,
Faßt bald des Knaben
Lockige Unschuld,
Bald auch den kahlen
Schuldigen Scheitel.

Nach ewigen, ehrnen,
Großen Gesetzen
Müssen wir alle
Unseres Daseins
Kreise vollenden.

Nur allein der Mensch
Vermag das Unmögliche:
Er unterscheidet,
Wählet und richtet;
Er kann dem Augenblick
Dauer verleihen.

Er allein darf
Den Guten lohnen,
Den Bösen strafen,
Heilen und retten,
Alles Irrende, Schweifende
Nützlich verbinden.

Und wir verehren
Die Unsterblichen,
Als wären sie Menschen,
Täten im Großen,
Was der Beste im Kleinen
Tut oder möchte.

So too does blind fortune
Grope through the crowd, now
Seizing a young boy's
Curly-haired innocence
And now the bald pate
Of the old and guilty.

As great, everlasting,
Adamantine laws
Dictate, we must all
Complete the cycles
Of our existence.

Only mankind
Can do the impossible:
He can distinguish,
He chooses and judges,
He can give permanence
To the moment.

He alone may
Reward the good
And punish the wicked;
He may heal and save
And usefully bind
All that strays and wanders.

And we revere
The immortals, as if
They were human beings
Who do on a great scale
What little the best of us
Does or endeavours.

1783

Der edle Mensch
Sei hilfreich und gut!
Unermüdet schaff er
Das Nützliche, Rechte,
Sei uns ein Vorbild
Jener geahneten Wesen!

22

Kennst du das Land, wo die Zitronen blühn,
Im dunkeln Laub die Gold-Orangen glühn,
Ein sanfter Wind vom blauen Himmel weht,
Die Myrte still und hoch der Lorbeer steht,
Kennst du es wohl?
 Dahin! Dahin
Möcht ich mit dir, o mein Geliebter, ziehn.

Kennst du das Haus? Auf Säulen ruht sein Dach,
Es glänzt der Saal, es schimmert das Gemach,
Und Marmorbilder stehn und sehn mich an:
Was hat man dir, du armes Kind, getan?
Kennst du es wohl?
 Dahin! Dahin
Möcht ich mit dir, o mein Beschützer, ziehn.

Kennst du den Berg und seinen Wolkensteg?
Das Maultier sucht im Nebel seinen Weg,
In Höhlen wohnt der Drachen alte Brut,
Es stürzt der Fels und über ihn die Flut;
Kennst du ihn wohl?
 Dahin! Dahin
Geht unser Weg! o Vater, laß uns ziehn!

Let the noble man
Be generous and good,
Tirelessly achieving
What is just and useful:
Let him be a model
For those beings whom he surmises.

22

Oh have you seen that land where lemons grow,
Where golden oranges through dark leaves glow,
Where gentle breezes stir in the blue sky,
Myrtle and baytree stand so still, so high?
Oh do you know it,
 Do you know?
There, there, beloved, you and I must go!

Oh do you know the house, the shining hall,
The gleaming room, the pillars straight and tall,
Where marble figures gaze at me all day:
What have they done to you, poor child? they say.
Oh have you seen them,
 Do you know?
There, my protector, you and I must go!

And do you know the mountain-pass, the road
Where mules must pick their way through mist and cloud,
The caves where dragons breed their ancient race,
The torrent crashing down the sheer cliff-face?
Oh do you know it,
 Do you know?
There is our land! Oh father, let us go!

23

Nur wer die Sehnsucht kennt,
Weiß, was ich leide!
Allein und abgetrennt
Von aller Freude,
Seh ich ans Firmament
Nach jener Seite.
Ach! der mich liebt und kennt,
Ist in der Weite.
Es schwindelt mir, es brennt
Mein Eingeweide.
Nur wer die Sehnsucht kennt,
Weiß, was ich leide!

24

Wer nie sein Brot mit Tränen aß,
Wer nie die kummervollen Nächte
Auf seinem Bette weinend saß,
Der kennt euch nicht, ihr himmlischen Mächte.

Ihr führt ins Leben uns hinein,
Ihr laßt den Armen schuldig werden,
Dann überlaßt ihr ihn der Pein:
Denn alle Schuld rächt sich auf Erden.

23

Only the lonely heart
Can feel my anguish!
Far away, far apart,
Joyless I languish,
Into the firmament
Gazing the way he went.
Where is my love, my friend?
He knows my anguish!
I faint, I swoon, oh what
Pain in me burns so hot!
Only the lonely heart
Knows how I languish!

24

Who never wept to eat his bread,
Who never sat through grievous hours
Of night in tears upon his bed,
He knows you not, you higher powers.

You lead us into life, to stray
Into our destined guilt, and then
Leave us to suffer and to pay
The debt all guilt exacts from mortal men.

ANAKREONS GRAB

Wo die Rose hier blüht, wo Reben um Lorbeer sich schlingen,
 Wo das Turtelchen lockt, wo sich das Grillchen ergetzt,
Welch ein Grab ist hier, das alle Götter mit Leben
 Schön bepflanzt und geziert? Es ist Anakreons Ruh.
Frühling, Sommer und Herbst genoß der glückliche Dichter;
 Vor dem Winter hat ihn endlich der Hügel geschützt.

ANACREON'S GRAVE

Here where the roses bloom, where laurel and vines intermingle,
 Turtle-doves call for their mates, crickets are chirping for joy:
Whose is this grave, this place all the gods have adorned like a garden
 With the beauty of life? It is Anacreon's rest.
Spring and summer and autumn, the lucky poet enjoyed them;
 Now from the winter at last under this mound he lies safe.

II

CLASSICAL AND MIDDLE YEARS

1786–1810

[II]

Saget, Steine, mir an, o sprecht, ihr hohen Paläste!
 Straßen, redet ein Wort! Genius, regst du dich nicht?
Ja, es ist alles beseelt in deinen heiligen Mauern,
 Ewige Roma; nur mir schweiget noch alles so still.
O wer flüstert mir zu, an welchem Fenster erblick ich
 Einst das holde Geschöpf, das mich versengend erquickt?
Ahn ich die Wege noch nicht, durch die ich immer und immer,
 Zu ihr und von ihr zu gehn, opfre die köstliche Zeit?
Noch betracht ich Kirch und Palast, Ruinen und Säulen,
 Wie ein bedächtiger Mann schicklich die Reise benutzt.
Doch bald ist es vorbei; dann wird ein einziger Tempel,
 Amors Tempel, nur sein, der den Geweihten empfängt.
Eine Welt zwar bist du, o Rom; doch ohne die Liebe
 Wäre die Welt nicht die Welt, wäre denn Rom auch nicht Rom.

[III]

Mehr als ich ahndete schön, das Glück, es ist mir geworden;
 Amor führte mich klug allen Palästen vorbei.
Ihm ist es lange bekannt, auch hab ich es selbst wohl erfahren,
 Was ein goldnes Gemach hinter Tapeten verbirgt.
Nennet blind ihn und Knaben und ungezogen, ich kenne,
 Kluger Amor, dich wohl, nimmer bestechlicher Gott!

[II]

Speak to me, stones, oh say, you lofty palaces, tell me –
 Streets, are you lost for a word? Genius, how idly you sleep!
Yes – though within your sacred walls, oh perennial city,
 All is alive and astir, still all is silent for me.
Who shall whisper the secret, and where one day at a window
 Shall I first see her, when first burn with love's life-giving fire?
Oh, those well-trodden paths that will lead me to her and from her,
 Squandering my hours away – can I not guess at them yet?
Still I am gazing at churches and palaces, ruins and columns,
 Carefully seeing the sights, as a good traveller should.
But all this will be over soon, and the city a temple –
 Love's great temple, and I'll be its initiate then.
Rome, though you are a whole world, yet a world without love would
 be no world,
 And if there were no love, Rome would not even be Rome.

27

[III]

More than I ever had hoped, what happiness I have been granted!
 Love led me wisely through Rome, passing its palaces by.
He has long known, and I myself have learnt it the hard way,
 What the fine tapestries hide in all those bedrooms of gold.
Call Eros blind if you like, and a boy, and wanton: I know him
 And his sagacity well, this incorruptible god.

from the ROMAN ELEGIES, 1788–90 65

Uns verführten sie nicht, die majestätschen Fassaden,
 Nicht der galante Balkon, weder das ernste Kortil.
Eilig ging es vorbei, und niedre zierliche Pforte
 Nahm den Führer zugleich, nahm den Verlangenden auf.
Alles verschafft er mir da, hilft alles und alles erhalten,
 Streuet jeglichen Tag frischere Rosen mir auf.
Hab ich den Himmel nicht hier? – Was gibst du, schöne Borghese,
 Nipotina, was gibst deinem Geliebten du mehr?
Tafel, Gesellschaft und Kors' und Spiel und Oper und Bälle,
 Amorn rauben sie nur oft die gelegenste Zeit.
Ekel bleibt mir Gezier und Putz, und hebet am Ende
 Sich ein brokatener Rock nicht wie ein wollener auf?
Oder will sie bequem den Freund im Busen verbergen,
 Wünscht er von alle dem Schmuck nicht schon behend sie befreit?
Müssen nicht jene Juwelen und Spitzen, Polster und Fischbein
 Alle zusammen herab, eh er die Liebliche fühlt?
Näher haben wir das! Schon fallt dein wollenes Kleidchen,
 So wie der Freund es gelöst, faltig zum Boden hinab.
Eilig trägt er das Kind, in leichter linnener Hülle,
 Wie es der Amme geziemt, scherzend aufs Lager hinan.
Ohne das seidne Gehäng und ohne gestickte Matratzen,
 Stehet es, zweien bequem, frei in dem weiten Gemach.
Nehme dann Jupiter mehr von seiner Juno, es lasse
 Wohler sich, wenn er es kann, irgend ein Sterblicher sein.
Uns ergötzen die Freuden des echten nacketen Amors
 Und des geschaukelten Betts lieblicher knarrender Ton.

Those majestic façades could not tempt us aside, nor the solemn
 Courtyards, the balconies well suited to nights of romance.
On we pressed, till at last a door both humble and charming
 Willingly welcomed the guide, welcomed the suppliant in.
Here there is nothing I lack, for he is a constant provider;
 Fresh are the roses that Love scatters each day on my path.
Is this not heaven itself? What more, fair Princess Borghese,
 Fair Nipotina, can you give for your lover's delight?
Dinners and parties, walks or drives down the Corso, or card-games,
 Operas, dances – they waste so much good love-making time!
I have grown sick of adornments and finery: are not, when all's done,
 Skirts of brocade and of wool equally easy to lift?
How can a woman embrace her lover in comfort unless she
 First, at his eager behest, sheds all her dainty array?
Will he not want those jewels and laces, that whalebone and quilted
 Satin discarded at once, freeing her for his caress?
We make short work of all that! – In a trice I unfasten this simple
 Woollen dress, and it drops, slips in its folds to the floor.
Quickly, cajolingly, like a good nurse, I carry my darling –
 Only a light linen shift covers her now – to the bed.
Here are no curtains of silk, no embroidered mattresses; freely
 In the wide bedroom it stands, ample in width to take two.
Now not Jupiter's pleasure in Juno's embraces is greater,
 And no mortal's content vies, I will wager, with mine!
Ours is the true, the authentic, the naked Love; and beneath us,
 Rocking in rhythm, the bed creaks the dear song of our joy.

from the ROMAN ELEGIES, 1788–90

[VII]

Froh empfind ich mich nun auf klassischem Boden begeistert;
 Vor- und Mitwelt spricht lauter und reizender mir.
Hier befolg ich den Rat, durchblättre die Werke der Alten
 Mit geschäftiger Hand, täglich mit neuem Genuß.
Aber die Nächte hindurch hält Amor mich anders beschäftigt;
 Werd ich auch halb nur gelehrt, bin ich doch doppelt beglückt.
Und belehr ich mich nicht, indem ich des lieblichen Busens
 Formen spähe, die Hand leite die Hüften hinab?
Dann versteh ich den Marmor erst recht; ich denk und vergleiche,
 Sehe mit fühlendem Aug, fühle mit sehender Hand.
Raubt die Liebste denn gleich mir einige Stunden des Tages,
 Gibt sie Stunden der Nacht mir zur Entschädigung hin.
Wird doch nicht immer geküßt, es wird vernünftig gesprochen;
 Überfallt sie der Schlaf, lieg ich und denke mir viel.
Oftmals hab ich auch schon in ihren Armen gedichtet
 Und des Hexameters Maß leise mit fingernder Hand
Ihr auf den Rücken gezählt. Sie atmet in lieblichem Schlummer,
 Und es durchglühet ihr Hauch mir bis ins Tiefste die Brust.
Amor schüret die Lamp indes und denket der Zeiten,
 Da er den nämlichen Dienst seinen Triumvirn getan.

[VII]

Now on classical soil I stand, inspired and elated:
 Past and present speak plain, charm me as never before.
Here I follow the counsels and busily thumb through the writings
 Of the ancients, and each day with increasing delight.
But at the love-god's behest, by night my business is different;
 Half of my scholarship's lost, yet I have double the fun.
And is not this education, to study the shape of her lovely
 Breasts, and down over her hip slide my adventuring hand?
Marble comes doubly alive for me then, as I ponder, comparing
 Seeing with vision that feels, feeling with fingers that see.
What if my darling deprive me of some few hours of daytime?
 Hours of night as a rich recompense she can bestow.
Though we spend some of them kissing, we spend others sensibly talking,
 And when she sinks into sleep, wakeful and thoughtful I lie.
Often I even compose my poetry in her embraces,
 Counting hexameter beats, tapping them out on her back
Softly, with one hand's fingers. She sweetly breathes in her slumber,
 Warmly the glow of her breath pierces the depths of my heart.
Eros recalls, as he tends our lamp, how he did the same service
 For his Triumvirs, the three poets of Love, long ago.

[xv]

Amor bleibet ein Schalk, und wer ihm vertraut, ist betrogen!
 Heuchelnd kam er zu mir: 'Diesmal nur traue mir noch.
Redlich mein ichs mit dir: du hast dein Leben und Dichten,
 Dankbar erkenn ich es wohl, meiner Verehrung geweiht.
Siehe, dir bin ich nun gar nach Rom gefolget; ich möchte
 Dir im fremden Gebiet gern was Gefälliges tun.
Jeder Reisende klagt, er finde schlechte Bewirtung;
 Welchen Amor empfiehlt, köstlich bewirtet ist er.
Du betrachtest mit Staunen die Trümmern alter Gebäude
 Und durchwandelst mit Sinn diesen geheiligten Raum.
Du verehrest noch mehr die werten Reste des Bildens
 Einziger Künstler, die stets ich in der Werkstatt besucht.
Diese Gestalten, ich formte sie selbst! Verzeih mir, ich prahle
 Diesmal nicht; du gestehst, was ich dir sage, sei wahr.
Nun du mir lässiger dienst, wo sind die schönen Gestalten,
 Wo die Farben, der Glanz deiner Erfindungen hin?
Denkst du nun wieder zu bilden, o Freund? Die Schule der Griechen
 Blieb noch offen, das Tor schlossen die Jahre nicht zu.
Ich, der Lehrer, bin ewig jung, und liebe die Jungen.
 Altklug lieb ich dich nicht! Munter! Begreife mich wohl!
War das Antike doch neu, da jene Glücklichen lebten!
 Lebe glücklich, und so lebe die Vorzeit in dir!
Stoff zum Liede, wo nimmst du ihn her? Ich muß dir ihn geben,
 Und den höheren Stil lehret die Liebe dich nur.'

Also sprach der Sophist. Wer widerspräch ihm? und leider
 Bin ich zu folgen gewöhnt, wenn der Gebieter befiehlt. –
Nun, verräterisch hält er sein Wort, gibt Stoff zu Gesängen,
 Ach! und raubt mir die Zeit, Kraft und Besinnung zugleich;

Eros was ever a rogue, and his promises fool the unwary.
 Subtly dissembling he came: 'Trust me just this once!' he said,
'I mean well by you – you have devoted your life and your writings
 To my service and fame, and this I gratefully note.
Now, having followed you even to Rome, as you see, in this foreign
 Country I should, in some way, like to do you a good turn.
Travellers always complain they are not treated as a guest should be;
 But they get all they could wish when they are sponsored by Love.
Here you stare with amazement at ancient buildings in ruins,
 And in this sacred place thoughtful and curious you roam;
Even more you revere the noble fragments of certain
 Rare creators, whom I often would visit at work –
For it was I who shaped and created for them! Forgive me,
 This is no idle boast; you must acknowledge its truth.
Since you became more lax in my service, have not your inventions
 Lost all their colour and form, lustre and beauty? My friend,
Would you now practise your art once more? The school of the Greeks is
 Open as ever; the years pass, yet its doors never closed.
I, the teacher, can never grow old; I love all who are youthful –
 Lively of heart, young in mind! be so, and mark my words well:
When they lived and enjoyed, it was new, that world you call ancient:
 Now, by enjoying your life, make the past live on in you!
Where shall you find a theme for your songs? It is Love who provides it,
 And in the loftier style there's no tuition like mine.'

Thus this sophist addressed me; and who should gainsay him? Alas, I
 Only too gladly obey when I receive his commands.
Well, he is true to his word, yet false! I have matter for poems;
 But where, alas, is my time, where are my senses and strength?

from the ROMAN ELEGIES, 1788–90 71

Blick und Händedruck, und Küsse, gemütliche Worte,
 Silben köstlichen Sinns wechselt ein liebendes Paar.
Da wird Lispeln Geschwätz, wird Stottern liebliche Rede:
 Solch ein Hymnus verhallt ohne prosodisches Maß.
Dich, Aurora, wie kannt ich dich sonst als Freundin der Musen!
 Hat, Aurora, dich auch Amor, der lose, verführt?
Du erscheinest mir nun als seine Freundin, und weckest
 Mich an seinem Altar wieder zum festlichen Tag.
Find ich die Fülle der Locken an meinem Busen! Das Köpfchen
 Ruhet und drücket den Arm, der sich dem Halse bequemt.
Welch ein freudig Erwachen! Erhieltet ihr ruhige Stunden
 Mir das Denkmal der Lust, die in den Schlaf uns gewiegt? –
Sie bewegt sich im Schlummer und sinkt auf die Breite des Lagers,
 Weggewendet; und doch läßt sie mir Hand noch in Hand.
Herzliche Liebe verbindet uns stets und treues Verlangen,
 Und den Wechsel behielt nur die Begierde sich vor.
Einen Druck der Hand, ich sehe die himmlischen Augen
 Wieder offen. – O nein! laßt auf der Bildung mich ruhn!
Bleibt geschlossen! ihr macht mich verwirrt und trunken, ihr raubet
 Mir den stillen Genuß reiner Betrachtung zu früh.
Diese Formen, wie groß! wie edel gewendet die Glieder!
 Schlief Ariadne so schön: Theseus, du konntest entfliehn?
Diesen Lippen ein einziger Kuß! O Theseus, nun scheide!
 Blick ihr ins Auge! Sie wacht! – Ewig nun hält sie dich fest.

Now two lovers, with pressure of hands, with glances and kisses,
 Murmur in tender exchange syllables precious to hear.
Lisping and stammering turn into talk, into sweetest of converse –
 Rhapsodies, hymns of a kind, but not the kind you can scan.
Goddess of Dawn, hitherto I have known you as 'friend of the Muses'!
 Have Love's blandishing wiles won the dawn-goddess as well?
Now you come to my window as his paramour, and I waken
 Here at his altar again, greeting the splendour of day.
Over my breast her locks fall full and abundant; her head droops
 Heavy, her neck fits snug on my encircling arm.
Here's an awakening indeed! Have these quiet hours preserved you,
 Has your memorial been raised, pleasure that rocked us to sleep?
In her slumber she moves and turns away from me, sinks down
 On the wide bed, but her hand still she leaves lying in mine.
Tenderest love is the bond between us, and faithfullest longing;
 Only our mutual desire varies, as appetites do.
If I so much as press on her hand, I shall see her enchanting
 Eyes reopen – ah no! let me still study her shape!
Eyes, stay closed! you make me confused and drunken, too soon you
 Bring to an end this pure, quiet, contemplative joy.
Look, how splendid these forms, how nobly moulded her limbs are!
 Did Ariadne sleep so? Theseus, oh how could you leave?
Only one kiss on those lovely lips – flee, Theseus! she wakes! Now
 You are her captive – her gaze holds you for ever in thrall.

[XVII]

Zwei gefährliche Schlangen, vom Chore der Dichter gescholten,
 Grausend nennt sie die Welt Jahre die tausende schon,
Python, dich, und dich, Lernäischer Drache! Doch seid ihr
 Durch die rüstige Hand tätiger Götter gefällt.
Ihr zerstöret nicht mehr mit feurigem Atem und Geifer
 Herde, Wiesen und Wald, goldene Saaten nicht mehr.
Doch welch ein feindlicher Gott hat uns im Zorne die neue
 Ungeheure Geburt giftigen Schlammes gesandt?
Überall schleicht er sich ein, und in den lieblichsten Gärtchen
 Lauert tückisch der Wurm, packt den Genießenden an.
Sei mir, hesperischer Drache, gegrüßt, du zeigtest dich mutig,
 Du verteidigtest kühn goldener Äpfel Besitz!
Aber dieser verteidiget nichts – und wo er sich findet,
 Sind die Gärten, die Frucht keiner Verteidigung wert.
Heimlich krümmet er sich im Busche, besudelt die Quellen,
 Geifert, wandelt in Gift Amors belebenden Tau.
O! wie glücklich warst du, Lucrez! du konntest der Liebe
 Ganz entsagen und dich jeglichem Körper vertraun.
Selig warst du, Properz! dir holte der Sklave die Dirnen
 Vom Aventinus herab, aus dem Tarpeischen Hain.
Und wenn Cynthia dich aus jenen Umarmungen schreckte,
 Untreu fand sie dich zwar; aber sie fand dich gesund.
Jetzt wer hütet sich nicht, langweilige Treue zu brechen!
 Wen die Liebe nicht halt, hält die Besorglichkeit auf.
Und auch da, wer weiß! gewagt ist jegliche Freude,
 Nirgend legt man das Haupt ruhig dem Weib in den Schoß.
Sicher ist nicht das Ehbett mehr, nicht sicher der Ehbruch;
 Gatte, Gattin und Freund, eins ist im andern verletzt.

30

[XVII]

You were two perilous serpents, reviled with one voice by the poets,
 And for long ages the world shuddered on hearing your names:
Python, and you, Lernaean Hydra! But luckily you're both
 Dead, struck down by the strong hands of adventuresome gods.
Now your fiery breath and your venomous spittle no longer
 Blast our forests and flocks, blight our rich acres of corn.
But, alas! what god in his fury and malice has sent us
 This new monster, this plague born of the poisonous mire?
Nowhere is safe from its creeping intrusion, it lurks in the loveliest
 Gardens, this treacherous worm strikes in the act of our joy!
Hail, Hesperian dragon! at least you bravely and fiercely
 Guarded those apples of gold, out in the uttermost west.
But this creature has nothing to guard, for gardens where he hides,
 And any fruit he has touched, they're not worth guarding at all.
Secretly there in the bushes he squirms, befouling the waters,
 Slavering poison and death into Love's life-giving dew.
Happy Lucretius! you could renounce romantic attachment,
 And without cause for alarm clasp any body you chose.
Slaves brought you your consenting bedmates, lucky Propertius,
 Down from the Aventine Hill, out of the Tarpeian Grove;
And if Cynthia caught you with one, then though you had wronged her
 By being faithless, at least nothing was wrong with your health.
Who does not hesitate now to break faith with a tedious mistress?
 Love may not hold us, but sheer caution will make us think twice.
Even at home, who knows! Not a single pleasure is risk-free;
 Who in his own wife's lap now lays a confident head?
Neither in wedlock now nor in bedlock can we be certain;
 Mutually noxious we are, husband and lover and wife.

O! der goldenen Zeit! da Jupiter noch, vom Olympus,
 Sich zu Semele bald, bald zu Kallisto begab.
Ihm lag selber daran, die Schwelle des heiligen Tempels
 Rein zu finden, den er liebend und mächtig betrat.
O! wie hätte Juno getobt, wenn im Streite der Liebe
 Gegen sie der Gemahl giftige Waffen gekehrt.
Doch wir sind nicht so ganz, wir alte Heiden, verlassen,
 Immer schwebet ein Gott über der Erde noch hin,
Eilig und geschäftig, ihr kennt ihn alle, verehrt ihn!
 Ihn den Boten des Zeus, Hermes, den heilenden Gott.
Fielen des Vaters Tempel zu Grund, bezeichnen die Säulen
 Paarweis kaum noch den Platz alter verehrender Pracht,
Wird des Sohnes Tempel doch stehn und ewige Zeiten
 Wechselt der Bittende stets dort mit dem Dankenden ab.
Eins nur fleh ich im stillen, an euch ihr Grazien wend ich
 Dieses heiße Gebet tief aus dem Busen herauf:
Schützet immer mein kleines, mein artiges Gärtchen, entfernet
 Jegliches Übel von mir; reichet mir Amor die Hand,
O! so gebet mir stets, sobald ich dem Schelmen vertraue,
 Ohne Sorgen und Furcht, ohne Gefahr den Genuß.

31

[XVIII]

Cäsarn wär ich wohl nie zu fernen Britannen gefolget,
 Florus hätte mich leicht in die Popine geschleppt!
Denn mir bleiben weit mehr die Nebel des traurigen Nordens,
 Als ein geschäftiges Volk südlicher Flöhe verhaßt.
Und noch schöner von heut an seid mir gegrüßet, ihr Schenken,
 Osterien, wie euch schicklich der Römer benennt;

Oh for that golden age, when Jove would descend from Olympus,
 Visiting Semele's place, paying Callisto a call!
He himself, in that sacred temple, required a clean welcome
 When he came to its door, entering in amorous might.
What a great fuss would Juno have made, if she'd found that with
 poisoned
 Weapons her husband fought, back in the conjugal bed! –
But we old heathen sinners are not completely abandoned;
 We can still call on one god – he hovers over the earth,
Busy and swift: you all know his name, so pay him due homage!
 He, Jove's messenger-boy, Mercury – he knows the cure.
Though his father's great temples have fallen, with pairs of old columns
 Scarcely still marking the place of the majestic old cult,
Yet young Mercury's temple will stand, and his suppliants enter
 Still, while others depart gratefully, world without end.
One petition to you, oh Graces, I offer in private!
 Grant this one fervent request, made from the depths of my heart:
Always protect the neat little garden I cherish, and always
 Fend off diseases from me; when I'm invited by Love
And when I trust myself to him, that rogue, may my pleasure be ever
 Carefree, and never with fear, never with danger be mixed!

31

[XVIII]

Caesar would hardly have got me to travel to far-away Britain;
 Florus's taverns in Rome would have been more to my taste.
If one must choose between mists of the dismal north and a host of
 Hard-working southern fleas, give me the fleas any day!
And I have now even greater cause to salute and to praise you,
 Osterie – as inns here are so fittingly called:

Denn ihr zeigtet mir heute die Liebste, begleitet vom Oheim,
 Den die Gute so oft, mich zu besitzen, betrügt.
Hier stand unser Tisch, den Deutsche vertraulich umgaben;
 Drüben suchte das Kind neben der Mutter den Platz,
Rückte vielmals die Bank und wußt es artig zu machen,
 Daß ich halb ihr Gesicht, völlig den Nacken gewann.
Lauter sprach sie, als hier die Römerin pfleget, kredenzte,
 Blickte gewendet nach mir, goß und verfehlte das Glas.
Wein floß über den Tisch, und sie, mit zierlichem Finger,
 Zog auf dem hölzernen Blatt Kreise der Feuchtigkeit hin.
Meinen Namen verschlang sie dem ihrigen; immer begierig
 Schaut ich dem Fingerchen nach, und sie bemerkte mich wohl.
Endlich zog sie behende das Zeichen der römischen Fünfe
 Und ein Strichlein davor. Schnell, und sobald ichs gesehn,
Schlang sie Kreise durch Kreise, die Lettern und Ziffern zu löschen;
 Aber die köstliche *Vier* blieb mir ins Auge geprägt.
Stumm war ich sitzen geblieben, und biß die glühende Lippe,
 Halb aus Schalkheit und Lust, halb aus Begierde, mir wund.
Erst noch so lange bis Nacht! dann noch vier Stunden zu warten!
 Hohe Sonne, du weilst, und du beschauest dein Rom!
Größeres sahest du nichts und wirst nichts Größeres sehen,
 Wie es dein Priester Horaz in der Entzückung versprach.
Aber heute verweile mir nicht, und wende die Blicke
 Von dem Siebengebirg fruher und williger ab!
Einem Dichter zuliebe verkürze die herrlichen Stunden,
 Die mit begierigem Blick selig der Maler genießt;
Glühend blicke noch schnell zu diesen hohen Fassaden,
 Kuppeln und Säulen zuletzt und Obelisken herauf;
Stürze dich eilig ins Meer, um morgen früher zu sehen,
 Was Jahrhunderte schon göttliche Lust dir gewährt:
Diese feuchten, mit Rohr so lange bewachsnen Gestade,
 Diese mit Bäumen und Busch düster beschatteten Höhn.
Wenig Hütten zeigten sie erst; dann sahst du auf einmal

For my darling today came to one of you, brought by her uncle,
 Whom so often she tricks when she finds ways to meet me.
Here was our table, with its familiar circle of Germans;
 And at a table near by, next to her mother, she sat.
Clever girl! she shifted the bench and so rearranged things
 That I could half see her face, and her whole neck was in view.
Raising her voice rather high for a Roman girl, she did the honours,
 Gave me a sidelong look, poured the wine, missing her glass.
Over the table it spilled, and with dainty finger she doodled –
 There, on the wet wooden page, circles of moisture she traced.
My name she mingled with hers; I eagerly followed her finger,
 Watching its every stroke, and she well knew that I did.
Quickly at last she inscribed a Roman 'five', with an upright
 'One' in front of it – then, when I had seen this, at once
With arabesque-like lines she effaced the letters and numbers,
 But left stamped on my mind's eye the delectable 'IV'.
I had sat speechless, biting my burning lip till it bled; half
 Mischievous pleasure I felt, half was aflame with desire.
Still so long until nightfall, and four more hours then of waiting!
 High sun, pausing to gaze down at your city of Rome,
Nothing you ever have seen has been greater, and nothing you will see;
 This was the truth that your priest, Horace, in rapture foretold.
Only today do not linger, consent to be brief in your survey,
 Sooner than usual to take leave of the fair Seven Hills!
Show a poet this favour, and shorten the hours of splendid
 Brightness, which painters' eyes drink so insatiably in;
Flash but a farewell glance at these lofty façades, at these columns;
 Gleam on the obelisks, gleam now on the domes, and begone!
Swiftly plunge into the sea and rise early tomorrow to hasten
 Back to this ageless sight, feast for the gaze of a god.
See, these moist river-banks that so long were covered with rushes,
 And these dark wooded hills, shadowed with bushes and trees –
Only a few huts stood there at first, then a flourishing tribe of

Sie vom wimmelnden Volk glücklicher Räuber belebt.
Alles schleppten sie drauf an diese Stätte zusammen;
 Kaum war das übrige Rund deiner Betrachtung noch wert.
Sahst eine Welt hier entstehn, sahst dann eine Welt hier in Trümmern,
 Aus den Trümmern aufs neu fast eine größere Welt!
Daß ich diese noch lange von dir beleuchtet erblicke,
 Spinne die Parze mir klug langsam den Faden herab.
Aber sie eile herbei, die schön bezeichnete Stunde! –
 Glücklich! hör ich sie schon? Nein; doch ich höre schon Drei.
So, ihr lieben Musen, betrogt ihr wieder die Länge
 Dieser Weile, die mich von der Geliebten getrennt.
Lebet wohl! Nun eil ich, und fürcht euch nicht zu beleidgen;
 Denn ihr Stolzen, ihr gebt Amorn doch immer den Rang.

32

[XXIII]

Zieret Stärke den Mann und freies mutiges Wesen,
 Oh! so ziemet ihm fast tiefes Geheimnis noch mehr.
Städtebezwingerin du, Verschwiegenheit! Fürstin der Völker!
 Teure Göttin, die mich sicher durchs Leben gefuhrt,
Welches Schicksal erfahr ich! Es löset scherzend die Muse,
 Amor löset, der Schalk, mir den verschlossenen Mund.
Ach, schon wird es so schwer, der Könige Schande verbergen!
 Weder die Krone bedeckt, weder ein phrygischer Bund
Midas' verlängertes Ohr; der nächste Diener entdeckt es,
 Und ihm ängstet und drückt gleich das Geheimnis die Brust.
In die Erde vergrüb er es gern, um sich zu erleichtern:
 Doch die Erde verwahrt solche Geheimnisse nicht;
Rohre sprießen hervor und rauschen und lispeln im Winde:
 Midas! Midas, der Fürst, trägt ein verlängertes Ohr!

Fortunate robbers arrived, peopling the place in a trice.
Here they gathered, and here their loot and wealth they assembled;
　This you observed – little else seemed to you worthy of note.
This was the birth of a world, and you saw it then perish in ruins,
　But from the ruins perhaps something still greater arose.
Oh, that I yet may for long behold this world in your radiance,
　Wisely and slow let the Fates spin out the thread of my life!
But that hour she so sweetly assigned, oh, let it come quickly!
　Does it already strike four? No; but with joy I hear three.
So, dear Muses, once more, as the tedious hours divided
　Me from my darling, how well you have beguiled them away!
Farewell now! I'll make haste to my tryst, and not fear to offend you;
　You may be proud, but you grant precedence always to Love.

32

[XXIII]

Strength, and a bold and liberal nature, are virtues a man needs;
　And even more, he must know how to keep things to himself.
Goddess Discretion! defeater of cities and ruler of peoples!
　Dear protectress, my sure guide through the perils of life,
See what a pass I am in! My lips are sealed, but the laughing
　Muse and the Love-god, that rogue, tempt me and loosen my tongue.
Ah, how hard it becomes to cover up royal disgraces!
　Midas needs more than a crown, more than a Phrygian cap
If he would hide his ass-ears. His closest servant has seen them,
　And a secret so dire heavily weighs on his mind.
He'd like to bury it deep in the earth, for that would relieve him;
　But such secrets as this even the earth will not keep.
Reeds spring up, and when the wind blows they rustle and murmur:
　'Midas, Midas the king, Midas has long pointed ears!'

from the ROMAN ELEGIES, 1788–90

Schwerer wird es nun mir, ein schönes Geheimnis zu wahren;
 Ach, den Lippen entquillt Fülle des Herzens so leicht!
Keiner Freundin darf ichs vertraun: sie möchte mich schelten;
 Keinem Freunde: vielleicht brächte der Freund mir Gefahr.
Mein Entzücken dem Hain, dem schallenden Felsen zu sagen,
 Bin ich endlich nicht jung, bin ich nicht einsam genug.
Dir, Hexameter, dir, Pentameter, sei es vertrauet,
 Wie sie des Tags mich erfreut, wie sie des Nachts mich beglückt.
Sie, von vielen Männern gesucht, vermeidet die Schlingen,
 Die ihr der Kühnere frech, heimlich der Listige legt;
Klug und zierlich schlüpft sie vorbei und kennet die Wege,
 Wo sie der Liebste gewiß lauschend begierig empfängt.
Zaudre, Luna, sie kommt! damit sie der Nachbar nicht sehe;
 Rausche, Lüftchen, im Laub! niemand vernehme den Tritt.
Und ihr, wachset und blüht, geliebte Lieder, und wieget
 Euch im leisesten Hauch lauer und liebender Luft,
Und entdeckt den Quiriten, wie jene Rohre geschwätzig,
 Eines glücklichen Paars schönes Geheimnis zuletzt.

33

[XXIV]

Hinten im Winkel des Gartens, da stand ich, der letzte der Götter,
 Rohgebildet, und schlimm hatte die Zeit mich verletzt.
Kürbisranken schmiegten sich auf am veralteten Stamme,
 Und schon krachte das Glied unter den Lasten der Frucht.
Dürres Gereisig neben mir an, dem Winter gewidmet,
 Den ich hasse, denn er schickt mir die Raben aufs Haupt,
Schändlich mich zu besudeln; der Sommer sendet die Knechte,
 Die, sich entladende, frech zeigen das rohe Gesäß.
Unflat oben und unten! ich mußte fürchten ein Unflat

Now it is growing harder for me to keep a sweet secret;
　　Ah, when the heart is so full, easily lips overflow!
Which of my friends can I tell? Not a woman, for she might reproach me;
　　Not a man either, for he might be a rival to fear.
And to confide my joy to the grove, to the rocks and their echoes –
　　That is for lonesome youth, that will not do at my age.
Listen, hexameter, listen, pentameter: you, then, shall hear it –
　　How she delights me by day, how she enchants me by night!
Many men seek her favours and try to ensnare her, the bold ones
　　Crudely, the cunning ones more subtly; but all she outwits.
Prudently, gracefully, she slips by, for she knows where her lover
　　Ardently listens and waits, knows hidden ways to his arms.
Moonlight, oh hesitate now – she is coming: no neighbour must see her!
　　Rustle the leaves, little breeze; no one must hear her approach!
And you, oh my beloved songs, may you blossom and flourish,
　　Swaying in love's warm winds, rocked by their gentlest breath;
Chatter as those reeds did, and at last tell Rome all about us:
　　Tell of two lovers whose glad secret is secret no more.

33

[XXIV]

Once in the garden's far corner I stood, the last and the least god
　　Coarsely carved, and ill-used by the rude ravage of time.
Gourd-plant tendrils entwined my perishing trunk, and already
　　My poor member had cracked under the weight of the fruit.
Broken branches lay by me, dry withered twigs for the winter;
　　How I hate winter! that's when ravens, detestable birds,
Drop all their filth on my head; and in summer the insolent gardeners
　　Squat here relieving themselves, showing their ugly backsides.
Shit from upstairs and downstairs! I feared even I would be turning

Selber zu werden, ein Schwamm, faules verlorenes Holz.
Nun, durch deine Bemühung, o! redlicher Künstler, gewinn ich
 Unter Göttern den Platz, der mir und andern gebührt.
Wer hat Jupiters Thron, den schlechterworbnen, befestigt?
 Farb und Elfenbein, Marmor und Erz und Gedicht.
Gern erblicken mich nun verständige Männer, und denken
 Mag sich jeder so gern, wie es der Künstler gedacht.
Nicht das Mädchen entsetzt sich vor mir, und nicht die Matrone,
 Häßlich bin ich nicht mehr, bin ungeheuer nur stark.
Dafür soll dir denn auch halbfußlang die prächtige Rute
 Strotzen vom Mittel herauf, wenn es die Liebste gebeut,
Soll das Glied nicht ermüden, als bis ihr die Dutzend Figuren
 Durchgenossen, wie sie künstlich Philänis erfand.

Into a spongy old turd, nothing but rotten waste wood.
Now, thanks to your good work, honest craftsman, I have been granted
 My due place among gods, fitting for me and for all.
What has kept Jove on his ill-gotten throne, and established it soundly?
 Colour and ivory, bronze, marble and poetry's art.
Now I'm a sight for intelligent men, they all like to imagine
 They themselves are as well made as the artist made me.
Girls are no longer shocked when they see me, and neither are matrons,
 For I'm not hideous now, I'm just enormously strong.
Therefore I bless your magnificent central rod, may it always
 Stand up half a foot tall at your beloved's behest.
May your member not tire, until you have both done the dozen
 Figures Philaenis describes, finished the dance of your joy.

[1]

Sarkophagen und Urnen verzierte der Heide mit Leben:
 Faunen tanzen umher, mit der Bacchantinnen Chor
Machen sie bunte Reihe; der ziegengefüßete Pausback
 Zwingt den heiseren Ton wild aus dem schmetternden Horn.
Zymbeln, Trommeln erklingen; wir sehen und hören den Marmor.
 Flatternde Vögel! wie schmeckt herrlich dem Schnabel die Frucht!
Euch verscheuchet kein Lärm, noch weniger scheucht er den Amor,
 Der in dem bunten Gewühl erst sich der Fackel erfreut.
So überwältiget Fülle den Tod; und die Asche da drinnen
 Scheint, im stillen Bezirk, noch sich des Lebens zu freun.
So umgebe denn spät den Sarkophagen des Dichters
 Diese Rolle, von ihm reichlich mit Leben geschmückt.

35

[9]

Gib mir statt 'Der Schwanz' ein ander Wort, o Priapus,
 Denn ich Deutscher, ich bin übel als Dichter geplagt.
Griechisch nenn ich dich φαλλός, das klänge doch prächtig den Ohren,
 Und lateinisch ist auch *mentula* leidlich ein Wort.
Mentula käme von *mens*, der Schwanz ist etwas von hinten,
 Und nach hinten war mir niemals ein froher Genuß.

34

[1]

Pagan burial-urns and sarcophagi, how they adorned them
　　With so much life! How they leap, Bacchants in chorus and fauns,
Alternating their dance, as the goatfooted satyr with cheeks puffed
　　Forces the harsh wild notes out of his loud braying horn!
Cymbals and drums resound; we are seeing and hearing the marble.
　　How the birds flutter, their beaks savouring wonderful fruit!
No noise startles them now, still less will the Love-god be startled
　　In this fine medley of joy where he can brandish his flame.
Thus mortality yields to abundance; the ashes within still
　　Seem, in this quiet place, to be alive and astir.
Thus, one day, may a poet's sarcophagus wear the adornment
　　Of this scroll of his words, filled with the beauty of life.

35

[9]

Give me, Priapus, another name for it! *Schwanz* is the German
　　Word, devil take it, for 'tail'; what's a poor poet to do?
Φαλλός I'd call it in Greek, that would be very fine and high-sounding;
　　And a Roman would say *mentula*; that too would serve;
It's from *mens*, I suppose, meaning 'mind'. But a *tail*'s on one's backside:
　　And backsidewise – well, that never was my kind of fun.

[16]

'Wär ich ein häusliches Weib, und hätte, was ich bedürfte,
　Treu sein wollt ich und froh, herzen und küssen den Mann.'
So sang, unter andern gemeinen Liedern, ein Dirnchen
　Mir in Venedig, und nie hört ich ein frömmer Gebet.

37

[21]

Wie von der künstlichsten Hand geschnitzt das liebe Figürchen,
　Weich und ohne Gebein, wie die Molluska nur schwimmt!
Alles ist Glied, und alles Gelenk, und alles gefallig,
　Alles nach Maßen gebaut, alles nach Willkür bewegt.
Menschen hab ich gekannt und Tiere, so Vögel als Fische,
　Manches besondre Gewürm, Wunder der großen Natur;
Und doch staun ich dich an, Bettine, liebliches Wunder,
　Die du alles zugleich bist, und ein Engel dazu.

38

[28]

Heraus mit dem Teile des Herrn! heraus mit dem Teile des Gottes!
　Rief ein unglücklich Geschöpf, blind für hysterischer Wut,
Als, die heiligen Reste Gründonnerstag Abends zu zeigen,
　In Sankt Markus ein Schelm über der Bühne sich wies.
Armes Mädchen, was soll dir ein Teil des gekreuzigten Gottes?
　Rufe den heilsamern Teil jenes von Lampsacus her.

36

[16]

'If I'd the husband I need, and if I kept house for him, I'd be
 Happy and faithful and true, hug him and kiss him all day.'
That was the song, among others more coarse, of a little Venetian
 Whore; and so pious a prayer never I heard in my life.

37

[21]

Dear little shape that might have been carved by the hand of an artist!
 Supple and boneless she seems, molluscoid, floating at ease.
All of her body is limbs, all joints, and all of it pleasing;
 All of it measured and made, all of it wilful and free.
Many the human and animal creatures, the birds and the fishes,
 Curious creeping things, wonders of nature I've known:
Yet you amaze me still, Bettina, sweet natural wonder!
 For you are all these at once, and a dear angel as well.

38

[28]

'Show us the parts of the Lord!' shrieked, blind with hysterical frenzy,
 An unfortunate girl: 'Show us the parts of our god!'
It was the evening of Holy Thursday, a priest was displaying
 (So the old charlatan claimed) relics of Christ in St Mark's.
Poor soul! Why do you cry out like this for the crucified god's parts?
 Cry for Priapus! That god's parts are the medicine you need.

39

[30]

Böcke, zur Linken mit euch! so ordnet künftig der Richter,
 Und ihr Schäfchen, ihr sollt ruhig zur Rechten mir stehn!
Wohl! Doch eines ist noch von ihm zu hoffen, dann sagt er:
 Seid, Vernünftige, mir grad gegenüber gestellt!

40

[33]

O, wie achtet ich sonst auf alle Zeiten des Jahres,
 Grüßte den kommenden Lenz, sehnte dem Herbste mich nach!
Aber nun ist nicht Sommer noch Winter, seit mich Beglückten
 Amors Fittich bedeckt, ewiger Frühling umschwebt.

41

[40]

Wonniglich ists, die Geliebte verlangend im Arme zu halten,
 Wenn ihr klopfendes Herz Liebe zuerst dir gesteht.
Wonniglicher, das Pochen des Neulebendigen fühlen,
 Das in dem lieblichen Schoß immer sich nährend bewegt.
Schon versucht es die Sprünge der raschen Jugend; es klopfet
 Ungeduldig schon an, sehnt sich nach himmlischem Licht.
Harre noch wenige Tage! Auf allen Pfaden des Lebens
 Führen die Horen dich streng, wie es das Schicksal gebeut.
Widerfahre dir, was dir auch will, du wachsender Liebling —
 Liebe bildete dich; werde dir Liebe zu teil!

39

[30]

'Goats, go and stand on my left!' so the Judge at the last day will order.
　　'And as for you, little sheep, come to my right, if you please.'
Excellent! But let us hope he will make one further announcement:
　　'Now, you men of good sense, face me, and stand straight ahead!'

40

[33]

Oh, how intently I used to observe all the year's four seasons,
　　Greeting the springtime's approach, longing for autumn to come!
Now I live neither in summer nor winter, now that the Love-god's
　　Wings caress me with joy, with a perpetual spring.

41

[40]

It is such joy to hug my beloved so close, to desire her,
　　And in her heartbeat to hear her first confession of love:
Joy still greater to feel life coming, another life pulsing
　　As it moves, as it thrives, in her dear nourishing womb!
Now already it leaps up boldly, in youthful impatience
　　Knocking and pushing its way, longing for heavenly light.
Wait for a few days longer! The Hours must strictly conduct you
　　On all the paths of your life, leading as Fate has decreed.
Let it decree for you what it will, little growing-up darling –
　　For you were fashioned by love; may you know love in your turn!

42

'Warum bin ich vergänglich, o Zeus?' So fragte die Schönheit.
 'Macht ich doch', sagte der Gott, 'nur das Vergängliche schön'.

43

Das ist die wahre Liebe, die immer und immer sich gleich bleibt,
 Wenn man ihr alles gewährt, wenn man ihr alles versagt.

44

Wem zu glauben ist, redlicher Freund, das kann ich dir sagen:
 Glaube dem Leben; es lehrt besser als Redner und Buch.

45

Immer strebe zum Ganzen, und kannst du selber kein Ganzes
 Werden, als dienendes Glied schließ an ein Ganzes dich an.

46

Gleich sei keiner dem andern; doch gleich sei jeder dem Höchsten.
 Wie das zu machen? Es sei jeder vollendet in sich.

42

'Why', asked Beauty, 'oh Zeus, must I wither and fade?' And the god said:
 'Why, I made you to adorn only what withers and fades!'

43

True love is love that stays constant for ever, whatever its fortune:
 Whether requited or scorned, filled or sent empty away.

44

Whom shall you trust, honest friend? Let me tell you, for I know the
 answer:
 Trust life itself; it knows more than any teacher or book.

45

Strive towards wholeness, and if in yourself you have failed to achieve it,
 Find something greater to serve, join in that whole as a part.

46

Let us not all be the same, but let each man resemble the highest.
 How so? Let each of us grow to the full height of himself.

Also sprachen die Männer sich unterhaltend. Die Mutter
Ging indessen, den Sohn erst vor dem Hause zu suchen,
Auf der steinernen Bank, wo sein gewöhnlicher Sitz war.
Als sie daselbst ihn nicht fand, so ging sie, im Stalle zu schauen
Ob er die herrlichen Pferde, die Hengste, selber besorgte,
Die er als Fohlen gekauft und die er niemand vertraute.
Und es sagte der Knecht: Er ist in den Garten gegangen.
Da durchschritt sie behende die langen doppelten Höfe,
Ließ die Ställe zurück und die wohlgezimmerten Scheunen,
Trat in den Garten, der weit bis an die Mauern des Städtchens
Reichte, schritt ihn hindurch, und freute sich jegliches
 Wachstums,
Stellte die Stützen zurecht, auf denen beladen die Äste
Ruhten des Apfelbaums, wie des Birnbaums lastende Zweige,
Nahm gleich einige Raupen vom kräftig strotzenden Kohl weg;
Denn ein geschäftiges Weib tut keine Schritte vergebens.
Also war sie ans Ende des langen Gartens gekommen,
Bis zur Laube mit Geisblatt bedeckt; nicht fand sie den Sohn da,
Ebensowenig als sie bis jetzt ihn im Garten erblickte.
Aber nur angelehnt war das Pförtchen, das aus der Laube,
Aus besonderer Gunst, durch die Mauer des Städtchens
 gebrochen
Hatte der Ahnherr einst, der würdige Burgemeister.
Und so ging sie bequem den trocknen Graben hinüber,
Wo an der Straße sogleich der wohlumzäunete Weinberg
Aufstieg steileren Pfads, die Fläche zur Sonne gekehret.
Auch den schritt sie hinauf, und freute der Fülle der Trauben
Sich im Steigen, die kaum sich unter den Blättern verbargen.
Schattig war und bedeckt der hohe mittlere Laubgang,
Den man auf Stufen erstieg von unbehauenen Platten.

Thus the men talked and conversed with each other. The mother went
 meanwhile
Seeking her son, and tried to find him in front of the house first,
On the stone bench where he usually sat. When she saw he was not there
She went on to the stables to look for him, thinking he might have
Come there himself to see to the splendid horses, the stallions
Which he had bought as foals and allowed no one else to look after.
And the stableman told her that he had gone into the garden.
Quickly she passed through the length of one courtyard, then of another,
Leaving the stables behind her, and leaving the well-timbered barns; then
Entered the garden, which ran right out to the walls of the small town.
Through it she walked, and was glad as she saw all the things that were
 growing;
Straightened as she went by the props that supported the burdened
Apple-tree's branches, and the well-laden boughs of the pear-tree;
Picked as she passed some grubs from the sprouting leaves of the cabbage;
For a well-occupied wife never takes a step to no purpose.
Thus she walked through the whole of the garden and came to its far end,
Came to the arbour covered with columbine; Hermann was not there,
Nor had she yet caught sight of him anywhere else in the garden.
But from the arbour a little gate led, which her family's worthy
Forebear, the burgomaster, had made by favour and privilege
Here in the little town's wall; and it now stood ajar. So she passed through,
Crossing easily over the waterless moat; and beyond this,
Close to the road, was the well-fenced vineyard, sloping up steeply,
Turning its face to the sun; and upwards through it a path went.
This she took, and was glad as she passed to see the abundant
Grapes all round her that scarcely could hide themselves under the
 vineleaves.
Roofed and shady it was, the vineyard's high middle pathway,
And there were rough-hewn slabs as steps to make climbing it easy.

Und es hingen herein Gutedel und Muskateller,
Rötlich blaue daneben von ganz besonderer Größe,
Alle mit Fleiße gepflanzt, der Gäste Nachtisch zu zieren.
Aber den übrigen Berg bedeckten einzelne Stöcke,
Kleinere Trauben tragend, von denen der köstliche Wein kommt.
Also schritt sie hinauf, sich schon des Herbstes erfreuend
Und des festlichen Tags, an dem die Gegend im Jubel
Trauben lieset und tritt, und den Most in die Fässer versammelt,
Feuerwerke des Abends von allen Orten und Enden
Leuchten und knallen, und so der Ernten schönste geehrt wird.
Doch unruhiger ging sie, nachdem sie dem Sohne gerufen
Zwei- auch dreimal, und nur das Echo vielfach zurückkam,
Das von den Türmen der Stadt, ein sehr geschwätziges, herklang.
Ihn zu suchen war ihr so fremd; er entfernte sich niemals
Weit, er sagt' es ihr denn, um zu verhüten die Sorge
Seiner liebenden Mutter und ihre Furcht vor dem Unfall.
Aber sie hoffte noch stets, ihn doch auf dem Wege zu finden;
Denn die Türen, die untre, sowie die obre, des Weinbergs
Standen gleichfalls offen. Und so nun trat sie ins Feld ein,
Das mit weiter Fläche den Rücken des Hügels bedeckte.
Immer noch wandelte sie auf eigenem Boden, und freute
Sich der eigenen Saat und des herrlich nickenden Kornes,
Das mit goldener Kraft sich im ganzen Felde bewegte.
Zwischen den Äckern schritt sie hindurch, auf dem Raine, den Fußpfad,
Hatte den Birnbaum im Auge, den großen, der auf dem Hügel
Stand, die Grenze der Felder, die ihrem Hause gehörten.
Wer ihn gepflanzt, man konnt es nicht wissen. Er war in der Gegend
Weit und breit gesehn, und berühmt die Früchte des Baumes.
Unter ihm pflegten die Schnitter des Mahls sich zu freuen am Mittag,
Und die Hirten des Viehs in seinem Schatten zu warten;
Bänke fanden sie da von rohen Steinen und Rasen.
Und sie irrte nicht; dort saß ihr Hermann und ruhte,
Saß mit dem Arme gestützt und schien in die Gegend zu schauen

Chasselas grapes and muscatel grapes hung down through the arches,
And among them the purple berries of extra-large size, all
Carefully grown to be served as dessert for guests after dinner.
But from the smaller grapes on the rows of separate vine-plants
Comes the exquisite wine, and these covered the rest of the vineyard.
Thus she walked on, and was glad already to think of the autumn
And the great festive day, with the folk from all over the district
Picking and treading the grapes, and the young wine gathered in barrels,
And the flashing and cracking of firework-displays in the evening,
Far and wide, to do honour to this, the finest of harvests.
But she grew more uneasy when two or three times she had called out
To her son and heard no reply but the multiple echo
Which from the towers of the town gave back its chattering answer.
She was not used to looking for him, for he never went far from
Her without telling her where he had gone, to prevent her from worrying
Like an affectionate mother so apprehensive of mishaps.
But she still kept on hoping that on her way she would find him,
For both the doors of the vineyard were open, the one at the bottom
And the top one as well. So now she entered the cornfields;
Many wide acres they were, and covered the whole of the hillside.
She was still walking on land that was hers, and was glad as she walked to
See her own crop of such splendid grain that nodded all round her,
Rich and golden and rippling in waves all over the corn-land.
On she walked through the separate fields, by the path on the unploughed
Border, making her way to the great pear-tree on the hill-top;
It was the boundary-mark of the land that belonged to her household.
Nobody knew who had planted it there; one could see it from far and
Wide, and the fruit of this tree was famous all over the district.
Under its shade the reapers would sit enjoying their dinner,
And the herdsman would sit there too looking after the cattle,
For there was soft grass there, and rough stone benches to rest on.
And she was not mistaken, for there her Hermann was seated,
Leaning his head on one arm, and gazing, it seemed, at the mountains

Jenseits, nach dem Gebirg, er kehrte der Mutter den Rücken.
Sachte schlich sie hinan, und rührt' ihm leise die Schulter.
Und er wandte sich schnell; da sah sie ihm Tränen im Auge.
Mutter, sagt' er betroffen, ihr überrascht mich! Und eilig
Trocknet' er ab die Träne, der Jüngling edlen Gefühles.
Wie? du weinest, mein Sohn? versetzte die Mutter betroffen:
Daran kenn ich dich nicht! ich habe das niemals erfahren!
Sag, was beklemmt dir das Herz? was treibt dich, einsam zu sitzen
Unter dem Birnbaum hier? was bringt dir Tränen ins Auge?

48

Also gingen die zwei entgegen der sinkenden Sonne,
Die in Wolken sich tief, gewitterdrohend, verhüllte,
Aus dem Schleier, bald hier bald dort, mit glühenden Blicken
Strahlend über das Feld die ahnungsvolle Beleuchtung.
Möge das drohende Wetter, so sagte Hermann, nicht etwa
Schloßen uns bringen und heftigen Guß; denn schön ist die Ernte.
Und sie freuten sich beide des hohen wankenden Kornes,
Das die Durchschreitenden fast, die hohen Gestalten, erreichte.
Und es sagte darauf das Mädchen zum leitenden Freunde:
Guter, dem ich zunächst ein freundlich Schicksal verdanke,
Dach und Fach, wenn im Freien so manchem Vertriebnen der Sturm
 dräut!
Saget mir jetzt vor allem, und lehret die Eltern mich kennen,
Denen ich künftig zu dienen von ganzer Seele geneigt bin;
Denn kennt jemand den Herrn, so kann er ihm leichter genug tun,
Wenn er die Dinge bedenkt, die jenem die wichtigsten scheinen,
Und auf die er den Sinn, den festbestimmten, gesetzt hat.
Darum saget mir doch: wie gewinn ich Vater und Mutter?

On the far side of the valley; his back was turned to his mother.
Softly she came up behind him and laid her hand on his shoulder;
Quickly he turned, and she saw he had tears in his eyes.

'Why, mother!'
He exclaimed in confusion, 'I wasn't expecting to see you.'
Quickly he dried his eyes, like a young man of sensitive feeling.
'What! are you crying?' his mother replied, confused and astonished.
'That is not like you, my son: I have never before known you do so.
Tell me, what makes you so sad? What has driven you here, to be sitting
Under the pear-tree all by yourself? and what do these tears mean?'

48

So together they walked towards the west and the sunset.
Deeply the sun was veiling its face in threatening storm-clouds,
Though it still gleamed here and there, its fiery eye was still flashing,
Glinting across the fields, as a luminous omen of thunder.
'This is dangerous weather,' said Hermann, 'I hope we shall not have
Violent rain or hail, for the harvest should be a fine one.'
And they were glad as they looked at the ripe grain nodding and
 swaying,
Almost as tall as themselves, as they walked on over the cornfields.
Then the young maiden spoke and addressed her escorting companion:
'It's to your kindness I owe the good fortune of somewhere to shelter
From this threatening storm, unlike many folk who are homeless.
Now I must ask you at once to tell me something about your
Parents, for I now truly look forward to being their servant,
And if one knows one's master, that makes it easier to please him,
For one can then take note of what he considers important
And remember the various things that he sets his whole heart on.
So will you tell me: how shall I please your father and mother?'

Und es versetzte dagegen der gute verständige Jüngling:
O, wie geb ich dir recht, du kluges treffliches Mädchen,
Daß du zuvörderst dich nach dem Sinne der Eltern befragest!
Denn so strebt ich bisher vergebens, dem Vater zu dienen,
Wenn ich der Wirtschaft mich als wie der meinigen annahm,
Früh den Acker und spät und so besorgend den Weinberg.
Meine Mutter befriedigt ich wohl, sie wußt es zu schätzen;
Und so wirst du ihr auch das trefflichste Mädchen erscheinen,
Wenn du das Haus besorgst, als wenn du das deine bedächtest.
Aber dem Vater nicht so; denn dieser liebet den Schein auch.
Gutes Mädchen, halte mich nicht für kalt und gefühllos,
Wenn ich den Vater dir sogleich, der Fremden, enthülle.
Ja, ich schwör es, das erstemal ists, daß frei mir ein solches
Wort die Zunge verläßt, die nicht zu schwatzen gewohnt ist;
Aber du lockst mir hervor aus der Brust ein jedes Vertrauen.
Einige Zierde verlangt der gute Vater im Leben,
Wünschet äußere Zeichen der Liebe, sowie der Verehrung,
Und er würde vielleicht vom schlechteren Diener befriedigt,
Der dies wüßte zu nutzen, und würde dem besseren gram sein.

Freudig sagte sie drauf, zugleich die schnelleren Schritte
Durch den dunkelnden Pfad verdoppelnd mit leichter Bewegung:
Beide zusammen hoff ich fürwahr zufrieden zu stellen;
Denn der Mutter Sinn ist wie mein eigenes Wesen,
Und der äußeren Zierde bin ich von Jugend nicht fremde.
Unsere Nachbarn, die Franken, in ihren früheren Zeiten
Hielten auf Höflichkeit viel; sie war dem Edlen und Bürger
Wie den Bauern gemein, und jeder empfahl sie den Seinen.
Und so brachten bei uns auf deutscher Seite gewöhnlich
Auch die Kinder des Morgens mit Händeküssen und Knixchen
Segenswünsche den Eltern, und hielten sittlich den Tag aus.
Alles, was ich gelernt und was ich von jung auf gewohnt bin,
Was von Herzen mir geht – ich will es dem Alten erzeigen.

And the good, intelligent boy replied to her question:
'Why, you clever and excellent girl, how sensible of you
That you enquire straight away about how to get on with my parents!
So far, I have had little success in serving my father;
I've tried hard to look after his land as if it were my land,
Working at all hours out in the fields and out in the vineyard;
Mother of course was pleased, she appreciates what I've been doing,
And that's why she will form a high opinion of you too,
If you look after the house just as well as if it were your own house;
But my father is very keen also on outward appearance.
Please, dear girl, I hope you won't think I am cold and unfeeling,
Talking so frankly at once to a stranger about my own father.
And indeed, I can swear that this is the very first time that
I've ever said such a thing, for I'm not a talkative person;
But you entice it all out of my heart, I know I can trust you.
My dear father has rather a liking for airs and for graces;
He's very fond of the outward signs of respect and affection,
And I would guess that a less good servant who knew how to show these
Would give him more satisfaction than better service without them.'

Thus he spoke, and she smiled, and with light, high-spirited movements
Quickened her pace on the darkening path as she made him her answer:
'Well, I am quite sure now I shall give them both satisfaction,
For it's clear that your mother and I have similar natures;
And from my childhood I've been accustomed to airs and to graces,
For the French were our neighbours, and they in that earlier epoch
Set much store by politeness, and not the nobility only:
Townsfolk and peasants as well, and they made their families learn it.
So we Germans were used to it too, and the children each morning
Came to wish their parents good health, and made little curtsies,
Kissing their hands, and passed the whole day in seemly behaviour.
All that I learnt as a child and have practised ever since childhood
So that it comes from my heart – all this I'll show to your father.

Aber wer sagt mir nunmehr: wie soll ich dir selber begegnen,
Dir, dem einzigen Sohn, und künftig meinem Gebieter?

Also sprach sie, und eben gelangten sie unter den Birnbaum.
Herrlich glänzte der Mond, der volle, vom Himmel herunter;
Nacht wars, völlig bedeckt das letzte Schimmern der Sonne.
Und so lagen vor ihnen in Massen gegeneinander,
Lichter, hell wie der Tag, und Schatten dunkeler Nächte;
Und es hörte die Frage, die freundliche, gern in dem Schatten
Hermann des herrlichen Baums, am Orte, der ihm so lieb war,
Der noch heute die Tränen um seine Vertriebne gesehen.
Und indem sie sich nieder ein wenig zu ruhen gesetzet,
Sagte der liebende Jüngling, die Hand des Mädchens ergreifend:
Laß dein Herz dir es sagen, und folg ihm frei nur in allem.
Aber er wagte kein weiteres Wort, so sehr auch die Stunde
Günstig war; er fürchtete, nur ein Nein zu ereilen,
Ach, und er fühlte den Ring am Finger, das schmerzliche Zeichen.
Also saßen sie still und schweigend nebeneinander;
Aber das Mädchen begann und sagte: Wie find ich des Mondes
Herrlichen Schein so süß! er ist der Klarheit des Tags gleich.
Seh ich doch dort in der Stadt die Häuser deutlich und Höfe,
An dem Giebel ein Fenster; mich deucht, ich zähle die Scheiben.

Was du siehst, versetzte darauf der gehaltene Jüngling,
Das ist unsere Wohnung, in die ich nieder dich führe,
Und dies Fenster dort ist meines Zimmers im Dache,
Das vielleicht das deine nun wird; wir verändern im Hause.
Diese Felder sind unser, sie reifen zur morgenden Ernte.
Hier im Schatten wollen wir ruhn und des Mahles genießen.
Aber laß uns nunmehr hinab durch Weinberg und Garten
Steigen; denn sieh, es rückt das schwere Gewitter herüber,
Wetterleuchtend und bald verschlingend den lieblichen Vollmond.
Und so standen sie auf und wandelten nieder, das Feld hin,

But I've been wondering now: what should my behaviour to you be,
Who as the son of the house will one day be my lord and my master?'

Thus she spoke, and at that very moment they came to the pear-tree.
Splendidly now the moon shone down from the sky in its fullness;
Night had fallen, the sun's last glow was hidden completely.
So before them lay darkness and light in masses contrasting,
Light as bright as the day, and darkening shadows of night-time.
Hermann listened with joy as she made her kindly enquiry,
Here in the shade of that splendid tree, in this place that he loved, where
Only to-day he had wept such tears for his refugee sweetheart.
So they sat down for a moment, to rest for a little, and Hermann
Said, as he lovingly seized her hand and tenderly held it:
'Your own heart will guide you in that, just do as it tells you.'
But he dared not say more, though a better moment for speaking
He'd never had; for he feared by haste to court a refusal,
And on her finger he felt the ring, that token of anguish.
So they sat there resting in silence beside one another.
Then again the girl spoke: 'How sweetly the moon here is shining!
It's so clear and so bright, you'd almost think it was daytime.
There in the town I can see the houses and courtyards distinctly;
There in that gable's a window, its panes are so clear I could count them.'

'That's our house!' said the boy, with an effort restraining his ardour;
'That's the one you can see down there; that's where we are going.
And that window up there in the gable's the window of my room,
Which perhaps will be your room now – we're making some changes.
These ripe fields are all ours; we're beginning the harvest tomorrow.
Here in the shade of this tree we'll be resting and having our dinner.
But come along now, we must go down through the vineyard and garden.
Look, the storm's drawing nearer, I think it's going to be heavy;
Lightning's flashing, and soon the clouds will have covered the full moon.'
Thus he spoke, and they rose then and walked on down through the
 cornfield,

Durch das mächtige Korn, der nächtlichen Klarheit sich freuend;
Und sie waren zum Weinberg gelangt und traten ins Dunkel.

Und so leitet' er sie die vielen Platten hinunter,
Die, unbehauen gelegt, als Stufen dienten im Laubgang.
Langsam schritt sie hinab, auf seinen Schultern die Hände;
Und mit schwankenden Lichtern, durchs Laub, überblickte der
 Mond sie,
Eh er, von Wetterwolken umhüllt, im Dunkeln das Paar ließ.
Sorglich stützte der Starke das Mädchen, das über ihn herhing;
Aber sie, unkundig des Steigs und der roheren Stufen,
Fehlte tretend, es knackte der Fuß, sie drohte zu fallen.
Eilig streckte gewandt der sinnige Jüngling den Arm aus,
Hielt empor die Geliebte; sie sank ihm leis auf die Schulter,
Brust war gesenkt an Brust und Wang an Wange. So stand er,
Starr wie ein Marmorbild, vom ernsten Willen gebändigt,
Drückte nicht fester sie an, er stemmte sich gegen die Schwere.
Und so fühlt' er die herrliche Last, die Wärme des Herzens,
Und den Balsam des Atems, an seinen Lippen verhauchet,
Trug mit Mannesgefühl die Heldengröße des Weibes.

Doch sie verhehlte den Schmerz, und sagte die scherzenden Worte:
Das bedeutet Verdruß, so sagen bedenkliche Leute,
Wenn beim Eintritt ins Haus, nicht fern von der Schwelle, der Fuß
 knackt.
Hätt ich mir doch fürwahr ein besseres Zeichen gewünschet!
Laß uns ein wenig verweilen, damit dich die Eltern nicht tadeln
Wegen der hinkenden Magd, und ein schlechter Wirt du erscheinest.

Passing the teeming grain, and glad of the radiant night-time.
So they came to the vineyard, and entered the shadowy darkness.

And he guided her down the pathway, under the arching
Vineleaves, down its numerous steps made of roughly-hewn flagstones.
Slowly she walked behind him, and braced both hands on his shoulders;
Moonlight flickered and gleamed on them, down through the foliage
 and branches,
Till it was hidden by gathering clouds, and darkness enclosed them.
Careful and strong, he supported her weight as she clung close behind him;
But there were some rough steps, and the pathway was unfamiliar,
And she stumbled, missing her foothold; just as she was falling
Hermann quickly, with presence of mind, turned round, put his arm out,
Caught his beloved and held her, and gently she sank on his shoulder;
Breast upon breast they were, cheek upon cheek. But he stood there as
 steadfast
As any marble statue, for sternly his will so commanded,
And he supported her weight, but pressed her no closer against him.
Thus his splendid burden he felt, and the warmth of her heartbeat,
And her breath was close to his lips like balmiest fragrance,
And with masculine strength he bore her magnificent stature.

But she made light of the pain, and smiled and jestingly spoke thus:
'It's an unfortunate sign (or so wise people have told me)
Stumbling and twisting one's foot just before first crossing the threshold:
I must say, I could really have done with a luckier omen!
Let's stay here for a little; what would your parents be thinking
If you brought them a limping maid, you improvident master!'

49

ZUEIGNUNG

Ihr naht euch wieder, schwankende Gestalten,
Die früh sich einst dem trüben Blick gezeigt.
Versuch ich wohl, euch diesmal festzuhalten?
Fühl ich mein Herz noch jenem Wahn geneigt?
Ihr drängt euch zu! nun gut, so mögt ihr walten,
Wie ihr aus Dunst und Nebel um mich steigt;
Mein Busen fühlt sich jugendlich erschüttert
Vom Zauberhauch, der euren Zug umwittert.

Ihr bringt mit euch die Bilder froher Tage,
Und manche liebe Schatten steigen auf;
Gleich einer alten, halbverklungnen Sage
Kommt erste Lieb und Freundschaft mit herauf;
Der Schmerz wird neu, es wiederholt die Klage
Des Lebens labyrinthisch irren Lauf
Und nennt die Guten, die, um schöne Stunden
Vom Glück getäuscht, vor mir hinweggeschwunden.

Sie hören nicht die folgenden Gesänge,
Die Seelen, denen ich die ersten sang;
Zerstoben ist das freundliche Gedränge,
Verklungen, ach! der erste Widerklang.
Mein Leid ertönt der unbekannten Menge,
Ihr Beifall selbst macht meinem Herzen bang,
Und was sich sonst an meinem Lied erfreuet,
Wenn es noch lebt, irrt in der Welt zerstreuet.

Und mich ergreift ein langst entwöhntes Sehnen
Nach jenem stillen, ernsten Geisterreich,
Es schwebet nun in unbestimmten Tönen

DEDICATION

Uncertain shapes, visitors from the past
At whom I darkly gazed so long ago,
My heart's mad fleeting visions – now at last
Shall I embrace you, must I let you go?
Again you haunt me: come then, hold me fast!
Out of the mist and murk you rise, who so
Besiege me, and with magic breath restore,
Stirring my soul, lost youth to me once more.

You bring back memories of happier days
And many a well-loved ghost again I greet;
As when some old half-faded legend plays
About our ears, sorrowing strains repeat
My journey through life's labyrinthine maze,
Old griefs revive, old friends, old loves I meet,
Those dear companions, by their fate's unkind
Decree cut short, who left me here behind.

They cannot hear my present music, those
Few souls who listened to my early song;
They are far from me now who were so close,
And their first answering echo has so long
Been silent. My lament is heard, who knows
By whom? I shudder as the nameless throng
Applauds it. Are they living still, those friends
Whom once it moved, scattered to the world's ends?

And I am seized by long unwonted yearning
For that still, solemn spirit-realm which then
Was mine; its hovering lisping tones returning

from FAUST *Part One*, 1797–1808

Mein lispelnd Lied, der Äolsharfe gleich,
Ein Schauer faßt mich, Träne folgt den Tränen,
Das strenge Herz, es fühlt sich mild und weich;
Was ich besitze, seh ich wie im Weiten,
Und was verschwand, wird mir zu Wirklichkeiten.

50

[GESANG DER ERZENGEL]

RAPHAEL Die Sonne tönt nach alter Weise
In Brudersphären Wettgesang,
Und ihre vorgeschriebne Reise
Vollendet sie mit Donnergang.
Ihr Anblick gibt den Engeln Stärke,
Wenn keiner sie ergründen mag;
Die unbegreiflich hohen Werke
Sind herrlich wie am ersten Tag.

GABRIEL Und schnell und unbegreiflich schnelle
Dreht sich umher der Erde Pracht;
Es wechselt Paradieseshelle
Mit tiefer, schauervoller Nacht;
Es schäumt das Meer in breiten Flüssen
Am tiefen Grund der Felsen auf,
Und Fels und Meer wird fortgerissen
In ewig-schnellem Sphärenlauf.

MICHAEL Und Stürme brausen um die Wette
Vom Meer aufs Land, vom Land aufs Meer,
Und bilden wütend eine Kette
Der tiefsten Wirkung ringsumher.
Da flammt ein blitzendes Verheeren

Sigh as from some Aeolian harp, as when
I sang them first; I tremble, and my burning
Tears flow, my stern heart melts to love again.
All that I now possess seems far away
And vanished worlds are real to me today.

50

[SONG OF THE ARCHANGELS]

RAPHAEL The sun proclaims its old devotion
In rival song with brother spheres
And still completes in thunderous motion
The circuits of its destined years.
Angelic powers, uncomprehending,
Are strengthened as they gaze their fill;
Thy works, unfathomed and unending,
Retain the first day's splendour still.

GABRIEL The glorious earth, with mind-appalling
Swiftness, upon itself rotates,
And with the dark night's dreadful falling
Its primal radiance alternates.
High cliffs stand deep in ocean weather,
Wide foaming waves flood out and in,
And cliffs and seas rush on together
Caught in the globe's unceasing spin.

MICHAEL And turn by turn the tempests raging
From sea to land, from land to sea,
Build up, in passion unassuaging,
Their chain of furious energy.
The thunder strikes, its flash is faster,

Dem Pfade vor des Donnerschlags;
Doch deine Boten, Herr, verehren
Das sanfte Wandeln deines Tags.

ZU DREI Der Anblick gibt den Engeln Stärke,
Da keiner dich ergründen mag,
Und alle deine hohen Werke
Sind herrlich wie am ersten Tag.

51

FAUST Vom Eise befreit sind Strom und Bäche
Durch des Frühlings holden, belebenden Blick,
Im Tale grünet Hoffnungsglück;
Der alte Winter, in seiner Schwäche,
Zog sich in rauhe Berge zurück.
Von dorther sendet er, fliehend, nur
Ohnmächtige Schauer körnigen Eises
In Streifen über die grünende Flur;
Aber die Sonne duldet kein Weißes:
Überall regt sich Bildung und Streben,
Alles will sie mit Farben beleben;
Doch an Blumen fehlts im Revier:
Sie nimmt geputzte Menschen dafür.
Kehre dich um, von diesen Höhen
Nach der Stadt zurückzusehen!
Aus dem hohlen, finstern Tor
Dringt ein buntes Gewimmel hervor.
Jeder sonnt sich heute so gern.
Sie feiern die Auferstehung des Herrn;
Denn sie sind selber auferstanden:

It spreads destruction on its way —
But we, thy messengers, O master,
Revere thy gently circling day.

ALL THREE And each of us, uncomprehending,
Is strengthened as we gaze our fill,
For all thy works, sublime, unending,
Retain their first day's splendour still.

51

FAUST Ice thaws on the river, ice melts on the streams,
They are freed again as the spring sun gleams.
The valley is green with new life, new hopes;
Old winter is beaten — see how it withdrew
To skulk up there on rough mountain-slopes!
And now in its weakness all it can do
Is to scatter hail in impotent showers
Over the meadows as they turn green.
But the sun will allow no white to be seen:
It calls for colours as the earth revives,
As everything grows and stirs and strives;
And the countryside is still short of flowers,
So the people instead, dressed up so fine,
Are lured out into the sweet sunshine.
Look back at the town from where we stand,
Look down at its hollow, gloomy gate,
Where the glad throng pours out over the land!
They have something today to celebrate,
For the Lord's resurrection is theirs as well:
Today they have risen and been set free

from FAUST *Part One*, 1797–1808

Aus niedriger Häuser dumpfen Gemächern,
Aus Handwerks- und Gewerbesbanden,
Aus dem Druck von Giebeln und Dächern,
Aus der Straßen quetschender Enge,
Aus der Kirchen ehrwürdiger Nacht
Sind sie alle ans Licht gebracht.
Sieh nur, sieh! wie behend sich die Menge
Durch die Gärten und Felder zerschlägt,
Wie der Fluß in Breit und Länge
So manchen lustigen Nachen bewegt,
Und, bis zum Sinken überladen,
Entfernt sich dieser letzte Kahn.
Selbst von des Berges fernen Pfaden
Blinken uns farbige Kleider an.
Ich höre schon des Dorfs Getümmel,
Hier ist des Volkes wahrer Himmel,
Zufrieden jauchzet groß und klein:
'Hier bin ich Mensch, hier darf ichs sein!'

52

FAUST Geschrieben steht: 'Im Anfang war das Wort!'
Hier stock ich schon! Wer hilft mir weiter fort?
Ich kann das Wort so hoch unmöglich schätzen,
Ich muß es anders übersetzen,
Wenn ich vom Geiste recht erleuchtet bin.
Geschrieben steht: Im Anfang war der Sinn.
Bedenke wohl die erste Zeile,
Daß deine Feder sich nicht übereile!
Ist es der Sinn, der alles wirkt und schafft?
Es sollte stehn: Im Anfang war die Kraft!

From the mean damp houses where they dwell,
From their trades and crafts and drudgery,
From the gabled roofs' oppressive gloom,
From the choking streets where they fight for room,
From the churches' solemn devotional night –
They all have risen into the light!
Oh, look how so many are nimbly dispersing
Over the gardens, across the fields,
And the boats on the river happily coursing;
How the wide stream flows, how the water yields!
And that last one setting off, almost foundering
Under its load; and even up there
On the far-off hills there are people wandering,
We can see them by the bright colours they wear.
We're nearing the village, I hear the noise.
These are the simple folk's real joys.
They shout with delight, the whole motley crowd:
Here I am human, here it's allowed!

52

FAUST 'In the beginning was the Word': why, now
I'm stuck already! I must change that; how?
Is then 'the word' so great and high a thing?
There is some other rendering,
Which with the spirit's guidance I must find.
We read: 'In the beginning was the Mind.'
Before you write this first phrase, think again;
Good sense eludes the overhasty pen.
Does 'mind' set worlds on their creative course?
It means: 'In the beginning was the Force'.

from FAUST *Part One, 1797–1808*

Doch auch indem ich dieses niederschreibe,
Schon warnt mich was, daß ich dabei nicht bleibe.
Mir hilft der Geist! auf einmal seh ich Rat
Und schreibe getrost: Im Anfang war die Tat! –

*

53

DER GOTT UND DIE BAJADERE

Mahadöh, der Herr der Erde,
Kommt herab zum sechsten Mal,
Daß er unsersgleichen werde,
Mit zu fühlen Freud und Qual.
Er bequemt sich, hier zu wohnen,
Läßt sich alles selbst geschehn.
Soll er strafen oder schonen,
Muß er Menschen menschlich sehn.
Und hat er die Stadt sich als Wandrer betrachtet,
Die Großen belauert, auf Kleine geachtet,
Verläßt er sie abends, um weiter zu gehn.

Als er nun hinausgegangen,
Wo die letzten Häuser sind,
Sieht er, mit gemalten Wangen,
Ein verlornes schönes Kind.
Grüß dich, Jungfrau! – Dank der Ehre!
Wart, ich komme gleich hinaus –
Und wer bist du? – Bajadere,
Und dies ist der Liebe Haus.
Sie rührt sich, die Zimbeln zum Tanze zu schlagen,
Sie weiß sich so lieblich im Kreise zu tragen,
Sie neigt sich und biegt sich, und reicht ihm den Strauß.

So it should be – but as I write this too,
Some instinct warns me that it will not do.
The spirit speaks! I see how it must read,
And boldly write: 'In the beginning was the Deed!'

*

53

THE GOD AND THE DANCING-GIRL

Lord of worlds, great Mahadiwa,
For the sixth time visiting,
Trod this earth to be as we were,
Tried what mortal fate might bring.
He has deigned to come down to us,
Joy and woe like us to find:
For to judge us he must know us,
Mix as man with humankind.
In wanderer's disguise he will pass through a city,
The great folk he'll watch and the humble he'll pity,
Then move on at nightfall and leave it behind.

In the outskirts thus he meets her,
Notes the pretty painted face
Of a fallen woman, greets her
Kindly. 'Thank you, sir! This place
Is love's house, and my employment,
Which you honour, is to dance
As a bayadère. One moment!
I will let you in at once.'
She strikes up the cymbals, her talent displaying;
She gives him the garland, and stooping and swaying
Weaves circles about him to charm and entrance.

Schmeichelnd zieht sie ihn zur Schwelle,
Lebhaft ihn ins Haus hinein.
Schöner Fremdling, lampenhelle
Soll sogleich die Hütte sein.
Bist du müd, ich will dich laben,
Lindern deiner Füße Schmerz.
Was du willst, das sollst du haben,
Ruhe, Freuden oder Scherz.
Sie lindert geschäftig geheuchelte Leiden.
Der Göttliche lächelt; er siehet mit Freuden
Durch tiefes Verderben ein menschliches Herz.

Und er fordert Sklavendienste;
Immer heitrer wird sie nur,
Und des Mädchens frühe Künste
Werden nach und nach Natur.
Und so stellet auf die Blüte
Bald und bald die Frucht sich ein;
Ist Gehorsam im Gemüte,
Wird nicht fern die Liebe sein.
Aber, sie schärfer und schärfer zu prüfen,
Wählet der Kenner der Höhen und Tiefen
Lust und Entsetzen und grimmige Pein.

Und er küßt die bunten Wangen,
Und sie fühlt der Liebe Qual,
Und das Mädchen steht gefangen,
Und sie weint zum erstenmal;
Sinkt zu seinen Füßen nieder,
Nicht um Wollust noch Gewinst,
Ach! und die gelenken Glieder,
Sie versagen allen Dienst.
Und so zu des Lagers vergnüglicher Feier
Bereiten den dunklen behaglichen Schleier
Die nächtlichen Stunden, das schöne Gespinst.

Flatteringly he is invited
In, by eager hands drawn near:
'Come! my lamps shall all be lighted
Now so fine a stranger's here!
Are you tired? My house refreshes;
Footsore? You may take your ease.
I'll provide for all your wishes:
Rest, or love, or what you please.'
She soothes his feigned hurts, and the wise god rejoices;
He smiles, for through all her corruptions and vices,
Deep buried, a heart that's still human he sees.

Slavish tasks that he commands her
She performs with cheerful skill;
Arts for which her trade intends her
Turn to innocence of will.
So by nature's own maturing
Fruit from flower must appear,
And the obedient heart's enduring
Turns to love, for love is near.
Yet he must test her, more fiercely than ever:
He knows the heights and the depths, he must give her
Ecstasy, torment and bitterest fear.

And her painted cheeks he kisses:
Tears till now she never knew.
Now she sheds them, and confesses
An affection strange and new;
Falls before his feet in anguish,
Seeks no pleasure now nor gain,
And her agile limbs, they languish
Now so numb and weak and vain!
And thus the night weaves for the bed of these lovers
Its veil of sweet darkness that comforts and covers
Their festive encounter, their joy and their pain.

1797 117

Spät entschlummert unter Scherzen,
Früh erwacht nach kurzer Rast,
Findet sie an ihrem Herzen
Tot den vielgeliebten Gast.
Schreiend stürzt sie auf ihn nieder,
Aber nicht erweckt sie ihn;
Und man trägt die starren Glieder
Bald zur Flammengrube hin.
Sie höret die Priester, die Totengesänge,
Sie raset und rennet und teilet die Menge.
Wer bist du? was drängt zu der Grube dich hin?

Bei der Bahre stürzt sie nieder,
Ihr Geschrei durchdringt die Luft:
Meinen Gatten will ich wieder!
Und ich such ihn in der Gruft.
Soll zu Asche mir zerfallen
Dieser Glieder Götterpracht?
Mein! er war es, mein vor allen!
Ach, nur Eine süße Nacht!
Es singen die Priester: Wir tragen die Alten,
Nach langem Ermatten und spätem Erkalten
Wir tragen die Jugend, noch eh sies gedacht.

Höre deiner Priester Lehre:
Dieser war dein Gatte nicht.
Lebst du doch als Bajadere,
Und so hast du keine Pflicht.
Nur dem Körper folgt der Schatten
In das stille Totenreich;
Nur die Gattin folgt dem Gatten:
Das ist Pflicht und Ruhm zugleich.
Ertöne, Drommete, zu heiliger Klage!
O nehmet, ihr Götter! die Zierde der Tage,
O nehmet den Jüngling in Flammen zu euch!

Late she sinks to sleep from loving,
Starts up soon from briefest rest,
Finds him at her side unmoving,
Cold and stiff, her much-loved guest:
He is dead, she cannot wake him.
Her distracted cries resound
Vainly. Soon men come and take him
To the burning funeral-ground.
She hears the priests chanting, their dirges intoning,
She breaks through the crowd, in a wild frenzy running:
'Who are you, who dares our great rite to confound?'

By the pyre she falls heart-broken,
Rends the air with pleas: 'I come
For the husband you have taken
From me, I will share his tomb!
Must I watch these flames devour him,
Burn to ash his limbs divine?
He was mine, like none before him:
Only one sweet night, but mine!'
The priests sing: 'We carry them, carry the old ones,
The slowly declining, the late and the cold ones,
The unthinking young: all to fire we consign.

Hear your priests and learn their answer:
You were not this dead man's wife.
Nothing binds you, as a dancer-
Prostitute, to give your life.
Only bodies take their shadows
With them to the realms below:
Only husbands take their widows:
Law and honour bid it so.
You trumpets, lament! and you blessed Immortals,
Receive this fair youth at your heavenly portals:
We send him to you in this funeral glow.'

So das Chor, das ohn Erbarmen
Mehret ihres Herzens Not;
Und mit ausgestreckten Armen
Springt sie in den heißen Tod.
Doch der Götter-Jüngling hebet
Aus der Flamme sich empor,
Und in seinen Armen schwebet
Die Geliebte mit hervor.
Es freut sich die Gottheit der reuigen Sünder;
Unsterbliche heben verlorene Kinder
Mit feurigen Armen zum Himmel empor.

54

DAUER IM WECHSEL

Hielte diesen frühen Segen
Ach, nur Eine Stunde fest!
Aber vollen Blütenregen
Schüttelt schon der laue West.
Soll ich mich des Grünen freuen,
Dem ich Schatten erst verdankt?
Bald wird Sturm auch das zerstreuen,
Wenn es falb im Herbst geschwankt.

Willst du nach den Früchten greifen,
Eilig nimm dein Teil davon!
Diese fangen an zu reifen,
Und die andern keimen schon;
Gleich mit jedem Regengusse
Ändert sich dein holdes Tal,
Ach, und in demselben Flusse
Schwimmst du nicht zum zweitenmal.

And for all her grief uncaring
Thus they chant, the priestly choir;
She, with arms flung wide, despairing,
Plunges to her doom of fire.
But the young god rises, raises
Her aloft, and up they fly
From the flames, as his embraces
Bear her soaring to the sky.
Let sinners repent, for the great gods in heaven
Rejoice in them then, and lost souls are forgiven;
In fiery arms they are carried on high.

54

PERMANENCE IN CHANGE

Shall these blossoms' early blessing
Last not even one short hour?
In the warm west wind's caressing
They are scattered like a shower.
And the green leaves too, that gladden
Still and shade me, soon they all,
Withering, yellowing in a sudden
Autumn storm, must shake and fall.

Pluck the fruit that hangs before you:
Take your share, it will not wait!
Some already ripens for you,
Some begins to germinate.
Look: your pleasant valley ever
Varies with each burst of rain;
Think: in one and the same river
You bathe once, but not again.

Du nun selbst! Was felsenfeste
Sich vor dir hervorgetan,
Mauern siehst du, siehst Paläste
Stets mit andern Augen an.
Weggeschwunden ist die Lippe,
Die im Kusse sonst genas,
Jener Fuß, der an der Klippe
Sich mit Gemsenfreche maß,

Jene Hand, die gern und milde
Sich bewegte wohlzutun,
Das gegliederte Gebilde,
Alles ist ein andres nun.
Und was sich an jener Stelle
Nun mit deinem Namen nennt,
Kam herbei wie eine Welle,
Und so eilts zum Element.

Laß den Anfang mit dem Ende
Sich in Eins zusammenziehn!
Schneller als die Gegenstände
Selber dich vorüberfliehn.
Danke, daß die Gunst der Musen
Unvergängliches verheißt,
Den Gehalt in deinem Busen
Und die Form in deinem Geist.

What of you yourself? They met you,
Castle walls and towers that rise
Hard and firm and constant, yet you
See them too with changing eyes.
Lips that once were healed by kisses
Wasted now and worn away;
Feet that leapt up mountain passes
Bold as wild goats, where are they?

Where the hand, outheld so kindly,
Gladly, to give pleasure? How
Subtly structured, formed so finely!
What is this, so different now?
All still known as you replacing,
All still you and none the same,
To the elements is racing,
Wave to wave as once it came.

Let your end and your beginning
To a single point unite!
All things fleeting, all things running,
Pass them in your own swift flight!
Thank the Muses for their favour:
They have promised for your heart's
Theme a union forged for ever
With the form your mind imparts.

NATUR UND KUNST

Natur und Kunst sie scheinen sich zu fliehen,
Und haben sich, eh man es denkt, gefunden;
Der Widerwille ist auch mir verschwunden,
Und beide scheinen gleich mich anzuziehen.

Es gilt wohl nur ein redliches Bemühen!
Und wenn wir erst in abgemeßnen Stunden
Mit Geist und Fleiß uns an die Kunst gebunden,
Mag frei Natur im Herzen wieder glühen.

So ists mit aller Bildung auch beschaffen:
Vergebens werden ungebundne Geister
Nach der Vollendung reiner Höhe streben.

Wer Großes will, muß sich zusammenraffen;
In der Beschränkung zeigt sich erst der Meister,
Und das Gesetz nur kann uns Freiheit geben.

NATURE AND ART

Nature and Art, they go their separate ways,
It seems; yet all at once they find each other.
Even I no longer am a foe to either;
Both equally attract me nowadays.

Some honest toil's required; then, phase by phase,
When diligence and wit have worked together
To tie us fast to Art with their good tether,
Nature again may set our hearts ablaze.

All culture is like this: the unfettered mind,
The boundless spirit's mere imagination,
For pure perfection's heights will strive in vain.

To achieve great things, we must be self-confined:
Mastery is revealed in limitation
And law alone can set us free again.

56

NACHTGESANG

O gib, vom weichen Pfühle,
Träumend, ein halb Gehör!
Bei meinem Saitenspiele
Schlafe! was willst du mehr?

Bei meinem Saitenspiele
Segnet der Sterne Heer
Die ewigen Gefühle;
Schlafe! was willst du mehr?

Die ewigen Gefühle
Heben mich, hoch und hehr,
Aus irdischem Gewühle;
Schlafe! was willst du mehr?

Vom irdischen Gewühle
Trennst du mich nur zu sehr,
Bannst mich in diese Kühle
Schlafe! was willst du mehr?

Bannst mich in diese Kühle,
Gibst nur im Traum Gehör.
Ach, auf dem weichen Pfühle
Schlafe! was willst du mehr?

NOCTURNE

Where you are softly lying,
Half in your dreams, oh hear!
Notes of my lute are sighing:
Sleep! all you want is here.

Notes of my lute are sighing
As the great starry sphere
Blesses our love undying:
Sleep! all you want is here.

Does not such love undying
Bless me and lift me clear,
Far from earth's turmoil flying?
Sleep! all you want is here.

Out of earth's turmoil flying
You lift me high and clear,
Spellbound in coolness lying:
Sleep! all you want is here.

Spellbound in coolness lying
Only in dreams you hear:
Oh sleep, so softly lying,
Sleep! all you want is here.

DAS TAGEBUCH

. . . aliam tenui, sed iam quum gaudia adirem,
admonuit dominae deseruitque Venus.

(Tibullus 1.5.39f.)

Wir hörens oft und glaubens wohl am Ende:
Das Menschenherz sei ewig unergründlich,
Und wie man auch sich hin und wider wende,
So sei der Christe wie der Heide sündlich.
Das Beste bleibt, wir geben uns die Hände
Und nehmens mit der Lehre nicht empfindlich;
Denn zeigt sich auch ein Dämon, uns versuchend,
So waltet was, gerettet ist die Tugend.

Von meiner Trauten lange Zeit entfernet,
Wies öfters geht, nach irdischem Gewinne,
Und was ich auch gewonnen und gelernet,
So hatt ich doch nur immer Sie im Sinne;
Und wie zu Nacht der Himmel erst sich sternet,
Erinnrung uns umleuchtet ferner Minne:
So ward im Federzug des Tags Ereignis
Mit süßen Worten Ihr ein freundlich Gleichnis.

Ich eilte nun zurück. Zerbrochen sollte
Mein Wagen mich noch eine Nacht verspäten;
Schon dacht ich mich, wie ich zu Hause rollte,
Allein da war Geduld und Werk vonnöten.
Und wie ich auch mit Schmied und Wagner tollte,
Sie hämmerten, verschmähten viel zu reden.
Ein jedes Handwerk hat nun seine Schnurren.
Was blieb mir nun? Zu weilen und zu murren.

THE DIARY

> I was with some other girl, but just short of the height of my pleasure
> Suddenly Venus withdrew, for I remembered my love.
>
> (Tibullus 1.5.39f.)

The saying goes – it's true enough, no doubt –
That man's heart is for ever fathomless:
That Christians, though they turn and turn about,
Are sinners still, like pagans. Let's confess
As much, and all shake hands! We carry out
What Virtue bids us, only rather less;
Why fret? For when by some wild imp we're tempted
Another force prevails, and sin's preempted.

It happened, as so often, travelling
For worldly profit, I'd been some time parted
From my true love; and many a useful thing
I'd done and learnt – but always, faithful-hearted,
Thinking of her. At night's first glittering
Of stars, remembered love's bright fire is started:
So too, I'd pen the doings of my day
In sweet words for my darling far away.

Now, hurrying back to her, misfortune struck
My homeward course: a broken wheel delayed me.
So soon I'd have been there! Now I was stuck.
O workmanship, what a droll trick you'd played me!
I cursed the smith, the wainwright and my luck;
They hammered on, and scant reply they made me.
I wait, they ply their mystery. What a crew!
But stay the night was all that I could do.

So stand ich nun! Der Stern des nächsten Schildes
Berief mich hin, die Wohnung schien erträglich.
Ein Mädchen kam, des seltensten Gebildes,
Das Licht erleuchtend. Mir ward gleich behäglich.
Hausflur und Treppe sah ich als ein Mildes,
Die Zimmerchen erfreuten mich unsäglich.
Den sündgen Menschen, der im Freien schwebet –
Die Schönheit spinnt, sie ists die ihn umwebet.

Nun setzt ich mich zu meiner Tasch und Briefen
Und meines Tagebuchs Genauigkeiten,
Um so wie sonst, wenn alle Menschen schliefen,
Mir und der Trauten Freude zu bereiten;
Doch weiß ich nicht, die Tintenworte liefen
Nicht so wie sonst in alle Kleinigkeiten:
Das Mädchen kam, des Abendessens Bürde
Verteilte sie gewandt mit Gruß und Würde.

Sie geht und kommt; ich spreche, sie erwidert.
Mit jedem Wort erscheint sie mir geschmückter.
Und wie sie leicht mir nun das Huhn zergliedert
Bewegend Hand und Arm, geschickt, geschickter –
Was auch das tolle Zeug in uns befiedert,
Genug, ich bin verworrner, bin verrückter,
Den Stuhl umwerfend spring ich auf und fasse
Das schöne Kind; sie lispelt: Lasse, lasse!

Die Muhme drunten lauscht, ein alter Drache,
Sie zählt bedächtig des Geschäfts Minute;
Sie denkt sich unten, was ich oben mache,
Bei jedem Zögern schwenkt sie frisch die Rute.
Doch schließe deine Türe nicht und wache,
So kommt die Mitternacht uns wohl zu Gute.
Rasch meinem Arm entwindet sie die Glieder,
Und eilet fort und kommt nur dienend wieder;

So there I stood. The nearest hostelry
Was called 'The Star'; it looked a decent place.
A girl appeared – a shapely rarity –
With lamp and light; my spirits rose apace.
The hallway and the stairs delighted me,
The little rooms seemed full of charm and grace.
When sinful mortals wander far from home,
Beauty's fine web may catch them as they roam.

So I sat down to my portfolio,
My letters, and my diary's exact
Reports: nocturnal words, which I would show
As always to my dearest. Yet they lacked
Somehow tonight their usual easy flow;
The ink ran sluggish round each trifling fact.
The girl brought in my supper, greeted me
And laid it out with skill and dignity.

She comes and goes, and as we talk I'm stricken
With growing admiration for her charm.
I watch how cleverly she carves my chicken
With quick, deft movements of her hand and arm:
How my mad feathers sprout, my pulses quicken!
In short, my head's confused, my heart is warm,
And up I jump, knock the chair over, seize
The pretty creature – but she whispers: 'Please,

Not now! My aunt's downstairs, she listens when
I serve up here, and checks how long I stay;
She brandishes her cane, the old harridan,
And punishes each minute of delay.
But stay awake, don't lock your door, and then
When midnight comes, maybe we'll find a way.'
She wriggles free from my embrace, and slips
Back to her work; soon in again she trips

Doch blickend auch! so daß aus jedem Blicke
Sich himmlisches Versprechen mir entfaltet.
Den stillen Seufzer drängt sie nicht zurücke,
Der ihren Busen herrlicher gestaltet.
Ich sehe, daß am Ohr, um Hals und Gnicke
Der flüchtgen Röte Liebesblüte waltet,
Und da sie nichts zu leisten weiter findet,
Geht sie und zögert, sieht sich um, verschwindet.

Der Mitternacht gehören Haus und Straßen,
Mir ist ein weites Lager aufgebreitet,
Wovon den kleinsten Teil mir anzumaßen
Die Liebe rät, die alles wohl bereitet.
Ich zaudre noch, die Kerzen auszublasen,
Nun hör ich sie, wie leise sie auch gleitet,
Mit giergem Blick die Hochgestalt umschweif ich,
Sie legt sich bei, die Wohlgestalt ergreif ich.

Sie macht sich los: Vergönne, daß ich rede,
Damit ich dir nicht völlig fremd gehöre.
Der Schein ist wider mich; sonst war ich blöde,
Stets gegen Männer setzt ich mich zur Wehre.
Mich nennt die Stadt, mich nennt die Gegend spröde;
Nun aber weiß ich, wie das Herz sich kehre:
Du bist mein Sieger, laß dichs nicht verdrießen,
Ich sah, ich liebte, schwur dich zu genießen.

Du hast mich rein, und wenn ichs besser wüßte,
So gäb ichs dir, ich tue was ich sage.
So schließt sie mich an ihre süßen Brüste,
Als ob ihr nur an meiner Brust behage.
Und wie ich Mund und Aug und Stirne küßte,
So war ich doch in wunderbarer Lage:
Denn der so hitzig sonst den Meister spielet
Weicht schülerhaft zurück und abgekühlet.

To serve me – but her looks, how much they tell!
A heavenly promise blossoms from her eyes;
I watch her rounded bosom's splendid swell
As it is filled with little half-checked sighs;
And to her ears and throat and neck as well
I see the fleeting rosy love-flush rise.
She pauses then, finds all her duties done,
Hesitates, looks about her and is gone.

Now midnight's here; streets, houses are at rest;
My bed is wide, but I have settled for
The narrowest share of it, at the behest
Of Love, that all-foreseeing counsellor.
My candles burn still, as with daintiest
Of footfalls she comes gliding to my door.
Her lovely form I seize with eager eyes
And then with eager arms, as down she lies.

Still she withdraws: 'Something I must confess,
Or we shall still be strangers. I know how
All this must look to you; nevertheless,
I always have resisted men till now.
Everyone calls me cold. But you possess
My heart: I saw you, and I made a vow
That I'd be yours, that you'd be mine tonight!
Forgive me! But I loved you at first sight;

And I'm a virgin still – for otherwise
I'd not pretend. Take me, it's all I know!'
She hugs me close to her sweet breasts, and lies
There in my arms, happy at last. But though
I kissed her now, her mouth, her brow, her eyes,
I was in wondrous quandary even so:
My master player, hitherto so hot,
Shrinks, novice-like, its ardour quite forgot.

Ihr scheint ein süßes Wort, ein Kuß zu gnügen,
Als wär es alles was ihr Herz begehrte.
Wie keusch sie mir, mit liebevollem Fügen,
Des süßen Körpers Fülleform gewährte!
Entzückt und froh in allen ihren Zügen
Und ruhig dann, als wenn sie nichts entbehrte.
So ruht ich auch, gefallig sie beschauend,
Noch auf den Meister hoffend und vertrauend.

Doch als ich länger mein Geschick bedachte,
Von tausend Flüchen mir die Seele kochte,
Mich selbst verwünschend, grinsend mich belachte,
Nichts besser ward, wie ich auch zaudern mochte:
Da lag sie schlafend, schöner als sie wachte;
Die Lichter dämmerten mit langem Dochte.
Der Tages-Arbeit, jugendlicher Mühe
Gesellt sich gern der Schlaf und nie zu frühe.

So lag sie himmlisch an bequemer Stelle,
Als wenn das Lager ihr allein gehörte,
Und an die Wand gedrückt, gequetscht zur Hölle,
Ohnmächtig Jener, dem sie nichts verwehrte.
Vom Schlangenbisse fallt zunächst der Quelle
Ein Wandrer so, den schon der Durst verzehrte.
Sie atmet lieblich holdem Traum entgegen;
Er hält den Atem, sie nicht aufzuregen.

Gefaßt bei dem, was ihm noch nie begegnet,
Spricht er zu sich: So mußt du doch erfahren,
Warum der Bräutigam sich kreuzt und segnet,
Vor Nestelknüpfen scheu sich zu bewahren.
Weit lieber da, wos Hellebarden regnet,
Als hier im Schimpf! So war es nicht vor Jahren,
Als deine Herrin dir zum ersten Male
Vors Auge trat im prachterhellten Saale.

How chaste she was! for though she made me free
Of her sweet body, loving words, a kiss
Contented her; she nestled close to me,
Desiring, as it seemed, no more than this;
Happy she looked, peacefully, yieldingly
Satisfied, as if nothing were amiss.
So I too lay and watched her, glad of heart,
Still hoping, trusting in that master part.

But as I further pondered my mischance
I raged a thousandfold, my soul was rent
With cursing and self-mockery both at once:
Wait as I might, there was no betterment.
She slept, lovelier than waking innocence;
The candles flickered, their long wicks half-spent.
To youth, after a day's hard toil, the boon
Of willing slumber never comes too soon.

So the dear angel lies, and as if all
The bed were hers, spreads each commodious limb,
While he, still powerless, squashed against the wall,
Must forfeit what she freely offered him.
Thus a parched wanderer still is doomed to fall
By snakebite at the fountain's very rim.
She breathes in her sweet dreams, and for her sake
He holds his breath; she dreams and does not wake.

Resigned to this most novel accident
He muses ruefully: So now you know
Why bridegrooms cross themselves, and what is meant
By magic love-knots. Better a bloody foe
In battle than this shame! How different
Things once were with you, when long years ago
You met your lady, on that first of nights,
In that glad throng, under the festive lights!

Da quoll dein Herz, da quollen deine Sinnen,
So daß der ganze Mensch entzückt sich regte.
Zum raschen Tanze trugst du sie von hinnen,
Die kaum der Arm und schon der Busen hegte,
Als wolltest du dir selbst sie abgewinnen;
Vervielfacht war, was sich für sie bewegte:
Verstand und Witz und alle Lebensgeister
Und rascher als die andern jener Meister.

So immerfort wuchs Neigung und Begierde,
Brautleute wurden wir im fruhen Jahre,
Sie selbst des Maien schönste Blum und Zierde;
Wie wuchs die Kraft zur Lust im jungen Paare!
Und als ich endlich sie zur Kirche führte:
Gesteh ichs nur, vor Priester und Altare,
Vor deinem Jammerkreuz, blutrünstger Christe,
Verzeih mirs Gott! es regte sich der Iste.

Und ihr, der Brautnacht reiche Bettgehänge,
Ihr Pfühle, die sich uns so breit erstreckten,
Ihr Teppiche, die Lieb und Lustgedränge
Mit seidenweichen Fittichen bedeckten,
Ihr Käfigvögel, deren Zwitschersänge
Zu neuer Lust und nie zu früh uns weckten,
Ihr kanntet uns, von eurem Schutz umfriedet,
Teilnehmend sie, mich immer unermüdet.

Und wie wir oft sodann im Raub genossen
Nach Buhlenart des Ehstands heilge Rechte,
Von reifer Saat umwogt, vom Rohr umschlossen,
An manchem Unort, wo ichs mich erfrechte,
Wir waren augenblicklich, unverdrossen
Und wiederholt bedient vom braven Knechte!
Verfluchter Knecht, wie unerwecklich liegst du!
Und deinen Herrn ums schönste Glück betrügst du.

Oh then did not your soul and senses leap,
Was all of you not ecstasy at once?
Scarcely in your arms, already she was deep
Into your heart. Who clasped her in that dance
More jealously than you, as if to keep
Her even from yourself? Intelligence,
Wit, vital powers all doubled – but still faster
Was *its* increase, that little lord and master!

Thus still they grew, desire and tenderness;
We were betrothed in spring, and she was more
Lovely than any maytime's bloom; ah yes,
How strong it waxed, our youthful passion's store!
And when at last we wed, I do confess,
Before that altar and that priest, before
Thy wretched bloodstained cross, *domine Christe*,
God pardon me! it stirred, young master Iste.

And you, the bridal bed's rich furnishings,
You pillows soft and wide for nuptial nights,
You woven fabrics with your silk-soft wings
Sheltering our bliss, our urgent lovers' rites;
You little cage-birds whose first twitterings,
Never too soon, woke us to fresh delights –
You knew us well, you saw how that kind soul
Received me as I played my tireless role.

And then how often too, with wanton passion,
We'd furtively enjoy our married state!
Down in the waving corn, in shameless fashion,
Among the reeds our love we'd consummate,
And that good slave would give us double ration
Of service every time, early or late.
Now, thrice-accursed slave, limp, lifeless toy,
You cheat your master of his dearest joy!

Doch Meister Iste hat nun seine Grillen
Und läßt sich nicht befehlen noch verachten,
Auf einmal ist er da, und ganz im stillen
Erhebt er sich zu allen seinen Prachten.
So steht es nun dem Wandrer ganz zu Willen,
Nicht lechzend mehr am Quell zu übernachten.
Er neigt sich hin, er will die Schläfrin küssen,
Allein er stockt, er fühlt sich weggerissen.

Wer hat zur Kraft ihn wieder aufgestählet,
Als jenes Bild, das ihm auf ewig teuer,
Mit dem er sich in Jugendlust vermählet?
Dort leuchtet her ein frisch erquicklich Feuer,
Und wie er erst in Ohnmacht sich gequälet,
So wird nun hier dem Starken nicht geheuer.
Er schaudert weg, vorsichtig, leise, leise
Entzieht er sich dem holden Zauberkreise,

Sitzt, schreibt: Ich nahte mich der heimschen Pforte,
Entfernen wollten mich die letzten Stunden,
Da hab ich nun, am sonderbarsten Orte,
Mein treues Herz aufs neue dir verbunden.
Zum Schlusse findest du geheime Worte:
Die Krankheit erst bewähret den Gesunden.
Dies Büchlein soll dir manches Gute zeigen,
Das Beste nur muß ich zuletzt verschweigen.

Da kräht der Hahn. Das Mädchen schnell entwindet
Der Decke sich und wirft sich rasch ins Mieder.
Und da sie sich so seltsam wiederfindet,
So stutzt sie, blickt und schlägt die Augen nieder –
Und da sie ihm zum letzten Mal verschwindet,
Im Auge bleiben ihm die schönen Glieder.
Das Posthorn tönt, er wirft sich in den Wagen
Und läßt getrost sich zu der Liebsten tragen.

But wise Sir Iste, he has many a mood:
He'll not be bidden, he'll not be ignored.
For now, to his full, splendid magnitude,
He rears up quietly of his own accord;
Now sweet refreshment need not be eschewed,
Now the benighted wanderer's life's restored!
He turns to wake the maiden with a kiss –
But something checks him: what new scruple's this?

What (he reflects) has steeled his strength again
But *her* dear image, whom he took to wife
In lusty youth? He loves her, now as then;
From her it glows, this freshening fire of life.
So his new vigour troubles him – as when
He lay here helpless, he's once more in strife
Of mind. A certain dread now gives him pause;
From the charmed circle gently he withdraws,

Sits, writes: 'Nearing my homeward journey's end,
In these last hours I have suffered some delay,
But my heart's true to you once more, dear friend,
And binds me to you in the strangest way.
Here some mysterious words I shall append:
Sickness is the true proof of health, they say.
This book shall tell you many a good thing,
But must not mention the best news I bring.'

Now the day breaks. Quickly the girl leaps out
Of bed, throws on her clothes; waking in these
Strange circumstances, she's confused no doubt,
Looks up, and then looks down again. Now he's
Bidding goodbye to her; she turns about,
And as she leaves, her shapely limbs still please
His eye. The carriage waits, the posthorn's sound
Cheers him, he's soon homeward and wifeward bound.

Und weil zuletzt bei jeder Dichtungsweise
Moralien uns ernstlich fordern sollen,
So will auch ich in so beliebtem Gleise
Euch gern bekennen, was die Verse wollen:
Wir stolpern wohl auf unsrer Lebensreise,
Und doch vermögen in der Welt, der tollen,
Zwei Hebel viel aufs irdische Getriebe:
Sehr viel die Pflicht, unendlich mehr die Liebe.

But since the end of all poetic art
Is the improvement of the reader's mind
(Or so we're told), my verses for their part
Shall point the usual moral of their kind:
This life's a crazy journey, and our heart
May stumble, but two mighty powers, we'll find,
Can move the world and help us as we go:
To Duty much, to Love far more we owe.

III

THE LATER GOETHE

1810–1832

58

HEGIRA

Nord und West und Süd zersplittern,
Throne bersten, Reiche zittern,
Flüchte du, im reinen Osten
Patriarchenluft zu kosten,
Unter Lieben, Trinken, Singen
Soll dich Chisers Quell verjüngen.

Dort im Reinen und im Rechten
Will ich menschlichen Geschlechten
In des Ursprungs Tiefe dringen,
Wo sie noch von Gott empfingen
Himmelslehr in Erdesprachen,
Und sich nicht den Kopf zerbrachen.

Wo sie Väter hoch verehrten,
Jeden fremden Dienst verwehrten;
Will mich freun der Jugendschranke:
Glaube weit, eng der Gedanke,
Wie das Wort so wichtig dort war,
Weil es ein gesprochen Wort war.

Will mich unter Hirten mischen
An Oasen mich erfrischen,
Wenn mit Karawanen wandle,
Schal, Kaffee und Moschus handle;
Jeden Pfad will ich betreten
Von der Wüste zu den Städten.

Bösen Felsweg auf und nieder
Trösten, Hāfis, deine Lieder,

HEGIRA

North and west and south are breaking,
Thrones are shattered, empires shaking:
Flee to the pure East, and there
Taste its patriarchal air;
Love, wine, song are waiting for you,
Khiser's fountain shall restore you.

In that right world, in that pure world,
I'll dig deep into the sure world-
Origins of humankind,
And that simple lore I'll find
Which they learnt, unschooled, God-given,
Dropped in earthly tongues from heaven.

Theirs were fathers high-respected;
Alien thraldom they rejected.
Hail, glad early youth of man,
Faith wide-flung, thought's narrow span!
In their words a power unbroken
Dwelt, for all their words were spoken.

Herdsmen's company I'll keep
In oases fresh and deep,
Travel with the caravans,
Trade in musk through burning sands;
All the coffee-trails I'll wander,
Deserts here to cities yonder.

As we ride the steep and rocky
Paths, great Hāfiz, yours the lucky

Wenn der Führer mit Entzücken
Von des Maultiers hohem Rücken
Singt, die Sterne zu erwecken
Und die Räuber zu erschrecken.

Will in Bädern und in Schenken,
Heilger Hāfis, dein gedenken;
Wenn den Schleier Liebchen lüftet,
Schüttelnd Ambralocken düftet.
Ja des Dichters Liebeflüstern
Mache selbst die Huris lüstern.

Wolltet ihr ihm dies beneiden,
Oder etwa gar verleiden;
Wisset nur, daß Dichterworte
Um des Paradieses Pforte
Immer leise klopfend schweben
Sich erbittend ewges Leben.

59

LIED UND GEBILDE

Mag der Grieche seinen Ton
Zu Gestalten drücken,
An der eignen Hände Sohn
Steigern sein Entzücken;

Aber uns ist wonnereich
In den Euphrat greifen,
Und im flüßgen Element
Hin und wider schweifen.

Songs our leader sings, rejoicing
On his high-backed mule, enticing
All the stars from sleep, and scaring
Robbers from our rich wayfaring.

In the baths and taverns too,
Hāfiz, I'll remember you,
When some sweetheart lifts her veil,
Shakes her scented locks; the tale
Of our whispered love shall fashion
Even the Huris' hearts to passion.

Who shall envy me such pleasure?
Who would shorten its full measure?
Let him note: in words upsoaring,
Softly knocking and imploring,
Poets ever haunt heaven's portal,
Seeking, finding life immortal.

59

SINGING AND SHAPING

Let the Greek make shapes of clay
For his own delight,
Children of his skilful hands
To rejoice his sight.

But our pleasure is to plunge
In the Euphrates' stream,
Dipping, drifting to and fro
Through its liquid dream.

Löscht ich so der Seele Brand,
Lied es wird erschallen;
Schöpft des Dichters reine Hand,
Wasser wird sich ballen.

60

PHÄNOMEN

Wenn zu der Regenwand
Phöbus sich gattet,
Gleich steht ein Bogenrand
Farbig beschattet.

Im Nebel gleichen Kreis
Seh ich gezogen,
Zwar ist der Bogen weiß,
Doch Himmelsbogen.

So sollst du, muntrer Greis,
Dich nicht betrüben,
Sind gleich die Haare weiß,
Doch wirst du lieben.

61

IM GEGENWÄRTIGEN VERGANGENES

Ros und Lilie morgentaulich
Blüht im Garten meiner Nähe;
Hinten an, bebuscht und traulich,
Steigt der Felsen in die Höhe;

Water, quench my burning soul!
Crystal sphere, arise!
In a poet's hand, his pure
Song solidifies.

60

A PHENOMENON

Look! when the sun-god weds
A wall of rain,
That arch of colours spreads
Radiant again.

Another arch I see
When mist enfolds it:
White though this bow may be,
Yet heaven upholds it.

So, old man, let this bright
Image regale you:
Though your hair's snowy white,
Love will not fail you.

61

A PAST WITHIN THE PRESENT

Roses, lilies, dewed with daybreak,
Blossom in the garden round me,
And the wooded hill's familiar
Shape rears skyward there behind me;

Und mit hohem Wald umzogen,
Und mit Ritterschloß gekrönet,
Lenkt sich hin des Gipfels Bogen,
Bis er sich dem Tal versöhnet.

Und da duftets wie vor alters,
Da wir noch von Liebe litten,
Und die Saiten meines Psalters
Mit dem Morgenstrahl sich stritten;
Wo das Jagdlied aus den Büschen
Fülle runden Tons enthauchte,
Anzufeuern, zu erfrischen
Wies der Busen wollt und brauchte.

Nun die Wälder ewig sprossen,
So ermutigt euch mit diesen,
Was ihr sonst für euch genossen
Läßt in andern sich genießen.
Niemand wird uns dann beschreien,
Daß wirs uns alleine gönnen;
Nun in allen Lebensreihen
Müsset ihr genießen können.

Und mit diesem Lied und Wendung
Sind wir wieder bei Hāfisen,
Denn es ziemt des Tags Vollendung
Mit Genießern zu genießen.

Tall the forest, high the castle
Stands, the summit's outline crowning
As it sweeps, ascends, descends, the
Valley once again rejoining.

Lingers still this scent of all the
Past, of all the love we suffered
Long ago, as to the morning
Sun my youthful lyre I offered;
Through the trees the fine resounding
Notes of hunting-horns we heeded
As they fired us and refreshed us,
Stirred and moved us as we needed.

See, these forests grow for ever:
So rejoice in such renewing!
Lost delights are found again in
Their vicarious pursuing.
Who shall now decry us, who shall
Say we never share our pleasure?
Every life-stage seen in others
Is our own remembered treasure.

Let us then return to Hāfiz
With this song and this reflection,
And enjoy with an enjoyer,
As befits the day's perfection.

TALISMANE

Gottes ist der Orient!
Gottes ist der Okzident!
Nord- und südliches Gelände
Ruht im Frieden seiner Hände.

—

Er, der einzige Gerechte,
Will für jedermann das Rechte.
Sei, von seinen hundert Namen,
Dieser hochgelobet! Amen.

—

Mich verwirren will das Irren;
Doch du weißt mich zu entwirren.
Wenn ich handle, wenn ich dichte,
Gib du meinem Weg die Richte.

—

Ob ich Irdsches denk und sinne,
Das gereicht zu höherem Gewinne.
Mit dem Staube nicht der Geist zerstoben,
Dringet, in sich selbst gedrängt, nach oben.

—

Im Atemholen sind zweierlei Gnaden:
Die Luft einziehen, sich ihrer entladen;
Jenes bedrängt, dieses erfrischt;
So wunderbar ist das Leben gemischt.
Du danke Gott, wenn er dich preßt,
Und dank ihm, wenn er dich wieder entläßt.

TALISMANS

All the East to God belongs!
All the West to God belongs!
Northern lands and southern lands
Rest at peace, held in His hands.

—

He, the Only Just God, none but He
Gives us each a just decree.
Of His hundred names, let men
Chiefly praise this name. Amen.

—

In a tangle though I be
Yet you can untangle me.
Whether in action or in making
Show me the way I should be taking.

—

Though my thoughts are earthly, they are bent
To a higher purpose and intent.
Spirit is not scattered with the dust,
But grows denser in its ever-upward thrust.

—

The act of breathing's a twofold blessing:
First there's indrawing, then there's outpressing.
The second's refreshment, the first is constriction;
Life's such a wonder of contradiction.
Give thanks to God when he squeezes you so,
And thank him again when he lets you go.

from the WEST-EASTERN DIVAN, 1814–18

UNBEGRENZT

Daß du nicht enden kannst, das macht dich groß,
Und daß du nie beginnst, das ist dein Los.
Dein Lied ist drehend wie das Sterngewölbe,
Anfang und Ende immerfort dasselbe,
Und was die Mitte bringt ist offenbar
Das was zu Ende bleibt und anfangs war.

Du bist der Freuden echte Dichterquelle,
Und ungezählt entfließt dir Well auf Welle.
Zum Küssen stets bereiter Mund,
Ein Brustgesang der lieblich fließet,
Zum Trinken stets gereizter Schlund,
Ein gutes Herz das sich ergießet.

Und mag die ganze Welt versinken!
Hāfis, mit dir, mit dir allein
Will ich wetteifern! Lust und Pein
Sei uns den Zwillingen gemein!
Wie du zu lieben und zu trinken,
Das soll mein Stolz, mein Leben sein.

Nun töne Lied mit eignem Feuer!
Denn du bist älter, du bist neuer.

63

UNBOUNDED

That you can never end, that makes you great,
And to have no beginning is your fate.
Your circling song is like the vault of stars,
Its end is its beginning, and what was
Before all things and after all shall be
Moves in the midst of all for all to see.

From you, true poet, fountain of delight,
Wave upon wave flows, countless, infinite:
Your lips for ever poised to kiss,
Your soul outstreaming its sweet note,
Your loving heart outpoured, your throat
Thirsty for wine's deep mysteries.

Let the world perish, Hāfiz, so
I vie with you, only with you!
Let us be twin-born brothers, two
That share our joy and share our woe!
To love and drink as you would do:
This is my pride and my life too.

Now, song, with your own fire speak bolder,
For you are newer, you are older.

64

'Der Spiegel sagt mir ich bin schön!
Ihr sagt: zu altern sei auch mein Geschick.
Vor Gott muß alles ewig stehn,
In mir liebt Ihn, für diesen Augenblick.'

65

GEHEIMES

Über meines Liebchens Äugeln
Stehn verwundert alle Leute;
Ich, der Wissende, dagegen
Weiß recht gut was das bedeute.

Denn es heißt: ich liebe diesen,
Und nicht etwa den und jenen.
Lasset nur, ihr guten Leute,
Euer Wundern, euer Sehnen!

Ja, mit ungeheuren Mächten
Blicket sie wohl in die Runde;
Doch sie sucht nur zu verkünden
Ihm die nächste süße Stunde.

SULEIKA SPEAKS

The mirror says that I am beautiful,
You say: And shall grow old, by Fate's decree.
In God's eternity all things stand still:
Love him, then, for this moment and in me.

THE SECRET

When she casts her looks about her
There's surprise, and heads are shaken;
But I know my darling's meaning
And I know they're all mistaken.

For her message is: Dear people,
Waste no wondering to discover
Whom I love: not those ones, that one;
This one only is my lover.

Yes, indeed: her magic glances
Sweep around with mighty power;
But to me they are a signal
Speaking of our next sweet hour.

VERSUNKEN

Voll Locken kraus ein Haupt so rund!
Und darf ich dann in solchen reichen Haaren
Mit vollen Händen hin und wider fahren,
Da fühl ich mich von Herzensgrund gesund.
Und küß ich Stirne, Bogen, Auge, Mund,
Dann bin ich frisch und immer wieder wund.
Der fünfgezackte Kamm wo sollt er stocken?
Er kehrt schon wieder zu den Locken.
Das Ohr versagt sich nicht dem Spiel,
Hier ist nicht Fleisch, hier ist nicht Haut,
So zart zum Scherz, so liebeviel!
Doch wie man auf dem Köpfchen kraut,
Man wird in solchen reichen Haaren
Für ewig auf und nieder fahren.
So hast du, Hāfis, auch getan,
Wir fangen es von vornen an.

ENGULFED

So round, so full of curls your head! and when
In the abundance of these locks I bury
My hands and move them to and fro, the very
Depths of my heart are warmed and healed. Again
I kiss your brow and eyebrows, mouth and eyes,
And the still-freshening wound of love replies.
This five-pronged comb, where should it come to rest?
Back to your locks it goes, for they are best.
Your ear joins in the game as well: can this
Be skin, can this be flesh? So delicate
To each caress, so rich with love it is!
And so your head I fondle, fortunate
To plunge my hands in this abundant hair
And move them up and down for ever there.
This, Hāfiz, is what you did too:
We make a new start, imitating you.

Lieb um Liebe, Stund um Stunde,
Wort um Wort und Blick um Blick;
Kuß um Kuß, vom treusten Munde,
Hauch um Hauch und Glück um Glück.
So am Abend, so am Morgen!
Doch du fühlst an meinen Liedern
Immer noch geheime Sorgen;
Jussuphs Reize möcht ich borgen
Deine Schönheit zu erwidern.

An vollen Büschelzweigen,
Geliebte, sieh nur hin!
Laß dir die Früchte zeigen
Umschalet stachlig grün.

Sie hängen längst geballet,
Still, unbekannt mit sich,
Ein Ast, der schaukelnd wallet
Wiegt sie geduldiglich.

Doch immer reift von innen
Und schwillt der braune Kern,
Er möchte Luft gewinnen
Und säh die Sonne gern.

Die Schale platzt und nieder
Macht er sich freudig los;
So fallen meine Lieder
Gehäuft in deinen Schoß.

67

Love for love and hour for hour,
Words and looks in equal measure,
Kiss for kiss from lips so faithful,
Breath for breath, pleasure for pleasure.
So each nightfall, so each morrow!
Yet in this my song's recital
You may sense a secret sorrow:
Joseph's beauty I would borrow;
His for yours could make requital.

68

Beloved, let me show you
These branches: have you seen
These fruits that hang in clusters,
In prickly shells of green?

Long they have waited, silent,
Round, dense, self-unaware;
A bough that rocks them gently
Rocks in the gentle air.

But the brown kernels ripen
And swell from deep within,
Longing to see the sunlight,
To breathe, to burst their skin;

And now it bursts! How gladly
The nuts drop from the tree!
So too these songs of homage
Drop to your lap from me.

from the WEST-EASTERN DIVAN, 1814–18

69a

SULEIKA Als ich auf dem Euphrat schiffte,
Streifte sich der goldne Ring
Fingerab in Wasserklüfte,
Den ich jüngst von dir empfing.

Also träumt ich. Morgenröte
Blitzt ins Auge durch den Baum,
Sag Poete, sag Prophete!
Was bedeutet dieser Traum?

69b

HATEM Dies zu deuten bin erbötig!
Hab ich dir nicht oft erzählt,
Wie der Doge von Venedig
Mit dem Meere sich vermählt?

So von deinen Fingergliedern
Fiel der Ring dem Euphrat zu.
Ach zu tausend Himmelsliedern
Süßer Traum, begeisterst du!

Mich, der von den Indostanen
Streifte bis Damaskus hin,
Um mit neuen Karawanen
Bis ans Rote Meer zu ziehn,

Mich vermählst du deinem Flusse,
Der Terrasse, diesem Hain,
Hier soll bis zum letzten Kusse
Dir mein Geist gewidmet sein.

<center>69a</center>

SULEIKA As I sailed on the Euphrates
(So I dreamt) the ring of gold
You had given me, from my finger
Slipped, and to the depths it rolled.

So I woke. The morning sunlight
Flashed through branches from the sky.
Tell me, poet, prophet, tell me
What this dream can signify.

<center>69b</center>

HATEM This I'm happy to interpret!
There's a tale you've heard from me,
Telling of the Doge of Venice
And his marriage to the sea.

Thus your ring dropped from your finger
Into the Euphrates' stream.
Ah, what myriad songs of rapture
It inspires, your charming dream!

From the Hindustans I've wandered,
To Damascus then I came,
Changing caravans my travel,
The Red Sea my journey's aim;

To your river so you wed me,
To this terrace, to this grove,
And to you I pledge my spirit
Till the last embrace of love.

GINGO BILOBA

Dieses Baums Blatt, der von Osten
Meinem Garten anvertraut,
Gibt geheimen Sinn zu kosten,
Wies den Wissenden erbaut.

Ist es ein lebendig Wesen,
Das sich in sich selbst getrennt?
Sind es zwei, die sich erlesen,
Daß man sie als eines kennt?

Solche Frage zu erwidern
Fand ich wohl den rechten Sinn:
Fühlst du nicht an meinen Liedern,
Daß ich eins und doppelt bin?

VOLLMONDNACHT

Herrin, sag was heißt das Flüstern?
Was bewegt dir leis die Lippen?
Lispelst immer vor dich hin,
Lieblicher als Weines Nippen!
Denkst du deinen Mundgeschwistern
Noch ein Pärchen herzuziehn?
 'Ich will küssen! Küssen! sagt ich.'

GINKGO BILOBA

To my garden here translated,
Foliage of this eastern tree
Nourishes the initiated
With its meaning's mystery.

Is its leaf one self divided,
Forked into a shape of strife?
Or have two of them decided
On a symbiotic life?

This I answer without trouble
And am qualified to know:
I am single, I am double,
And my poems tell you so.

THE NIGHT OF THE FULL MOON

Lady, say, what are you whispering?
Still you move your lips and murmur
To yourself as soft as air;
Sips of wine were never sweeter.
Are your mouth's twin sisters seeking
To attract a matching pair?
 'Let me kiss him, kiss him, I was saying'.

Schau! Im zweifelhaften Dunkel
Glühen blühend alle Zweige,
Nieder spielet Stern auf Stern;
Und smaragden durchs Gesträuche
Tausendfältiger Karfunkel:
Doch dein Geist ist allem fern.
 'Ich will küssen! Küssen! sagt ich.'

Dein Geliebter, fern, erprobet
Gleicherweis im Sauersüßen,
Fühlt ein unglückselges Glück.
Euch im Vollmond zu begrüßen
Habt ihr heilig angelobet,
Dieses ist der Augenblick.
 'Ich will küssen! Küssen! sag ich.'

72

Ach, um deine feuchten Schwingen,
West, wie sehr ich dich beneide:
Denn du kannst ihm Kunde bringen
Was ich in der Trennung leide!

Die Bewegung deiner Flügel
Weckt im Busen stilles Sehnen;
Blumen, Augen, Wald und Hügel
Stehn bei deinem Hauch in Tränen.

Doch dein mildes sanftes Wehen
Kühlt die wunden Augenlider;
Ach, für Leid müßt ich vergehen,
Hofft ich nicht zu sehn ihn wieder.

Look, how in the doubtful darkness
All the branches glow and blossom,
Starshine plays, star gleams on star,
Through the undergrowth the emerald
Lights, a thousand gems are glittering:
But your thoughts have wandered far.
 'Let me kiss him, kiss him, I was saying'.

Even so this bitter-sweetness
He knows well, your far-off lover,
Feels a happiness of pain.
Solemnly you vowed to greet each
Other at the full moon's rising:
Now the moment comes again.
 'Let me kiss him, kiss him, I am saying'.

72

West wind, how I envy you your
Dewy wings, for to my lover
Far away they bear my message:
You can tell him how I suffer.

Swiftly speeds your flight and softly
Stirs the longing heart's emotion.
Eyes and flowers, hills and forest,
Weep to feel your breath's sweet motion.

Eyelids hot with tears your gentle
Breezes cool: oh, must I perish,
Or may I still hope to see him
Yet again, the hope I cherish?

from the WEST-EASTERN DIVAN, 1814–18

Eile denn zu meinem Lieben,
Spreche sanft zu seinem Herzen;
Doch vermeid ihn zu betrüben
Und verbirg ihm meine Schmerzen.

Sag ihm, aber sags bescheiden:
Seine Liebe sei mein Leben,
Freudiges Gefühl von beiden
Wird mir seine Nähe geben.

73

Behramgur, sagt man, hat den Reim erfunden,
Er sprach entzückt aus reiner Seele Drang;
Dilaram schnell, die Freundin seiner Stunden,
Erwiderte mit gleichem Wort und Klang.

Und so, Geliebte, warst du mir beschieden
Des Reims zu finden holden Lustgebrauch,
Daß auch Behramgur ich, den Sassaniden,
Nicht mehr beneiden darf: mir ward es auch.

Hast mir dies Buch geweckt, du hasts gegeben;
Denn was ich froh, aus vollem Herzen sprach,
Das klang zurück aus deinem holden Leben,
Wie Blick dem Blick, so Reim dem Reime nach.

Nun tön es fort zu dir, auch aus der Ferne,
Das Wort erreicht, und schwände Ton und Schall.
Ists nicht der Mantel noch gesäter Sterne?
Ists nicht der Liebe hochverklärtes All?

Hasten to my darling, bring these
Words to him, but soothing, healing,
For he must not grieve: speak gently
To his heart, my pain concealing.

Say, but say it mildly, wisely:
I am living if he loves me.
I shall have love, joy and life, when
All of these his presence gives me.

73

King Behramgur, they say, invented rhyme:
Words from his soul, out of his pure joy broke,
And Dilaram, she who beguiled his time,
Made answer, and the selfsame sounds she spoke.

Such was our destiny, beloved: you
Were given to me to find out rhyme's sweet strain.
Why envy now that Sassanid king? I too
Possess his gift, he speaks in me again.

In me you waked, to me you gave this book:
All my full heart's glad speech, all it could hold
From your sweet life came echoing back: each look
To look, each rhyme to rhyme the answer told.

Now may you hear it still, even from far;
Words reach their goal, though sound and music fade.
Is it not still the tent of scattered stars,
The high transfigured world that love has made?

SOMMERNACHT

DICHTER Niedergangen ist die Sonne,
Doch im Westen glänzt es immer;
Wissen möcht ich wohl, wie lange
Dauert noch der goldne Schimmer?

SCHENKE Willst du, Herr, so will ich bleiben,
Warten außer diesen Zelten;
Ist die Nacht des Schimmers Herrin,
Komm ich gleich es dir zu melden.

Denn ich weiß, du liebst, das Droben,
Das Unendliche zu schauen,
Wenn sie sich einander loben
Jene Feuer in dem Blauen.

Und das hellste will nur sagen:
'Jetzo glänz ich meiner Stelle;
Wollte Gott euch mehr betagen,
Glänztet ihr wie ich so helle.'

Denn vor Gott ist alles herrlich,
Eben weil er ist der Beste;
Und so schläft nun aller Vogel
In dem groß- und kleinen Neste.

Einer sitzt auch wohl gestängelt
Auf den Ästen der Zypresse,
Wo der laue Wind ihn gängelt,
Bis zu Taues luftger Nässe.

74a

SUMMER NIGHT

THE POET Now the westering sun's gone under,
 But there's still a glow and glimmer
 In the sky: how long, I wonder,
 Will it last, that golden shimmer?

THE CUPBEARER Sir, so please you, I'll be sitting
 Here outwith the tents and waiting,
 And I'll come at once to tell you,
 Soon as night is dominating.

 For I know you love to lift your
 Eyes and watch those endless spaces
 And those fires in the blue sky
 As they sing each other's praises.

 And the brightest of them only
 Says: 'I'm here to shine for ever:
 But you all would shine as I do
 If God gave you brighter favour.'

 For in God's eyes all is glorious,
 Just because he's best of any.
 Birds are nesting now and sleeping,
 Great and small birds, one and many.

 There's one sitting on the cypress
 Branches where warm winds are playing;
 Till the dew brings airy moisture
 He will perch there, rocking, swaying.

from the WEST-EASTERN DIVAN, 1814–18 171

Solches hast du mich gelehret,
Oder etwas auch dergleichen;
Was ich je dir abgehöret
Wird dem Herzen nicht entweichen.

Eule will ich deinetwegen
Kauzen hier auf der Terrasse,
Bis ich erst des Nordgestirnes
Zwillingswendung wohl erpasse.

Und da wird es Mitternacht sein,
Wo du oft zu früh ermunterst,
Und dann wird es eine Pracht sein,
Wenn das All mit mir bewunderst.

DICHTER Zwar in diesem Duft und Garten
Tönet Bulbul ganze Nächte;
Doch du könntest lange warten,
Bis die Nacht so viel vermöchte.

Denn in dieser Zeit der Flora,
Wie das Griechenvolk sie nennet,
Die Strohwitwe, die Aurora,
Ist in Hesperus entbrennet.

Sieh dich um! sie kommt! wie schnelle!
Über Blumenfelds Gelänge! –
Hüben hell und drüben helle,
Ja, die Nacht kommt ins Gedränge.

Und auf roten leichten Sohlen
Ihn, der mit der Sonn entlaufen,
Eilt sie irrig einzuholen;
Fühlst du nicht ein Liebe-Schnaufen?

That I think is what you've taught me;
Maybe not quite how you told it.
Every word I've heard you saying,
Safe and sure my heart will hold it.

I'm your owl, I'll squat here peering
Till the north stars' turn and twinning,
From your terrace I'll be watching
For the deepest dark's beginning.

That's the midnight hour, when often
You wake early from your dreaming;
Then we'll gaze at it together,
See the whole great star-world gleaming.

THE POET Well I know this fragrant garden:
Nightly Bulbul sings her story
Here, but such great nights come seldom,
You'll wait long to see that glory.

For as Greeks say, this is Flora's
Season, and the Dawn's forsaken
By her husband: now her fancy
By the evening star is taken.

Look behind you! Over summer
Fields she comes, so swiftly, brightly:
Both the east and west are shining
As the night is squeezed so tightly!

With the sun he fled, and rosy-
Footed after him she dances:
Can you feel the dawn wind blowing
As her breathless chase advances?

Geh nur, lieblichster der Söhne,
Tief ins Innre, schließ die Türen;
Denn sie möchte deine Schöne
Als den Hesperus entführen.

74b

DER SCHENKE *schläfrig*

So hab ich endlich von dir erharrt:
In allen Elementen Gottes Gegenwart.
Wie du mir das so lieblich gibst!
Am lieblichsten aber daß du liebst.

HATEM Der schläft recht süß und hat ein Recht zu schlafen.
Du guter Knabe hast mir eingeschenkt,
Vom Freund und Lehrer, ohne Zwang und Strafen,
So jung vernommen wie der Alte denkt.
Nun aber kommt Gesundheit holder Fülle
Dir in die Glieder daß du dich erneust.
Ich trinke noch, bin aber stille, stille,
Damit du mich, erwachend nicht, erfreust.

Go, sweet boy, into the house now,
Lock the doors, for that will make you
Safe: or she may see your beauty
And for Hesperus mistake you.

74b

THE CUPBEARER *sleepily*

Well, so at last I've learnt it all from you:
God's here in every element, I know that's true.
How dear you are to tell me all
These things! And yet your love's dearest of all.

HATEM Sweetly he sleeps, as is his right indeed.
So young, you have served my wine, and listened well
To your old friend and teacher's thoughts; no need,
Dear child, to force you, no need to compel.
And now it comes again, the sweet life pouring
Into your limbs, your wholesome youth restoring.
I sit and drink, but not a sound I make,
Still glad to watch you, glad you do not wake.

BEGÜNSTIGTE TIERE

Vier Tieren auch verheißen war
Ins Paradies zu kommen,
Dort leben sie das ewge Jahr
Mit Heiligen und Frommen.

Den Vortritt hier ein Esel hat
Er kommt mit muntern Schritten:
Denn Jesus zur Prophetenstadt
Auf ihm ist eingeritten.

Halb schüchtern kommt ein Wolf sodann,
Dem Mahomet befohlen:
'Laß dieses Schaf dem armen Mann,
Dem Reichen magst dus holen.'

Nun, immer wedelnd, munter, brav,
Mit seinem Herrn, dem braven,
Das Hündlein, das den Siebenschlaf
So treulich mitgeschlafen.

Abuherriras Katze hier
Knurrt um den Herrn und schmeichelt:
Denn immer ists ein heilig Tier
Das der Prophet gestreichelt.

PRIVILEGED ANIMALS

Four animals have qualified
For Paradise, I hear:
With saints and the devout they too
Shall live the eternal year.

A donkey here has precedence
And in he trots with pride,
For Jesus on his back into
Jerusalem did ride.

A shy old wolf is next, whom once
Muhammad put to shame:
'Don't touch that poor man's sheep!' he said.
'The rich man's is fair game.'

And now, tail wagging and bright-eyed,
The dog who kept the Seven
Sleepers such faithful company
Comes bounding into Heaven.

Abuherrira's cat's here too
And fawns about him purring.
The Prophet's hand has stroked the beast,
Full sanctity conferring.

HÖHERES UND HÖCHSTES

Daß wir solche Dinge lehren
Möge man uns nicht bestrafen:
Wie das alles zu erklären,
Dürft ihr euer Tiefstes fragen.

Und so werdet ihr vernehmen:
Daß der Mensch, mit sich zufrieden,
Gern sein Ich gerettet sähe,
So da droben wie hienieden.

Und mein liebes Ich bedürfte
Mancherlei Bequemlichkeiten,
Freuden wie ich hier sie schlürfte
Wünscht ich auch für ewge Zeiten.

So gefallen schöne Gärten,
Blum und Frucht und hübsche Kinder,
Die uns allen hier gefielen,
Auch verjüngtem Geist nicht minder.

Und so möcht ich alle Freunde,
Jung und alt, in eins versammeln,
Gar zu gern in deutscher Sprache
Paradiesesworte stammeln.

Doch man horcht nun Dialekten
Wie sich Mensch und Engel kosen,
Der Grammatik, der versteckten,
Deklinierend Mohn und Rosen.

HIGHER AND HIGHEST MATTERS

For the doctrines we are teaching
Do not censure us unduly:
Seek the answers deep within you
If you'd understand them truly.

There you'll find the ancient message:
Man, that self-contented wonder,
Seeks his own self-preservation
Whether here on earth or yonder.

As for my dear self, I'd gladly
Be permitted certain pleasures,
Certain comforts I have tasted
Here below in ample measures.

Gardens, flowers, fruit, fair maidens,
For example, here enchant us:
As rejuvenated spirits
These shall all no less content us.

And I'd dearly like my friends, both
Young and old, up there to gather,
All of us in German babbling
Paradisal words together.

Yet in other dialects men and
Angels make communication:
Secret grammars, speech of roses,
And the poppy's conjugation.

Mag man ferner auch in Blicken
Sich rhetorisch gern ergehen
Und zu himmlischem Entzücken
Ohne Klang und Ton erhöhen.

Ton und Klang jedoch entwindet
Sich dem Worte selbstverständlich,
Und entschiedener empfindet
Der Verklärte sich unendlich.

Ist somit dem Fünf der Sinne
Vorgesehn im Paradiese,
Sicher ist es, ich gewinne
Einen Sinn für alle diese.

Und nun dring ich aller Orten
Leichter durch die ewgen Kreise,
Die durchdrungen sind vom Worte
Gottes rein-lebendger Weise.

Ungehemmt mit heißem Triebe
Läßt sich da kein Ende finden,
Bis im Anschaun ewger Liebe
Wir verschweben, wir verschwinden.

Looks and glances too shall serve us,
Their mute rhetoric devising,
As to soundless, voiceless heights of
Joy celestial we are rising.

But all voice and sound must struggle
Free of words, our words transcending,
And transfiguration gives us
Surer hope of life unending.

If for each of my five senses
Paradise is thus provided,
Then, I think, they all will mingle
And be one and undivided.

Lightlier now I pass through all the
Timeless cycles God created
Which by his pure word and living
Motion all are penetrated.

Carried by resistless passion
There's no end to our exploring
Till in visions of eternal
Love we vanish, fading, soaring.

SELIGE SEHNSUCHT

Sagt es niemand, nur den Weisen,
Weil die Menge gleich verhöhnet:
Das Lebendge will ich preisen
Das nach Flammentod sich sehnet.

In der Liebesnächte Kühlung,
Die dich zeugte, wo du zeugtest,
Überfällt dich fremde Fühlung
Wenn die stille Kerze leuchtet.

Nicht mehr bleibest du umfangen
In der Finsternis Beschattung,
Und dich reißet neu Verlangen
Auf zu höherer Begattung.

Keine Ferne macht dich schwierig,
Kommst geflogen und gebannt,
Und zuletzt, des Lichts begierig,
Bist du Schmetterling verbrannt.

Und so lang du das nicht hast,
Dieses: Stirb und werde!
Bist du nur ein trüber Gast
Auf der dunklen Erde.

77

ECSTATIC LONGING

Tell it to the wisest only,
For the mob will mock such learning:
I will praise the living creature
That can long for death by burning.

As the candle's quiet gleaming
Cools your nights of hot surrender,
You are touched by strange emotion,
Born again as you engender.

You have passed beyond the shadows:
Snatched aloft, you shall discover
New desire and higher union:
Thrall of darkness now is over.

Distance tires you not nor hinders,
On you come with fated flight
Till, poor moth, at last you perish
In the flame, in love with light.

Die into becoming! Grasp
This, or sad and weary
Shall your sojourn ever be
On the dark earth dreary.

78

DAS ALTER

Das Alter ist ein höflich Mann:
Einmal übers andre klopft er an;
Aber nun sagt niemand: Herein!
Und vor der Türe will er nicht sein.
Da klinkt er auf, tritt ein so schnell,
Und nun heißts, er sei ein grober Gesell.

79

ANNONCE

'Ein Hündchen wird gesucht
Das weder murrt noch beißt,
Zerbrochene Gläser frißt
Und Diamanten scheißt.'

80

Wer aber recht bequem ist und faul,
Flög dem eine gebratne Taube ins Maul,
Er würde höchlich sichs verbitten,
Wär sie nicht auch geschickt zerschnitten.

81

Dem ist es schlecht in seiner Haut,
Der in seinen eignen Busen schaut.

78

OLD AGE

When old age comes, he arrives politely,
Knocks once or twice at the door quite quietly;
But no one welcomes him in so pat,
And to be left outside, well, he doesn't like that.
So he lifts the latch as quick as he can,
And now they say: What an ill-mannered man.

79

ADVERTISEMENT

'Wanted: a little dog
That will not growl or bite,
Eats broken glass, and shits
Diamonds instead of shite.'

80

If a man's dead idle, a roasted duck
Could fly into his mouth, and he'd curse his luck
And complain that it hadn't been properly served:
It must first be roasted, then neatly carved.

81

A man's a misfit in his own hide
If he studies himself and looks inside.

82

Am Jüngsten Tag, vor Gottes Thron,
Stand endlich Held Napoleon.
Der Teufel hielt ein großes Register
Gegen denselben und sein Geschwister,
War ein wundersam verruchtes Wesen;
Satan fing an, es abzulesen.

Gott Vater, oder Gott der Sohn,
Einer von beiden sprach vom Thron,
Wenn nicht etwa gar der Heilige Geist
Das Wort genommen allermeist:

'Wiederhols nicht vor göttlichen Ohren!
Du sprichst wie die deutschen Professoren.
Wir wissen alles, mach es kurz!
Am Jüngsten Tag ists nur ein Furz.
Getraust du dich, ihn anzugreifen,
So magst du ihn nach der Hölle schleifen.'

83

[FLIEGENTOD]

Sie saugt mit Gier verrätrisches Getränke
Unabgesetzt, vom ersten Zug verführt;
Sie fühlt sich wohl, und längst sind die Gelenke
Der zarten Beinchen schon paralysiert,
Nicht mehr gewandt, die Flügelchen zu putzen,
Nicht mehr geschickt, das Köpfchen aufzustutzen –

The hero Napoleon came to meet
His Maker before the Judgment Seat.
The Devil had catalogued many a sin
Against him and all his kith and kin,
An amazing list of infamous deeds
Which Satan now produces and reads.

But God the Father, or God the Son
Spoke, I'm not really sure which one,
Or maybe it was the Holy Ghost
That did the talking, or did most:

'Our divine ears have heard enough!
Don't give us this German professor stuff.
Cut it short! We know it all anyway!
It's not worth a fart on Judgment Day.
If you dare attack him, you have our permission
To carry him off to Hell and perdition.'

[THE DEATH OF A FLY]

How greedily he sucks the treacherous dregs
Without a pause, by a first sip lured on!
He feels no sickness, but his jointed legs
Are paralysed, their strength already gone;
Now they have lost the skill they had to clean
His delicate wings, his little head to preen –

Das Leben so sich im Genuß verliert.
Zum Stehen kaum wird noch das Füßchen taugen;
So schlürft sie fort, und mitten unterm Saugen
Umnebelt ihr der Tod die tausend Augen.

84

UM MITTERNACHT

Um Mitternacht ging ich, nicht eben gerne,
Klein, kleiner Knabe, jenen Kirchhof hin
Zu Vaters Haus, des Pfarrers; Stern am Sterne,
Sie leuchteten doch alle gar zu schön;
 Um Mitternacht.

Wenn ich dann ferner in des Lebens Weite
Zur Liebsten mußte, mußte, weil sie zog,
Gestirn und Nordschein über mir im Streite,
Ich gehend, kommend Seligkeiten sog;
 Um Mitternacht.

Bis dann zuletzt des vollen Mondes Helle
So klar und deutlich mir ins Finstere drang,
Auch der Gedanke willig, sinnig, schnelle
Sich ums Vergangne wie ums Künftige schlang;
 Um Mitternacht.

Thus life in pleasure ebbs away and dies.
He scarcely stands now on his failing feet;
Yet still he drinks, and as he sucks the sweet
Elixir down, death clouds his thousand eyes.

84

AT MIDNIGHT

At midnight past that churchyard I would go,
Rather unwillingly, a small small boy,
To father's house, the priest's house; all aglow
With shining stars, so splendid was the sky
 At midnight.

And further on in life, going to meet
My darling, drawn to her against my will,
I saw the Northern Lights and stars compete;
I came, I went, drinking her sweetness still
 At midnight.

Until at last the full moon's radiance gleamed
Into my darkness; and how well in place,
How willing and how swift my thoughts all seemed
As past and future lay in their embrace
 At midnight.

URWORTE. ORPHISCH

ΔΑΙΜΩΝ Dämon

Wie an dem Tag, der dich der Welt verliehen,
Die Sonne stand zum Gruße der Planeten,
Bist alsobald und fort und fort gediehen
Nach dem Gesetz, wonach du angetreten.
So mußt du sein, dir kannst du nicht entfliehen,
So sagten schon Sibyllen, so Propheten;
Und keine Zeit und keine Macht zerstückelt
Geprägte Form, die lebend sich entwickelt.

ΤΥΧΗ das Zufällige

Die strenge Grenze doch umgeht gefällig
Ein Wandelndes, das mit und um uns wandelt;
Nicht einsam bleibst du, bildest dich gesellig,
Und handelst wohl so, wie ein andrer handelt:
Im Leben ists bald hin-, bald widerfällig,
Es ist ein Tand und wird so durchgetandelt.
Schon hat sich still der Jahre Kreis geründet,
Die Lampe harrt der Flamme, die entzündet.

ΕΡΩΣ Liebe

Die bleibt nicht aus! – Er stürzt vom Himmel nieder,
Wohin er sich aus alter Öde schwang,
Er schwebt heran auf luftigem Gefieder
Um Stirn und Brust den Frühlingstag entlang,
Scheint jetzt zu fliehn, vom Fliehen kehrt er wieder:
Da wird ein Wohl im Weh, so süß und bang.
Gar manches Herz verschwebt im Allgemeinen,
Doch widmet sich das edelste dem Einen.

PRIMAL WORDS. ORPHIC

DAIMON Destiny

As on the day that gave you to the world,
As then the planets stood to greet the sun,
Even so since then your life has all unfurled
By that same law at that same hour begun.
You are, as seers and sibyls have foretold,
Yourself, and from yourself you cannot run;
For neither time nor any power can shatter
The evolving life-form of imprinted matter.

TYCHE Chance

And yet a pleasing, changeful element
Moves with us, round us, mitigates that stern
Restriction; you are not alone, you are meant
To do as others do, from them to learn.
Life is a toy, and toying it is spent;
It takes a lucky or an unlucky turn.
The quiet years have passed now, and time came
Full course; the lamp awaits the enkindling flame.

EROS Love

And sure enough, it comes! – That god who soared
Up from the primal chaos, swoops down now
On airy wings and hovering like a bird
Through the spring day about our breast and brow,
Fluttering and feigning, earthward, heavenward
And back again: joy, dread, sweet anguish, how
They mingle! – Many a heart strays far and wide:
The noblest knows one love and none beside.

ΑΝΑΓΚΗ Nötigung

Da ists denn wieder, wie die Sterne wollten:
Bedingung und Gesetz; und aller Wille
Ist nur ein Wollen, weil wir eben sollten,
Und vor dem Willen schweigt die Willkür stille;
Das Liebste wird vom Herzen weggescholten,
Dem harten Muß bequemt sich Will und Grille.
So sind wir scheinfrei denn, nach manchen Jahren
Nur enger dran, als wir am Anfang waren.

ΕΛΠΙΣ Hoffnung

Doch solcher Grenze, solcher ehrnen Mauer
Höchst widerwärtge Pforte wird entriegelt,
Sie stehe nur mit alter Felsendauer!
Ein Wesen regt sich leicht und ungezügelt:
Aus Wolkendecke, Nebel, Regenschauer
Erhebt sie uns, mit ihr, durch sie beflügelt,
Ihr kennt sie wohl, sie schwärmt durch alle Zonen –
Ein Flügelschlag – und hinter uns Äonen!

86

PARIA

Des Paria Gebet

Großer Brahma, Herr der Mächte!
Alles ist von deinem Samen,
Und so bist du der Gerechte!
Hast du denn allein die Brahmen,
Nur die Rajahs und die Reichen,
Hast du sie allein geschaffen?
Oder bist auch dus, der Affen
Werden ließ und unseresgleichen?

ANANKE Necessity

And then all's as it was: the stars' decree,
Necessity and law; our will's no more
Than willing what we had and have to be;
That will outwills us; wishes, wants, implore
It vainly, and we lose most cruelly
What we love most; our heart is dumb before
The strict command. Thus, seeming free, we know
Ourselves trapped faster than long years ago.

ELPIS Hope

Yet not for ever closed is the dread gate
Of such a barrier, such a brazen wall,
Though it may stand rock-fast like ancient fate!
There is a being, and you know her well:
Lightsome, unbridled, who on delicate
Wings lifts us high through clouds, fog, rain and all
That weighs us down: she flies both wide and far –
One wing-beat bears us where vast ages are!

86

THE PARIAH

The Pariah's Prayer

Great god Brahma, lord of spirits,
From your seed all life inherits,
And most just are all your ways.
Did you then create the holy
Brahmins, kings and rich folk only,
Did you make no other race?
Or did your almighty mind
Breed the apes and our base kind?

Edel sind wir nicht zu nennen:
Denn das Schlechte, das gehört uns,
Und was andre tödlich kennen,
Das alleine, das vermehrt uns.
Mag dies für die Menschen gelten,
Mögen sie uns doch verachten;
Aber du, du sollst uns achten,
Denn du könntest alle schelten.

Also, Herr, nach diesem Flehen,
Segne mich zu deinem Kinde;
Oder eines laß entstehen,
Das auch mich mit dir verbinde!
Denn du hast den Bajaderen
Eine Göttin selbst erhoben;
Auch wir andern, dich zu loben,
Wollen solch ein Wunder hören.

Legende

Wasser holen geht die reine
Schöne Frau des hohen Brahmen,
Des verehrten, fehlerlosen,
Ernstester Gerechtigkeit.
Täglich von dem heiligen Flusse
Holt sie köstlichstes Erquicken –
Aber wo ist Krug und Eimer?
Sie bedarf derselben nicht.
Seligem Herzen, frommen Händen
Ballt sich die bewegte Welle
Herrlich zu kristallner Kugel;
Diese trägt sie, frohen Busens,
Reiner Sitte, holden Wandelns,
Vor den Gatten in das Haus.

No one calls us noble creatures,
For the dirt cleaves to our natures;
Filthy food no others thrive on
Is all we may keep alive on;
So with men, if they concern us.
But you, master, need not spurn us,
For before you, we are sure,
None is perfect, none is pure.

Lord, now I have supplicated,
Bless me, make me your child too:
Or let something be created
Binding even me to you.
For you gave the bayadères
A great goddess of their own;
See, we bow before your throne:
Work this wonder, hear our prayers!

The Legend

Pure and lovely, to fetch water,
Goes the wife of the high brahmin
Honoured for his faultless justice,
Judge most noble and most grave.
Daily from the sacred river
She brings precious clear refreshment
Carried in no jug nor pitcher,
For she has no need of these.
When the heart and hands are guiltless
Then the moving water changes
To a splendid sphere of crystal.
This she carries, light of spirit,
Pure and gentle in her conduct,
To her husband and her house.

Heute kommt die morgendliche
Im Gebet zu Ganges' Fluten,
Beugt sich zu der klaren Fläche –
Plötzlich überraschend spiegelt,
Aus des höchsten Himmels Breiten
Über ihr vorübereilend,
Allerlieblichste Gestalt
Hehren Jünglings, den des Gottes
Uranfänglich schönes Denken
Aus dem ewgen Busen schuf.
Solchen schauend, fühlt ergriffen
Von verwirrenden Gefühlen
Sie das innere tiefste Leben,
Will verharren in dem Anschaun,
Weist es weg, da kehrt es wieder,
Und verworren strebt sie flutwärts,
Mit unsichrer Hand zu schöpfen;
Aber ach! sie schöpft nicht mehr!
Denn des Wassers heilige Welle
Scheint zu fliehn, sich zu entfernen,
Sie erblickt nur hohler Wirbel
Grause Tiefen unter sich.

Arme sinken, Tritte straucheln,
Ists denn auch der Pfad nach Hause?
Soll sie zaudern? soll sie fliehen?
Will sie denken, wo Gedanke,
Rat und Hilfe gleich versagt? –
Und so tritt sie vor den Gatten;
Er erblickt sie, Blick ist Urteil,
Hohen Sinns ergreift das Schwert er,
Schleppt sie zu dem Totenhügel,
Wo Verbrecher büßend bluten.
Wüßte sie zu widerstreben?

So today she comes in morning
Beauty to the river Ganges,
Bows in prayer to the bright surface –
Suddenly, from the high heavens,
As it flashes past above her,
In the stream a shape is mirrored:
The enchanting, noble form
Of a young man, god-engendered
From the eternal heart of beauty
In divine primordial thought.
As she sees him, her profoundest
Inner life is seized by over-
Powering chaos of emotions:
She would linger with the vision,
It returns when she rejects it.
And in her confusion stooping,
With uncertain hands, she vainly
Tries to lift the sacred water –
Can, alas, no longer do so!
For it swirls away, it flees her
Now, and she can gaze down only
Into eddying gulfs of dread.

See, her arms sink, her steps stumble:
Which way home? She scarcely finds it.
Shall she flee or shall she tarry?
How can she take thought or counsel?
There's no help nor counsel now.
So she comes before her husband,
So he sees her: sight is judgment.
High of mind, his sword he snatches,
To the Hill of Death he drags her,
Where the guilty pay their blood-debt.
How could she resist, and how could

Wüßte sie sich zu entschuldgen,
Schuldig, keiner Schuld bewußt?

Und er kehrt mit blutigem Schwerte
Sinnend zu der stillen Wohnung;
Da entgegnet ihm der Sohn.
'Wessen Blut ists? Vater! Vater!' –
Der Verbrecherin! – 'Mitnichten!
Denn es starret nicht am Schwerte
Wie verbrecherische Tropfen,
Fließt wie aus der Wunde frisch.
Mutter! Mutter! tritt heraus her!
Ungerecht war nie der Vater,
Sage, was er jetzt verübt.' –
Schweige! Schweige! 's ist das ihre! –
'Wessen ist es?' – Schweige! Schweige! –
'Wäre meiner Mutter Blut!!!

Was geschehen? was verschuldet?
Her das Schwert! ergriffen hab ichs;
Deine Gattin magst du töten,
Aber meine Mutter nicht!
In die Flammen folgt die Gattin
Ihrem einzig Angetrauten,
Seiner einzig teuren Mutter
In das Schwert der treue Sohn.'

Halt, o halte! rief der Vater,
Noch ist Raum, enteil, enteile!
Füge Haupt dem Rumpfe wieder,
Du berührest mit dem Schwerte,
Und lebendig folgt sie dir.

Eilend, atemlos erblickt er
Staunend zweier Frauen Körper
Überkreuzt, und so die Häupter –

She find words that would excuse her,
Guiltless–guilty as she is?

With the bloodstained blade and pensive
To his quiet house returning,
There the brahmin meets his son.
'Father! father! Whose blood is this?'
'Hers who sinned'. 'It cannot be so!
To your sword it is not sticking,
As the drops of miscreants' blood do:
Fresh as from the wound it flows.
Mother! Mother! Come! Where are you?
Was my father ever unjust?
Tell me now what he has done!'
'Hold your peace! The blood is her blood!'
'Whose blood did you say?' 'Be silent!'
'Can this be my mother's blood?

What has happened? How offended?
Give your sword to me! I'll have it!
Slay your wife, if you must do so:
Slay your wife, but not my mother!
To the flames a wife must follow
Her true husband: so a faithful
Son must follow his beloved
Precious mother to the sword!'

'Stop! oh, stop!' exclaimed his father.
'There's still time; go quickly, quickly!
Fit the head back to the torso;
Take the sword then, touch her with it.
That will bring her back to life.'

Hastening there, the son, amazed and
Breathless, finds two female corpses
Lying crosswise, and the heads too –

Welch Entsetzen! welche Wahl!
Dann der Mutter Haupt erfaßt er,
Küßt es nicht, das tot erblaßte;
Auf des nächsten Rumpfes Lücke
Setzt ers eilig, mit dem Schwerte
Segnet er das fromme Werk.

Aufersteht ein Riesenbildnis. –
Von der Mutter teuren Lippen,
Göttlich-unverändert-süßen,
Tönt das grausenvolle Wort:
Sohn, o Sohn! welch Übereilen!
Deiner Mutter Leichnam dorten,
Neben ihm das freche Haupt
Der Verbrecherin, des Opfers
Waltender Gerechtigkeit!
Mich nun hast du ihrem Körper
Eingeimpft auf ewige Tage:
Weisen Wollens, wilden Handelns
Werd ich unter Göttern sein;
Ja, des Himmelsknaben Bildnis
Webt so schön vor Stirn und Auge –
Senkt sichs in das Herz herunter,
Regt es tolle Wutbegier.

Immer wird es wiederkehren,
Immer steigen, immer sinken,
Sich verdüstern, sich verklären,
So hat Brahma dies gewollt.
Er gebot ja buntem Fittich,
Klarem Antlitz, schlanken Gliedern,
Göttlich-einzigem Erscheinen
Mich zu prüfen, zu verführen;
Denn von oben kommt Verführung,
Wenns den Göttern so beliebt.

What a horror! What a choice!
So his mother's head he seizes,
Does not kiss the death-pale features,
Sets it quickly on the nearest
Torso's wound, and his sword's blessing
Then completes the pious work.

A gigantic figure rises,
And his mother's dear beloved
Lips, unchanged in godlike sweetness,
Speak the horrifying words:
'Son, oh son, what haste! What error!
Over there your mother's corpse lies,
And in shamelessness beside it
Lies the head of a vile miscreant
Brought to justice for her crimes.
You have set me on her body,
Grafted me to her for ever:
Now among the gods I shall be
Wise in will and wild in action.
Yes, before my face and eyes that
Young god's image floats in beauty;
But when it sinks lower, with a
Raging lust it fills my heart.

It will always be returning,
Always rising, always sinking,
Now obscured and now transfigured:
This is the lord Brahma's will.
It was he who bade that boy's bright
Wings, his shining face, his slender
Limbs, his godlike rare appearance
Come to test me, to seduce me;
For seduction from on high can
Come, if the high gods so choose.

Und so soll ich, die Brahmane,
Mit dem Haupt im Himmel weilend,
Fühlen, Paria, dieser Erde
Niederziehende Gewalt.

Sohn, ich sende dich dem Vater!
Tröste! – Nicht ein traurig Büßen,
Stumpfes Harren, stolz Verdienen
Halt euch in der Wildnis fest;
Wandert aus durch alle Welten,
Wandelt hin durch alle Zeiten
Und verkündet auch Geringstem:
Daß ihn Brahma droben hört!

Ihm ist keiner der Geringste –
Wer sich mit gelähmten Gliedern,
Sich mit wild zerstörtem Geiste,
Düster, ohne Hilf und Rettung,
Sei er Brahma, sei er Paria,
Mit dem Blick nach oben kehrt,
Wirds empfinden, wirds erfahren:
Dort erglühen tausend Augen,
Ruhend lauschen tausend Ohren,
Denen nichts verborgen bleibt.

Heb ich mich zu seinem Throne,
Schaut er mich, die Grausenhafte,
Die er gräßlich umgeschaffen,
Muß er ewig mich bejammern,
Euch zugute komme das.
Und ich werd ihn freundlich mahnen,
Und ich werd ihm wütend sagen,
Wie es mir der Sinn gebietet,
Wie es mir im Busen schwellet.
Was ich denke, was ich fühle –
Ein Geheimnis bleibe das.'

So must I, a brahmin lady,
With my head still in the heavens,
Feel, as a pariah, how this
Earth has power to drag me down.

Son, I send you to your father!
Comfort him, but let no dismal
Penance, feats of proud endurance,
Keep you in the wilderness:
Wander forth through all the worlds now,
Journey on through all the ages,
And proclaim even to the humblest
That great Brahma hears his prayer!

For to him none is the humblest –
Any man may feel and learn this,
Be he brahmin or pariah,
Who in mental wild distraction,
Who with palsied limbs, from darkness
Where there is no help nor rescue,
Looks to heaven: for there a thousand
Eyes are burning, there a thousand
Ears in stillness listen: nothing
From those eyes and ears can hide.

Now, when I rise up to where he
Sees me from his throne, and sees this
Thing of horror he has made me,
He must pity me for ever:
All of you shall gain from this.
I will counsel him in friendship
And declare to him in fury
What my mind shall bid me tell him,
And my heart uprising in me.
But my thoughts, my feelings, let them
Dwell in secret evermore.'

Dank des Paria

Großer Brahma! nun erkenn ich,
Daß du Schöpfer bist der Welten!
Dich als meinen Herrscher nenn ich,
Denn du lässest alle gelten.

Und verschließest auch dem Letzten
Keines von den tausend Ohren;
Uns, die tief Herabgesetzten,
Alle hast du neu geboren.

Wendet euch zu dieser Frauen,
Die der Schmerz zur Göttin wandelt!
Nun beharr ich, anzuschauen
Den, der einzig wirkt und handelt.

87

TRILOGIE DER LEIDENSCHAFT

An Werther

Noch einmal wagst du, vielbeweinter Schatten,
Hervor dich an das Tageslicht,
Begegnest mir auf neu beblümten Matten,
Und meinen Anblick scheust du nicht.
Es ist, als ob du lebtest in der Frühe,
Wo uns der Tau auf Einem Feld erquickt
Und nach des Tages unwillkommner Mühe
Der Scheidesonne letzter Strahl entzückt;
Zum Bleiben ich, zum Scheiden du erkoren,
Gingst du voran – und hast nicht viel verloren.

The Pariah's Thanksgiving

Great lord Brahma, now as maker
Of all worlds I hail you truly,
And I name you as my master,
For you value all men duly.

All your thousand ears are open
To the lowest on the earth;
Even to us, the deep-degraded,
You have given a new birth.

Brothers, seek this Lady's favour:
To a goddess grief has made her.
I will gaze on one Creator
And his words and deeds for ever.

87

A TRILOGY OF PASSION

To Werther

And so you venture, much lamented shade,
Once more into the light of day;
On fresh green fields you meet me, unafraid
To face me and not turn away.
A visitor from earlier years you seem,
Those years when the same grass and dew, my friend,
Refreshed us both, and at day's toilful end
We both rejoiced in the sun's parting gleam.
Fate chose: you went before me, I remained –
Little you lost, and little I have gained.

Des Menschen Leben scheint ein herrlich Los:
Der Tag wie lieblich, so die Nacht wie groß!
Und wir, gepflanzt in Paradieses Wonne,
Genießen kaum der hocherlauchten Sonne,
Da kämpft sogleich verworrene Bestrebung
Bald mit uns selbst und bald mit der Umgebung;
Keins wird vom andern wünschenswert ergänzt,
Von außen düsterts, wenn es innen glänzt,
Ein glänzend Äußres deckt ein trüber Blick,
Da steht es nah – und man verkennt das Glück.

Nun glauben wirs zu kennen! Mit Gewalt
Ergreift uns Liebreiz weiblicher Gestalt:
Der Jüngling, froh wie in der Kindheit Flor,
Im Frühling tritt als Frühling selbst hervor,
Entzückt, erstaunt, wer dies ihm angetan?
Er schaut umher, die Welt gehört ihm an.
Ins Weite zieht ihn unbefangne Hast,
Nichts engt ihn ein, nicht Mauer, nicht Palast;
Wie Vögelschar an Wäldergipfeln streift,
So schwebt auch er, der um die Liebste schweift,
Er sucht vom Äther, den er gern verläßt,
Den treuen Blick, und dieser hält ihn fest.

Doch erst zu früh und dann zu spät gewarnt,
Fühlt er den Flug gehemmt, fühlt sich umgarnt.
Das Wiedersehn ist froh, das Scheiden schwer,
Das Wieder-Wiedersehn beglückt noch mehr,
Und Jahre sind im Augenblick ersetzt;
Doch tückisch harrt das Lebewohl zuletzt.

Du lächelst, Freund, gefühlvoll, wie sich ziemt:
Ein gräßlich Scheiden machte dich berühmt;
Wir feierten dein kläglich Mißgeschick,

How glorious seems a man's allotted time,
Each day delightful, and each night sublime!
But scarcely born into this Eden, still
Scarce blessed by the exalted sun, our will,
At once confused, plunges into self-strife
Or strife with our surroundings. Thus our life
Divides, not marrying to a whole; the light
That shines in us an outward gloom may blight,
Or outward splendour darken in our eyes
And nearby joy we fail to recognise.

But then we think we see it! Womankind
With sudden powerful charm enchants our mind:
Glad as in childhood's flower, in boyhood's spring,
Himself the spring, the young lover, wondering
What has bewitched him so, steps forth, looks round
At the delightful world that he has found.
An unchecked haste draws him afar, on high,
No walls confining him; and as birds fly
In flocks about the wooded mountain peaks,
So he round his beloved, as he seeks
From the ethereal sky to capture her,
Her lovely eyes that hold him prisoner.

Too soon comes warning, then too late: his flight
Is checked, he feels himself ensnared, the sight
Of her is joy, each parting is despair,
Seeing her yet again too sweet to bear;
For empty years one moment compensates,
But last of all a cruel farewell waits.

Sadly you smile, friend, as befits your fame
Who to a dreadful parting gave your name;
For good or ill you left us here behind,

Du ließest uns zu Wohl und Weh zurück.
Dann zog uns wieder ungewisse Bahn
Der Leidenschaften labyrinthisch an;
Und wir, verschlungen wiederholter Not,
Dem Scheiden endlich – Scheiden ist der Tod!
Wie klingt es rührend, wenn der Dichter singt,
Den Tod zu meiden, den das Scheiden bringt!
Verstrickt in solche Qualen, halbverschuldet,
Geb ihm ein Gott zu sagen, was er duldet.

Elegie

Und wenn der Mensch in seiner Qual verstummt,
Gab mir ein Gott zu sagen, was ich leide.

Was soll ich nun vom Wiedersehen hoffen,
Von dieses Tages noch geschloßner Blüte?
Das Paradies, die Hölle steht dir offen;
Wie wankelsinnig regt sichs im Gemüte! –
Kein Zweifeln mehr! Sie tritt ans Himmelstor,
Zu ihren Armen hebt sie dich empor.

So warst du denn im Paradies empfangen,
Als wärst du wert des ewig schönen Lebens;
Dir blieb kein Wunsch, kein Hoffen, kein Verlangen,
Hier war das Ziel des innigsten Bestrebens,
Und in dem Anschaun dieses einzig Schönen
Versiegte gleich der Quell sehnsüchtiger Tränen.

Wie regte nicht der Tag die raschen Flügel,
Schien die Minuten vor sich her zu treiben!
Der Abendkuß, ein treu verbindlich Siegel:
So wird es auch der nächsten Sonne bleiben.
Die Stunden glichen sich in zartem Wandern
Wie Schwestern zwar, doch keine ganz den andern.

Calling your pitiable fate to mind,
Until once more passion's uncertain maze
Drew us into its labyrinthine ways,
And love's repeated complicated pain;
So till the end – parting and death again.
How touchingly a poet can avoid
Parting and death! Yet by such anguish cloyed
And half to blame, may he find words to sing,
Taught by some god, that tell his suffering.

Elegy

> When in their anguish other men fall silent
> A god gave me the power to tell my pain.

What can I hope from this reunion, and
From the unopened blossom of this day?
Both paradise and hell, open they stand;
What hesitation stirs in me! Away,
Enough of it! To heaven's gate she comes
And raises me on high into her arms.

And so I entered paradise, somehow
I had deserved life in eternity;
No wish, no hope, no deep desire was now
Unsatisfied: here was reality,
And as I gazed at this one loveliness
My tears dried up, and gone was all distress.

How quickly the day passed, how its wings stirred
And seemed to drive the fleeting minutes on!
The kiss at evening, like a faithful word:
'So it shall be until tomorrow's sun!'
So gently the hours wandered, went and came,
Alike as sisters, yet none quite the same.

Der Kuß, der letzte, grausam süß, zerschneidend
Ein herrliches Geflecht verschlungner Minnen.
Nun eilt, nun stockt der Fuß, die Schwelle meidend,
Als trieb' ein Cherub flammend ihn von hinnen;
Das Auge starrt auf düstrem Pfad verdrossen,
Es blickt zurück, die Pforte steht verschlossen.

Und nun verschlossen in sich selbst, als hätte
Dies Herz sich nie geöffnet, selige Stunden
Mit jedem Stern des Himmels um die Wette
An ihrer Seite leuchtend nicht empfunden;
Und Mißmut, Reue, Vorwurf, Sorgenschwere
Belastens nun in schwüler Atmosphäre.

Ist denn die Welt nicht übrig? Felsenwände,
Sind sie nicht mehr gekrönt von heiligen Schatten?
Die Ernte, reift sie nicht? Ein grün Gelände,
Zieht sichs nicht hin am Fluß durch Busch und Matten?
Und wölbt sich nicht das überweltlich Große,
Gestaltenreiche, bald Gestaltenlose?

Wie leicht und zierlich, klar und zart gewoben
Schwebt, seraphgleich, aus ernster Wolken Chor,
Als glich' es ihr, am blauen Äther droben
Ein schlank Gebild aus lichtem Duft empor!
So sahst du sie in frohem Tanze walten,
Die lieblichste der lieblichsten Gestalten.

Doch nur Momente darfst dich unterwinden,
Ein Luftgebild statt ihrer festzuhalten;
Ins Herz zurück! dort wirst dus besser finden,
Dort regt sie sich in wechselnden Gestalten:
Zu Vielen bildet Eine sich hinüber,
So tausendfach, und immer, immer lieber.

Then the last kiss of all, cruelly sweet,
Tearing apart the splendid weft of love.
I fled the threshold now, with stumbling feet;
A fiery cherub seemed to come and drive
Me out; at the dark road I stared in pain;
The gate was locked, now I looked back in vain.

And so, imprisoned in itself, my heart
Felt it had never opened, never known
That blessedness so bright and heaven-starred
When I was with her. Heavy now as stone
It fills with self-reproach, remorse, despair,
Anxiety, choked in a sultry air.

Is not the world still here? The mountain's height,
Is it no longer crowned with sacred shade?
Does not corn ripen, or green countryside
By rivers lie, of trees and meadows made,
Or the great vault, greater than worlds, not fill
With shapes that vanish, but enrich it still?

There in the ethereal blue, where clouds stand by
In solemn chorus, there so clear and tender
She seems to float like a bright mist on high,
An angel spirit, delicate and slender!
Once as she danced I saw that vision blest:
Of loveliest forms she was the loveliest.

Yet only momentarily I dare
Hold fast an airy fiction in her place:
Better my own heart! Let me shelter there,
For there she dwells, an ever-changing face,
One and yet self-transformed a thousandfold,
Ever more dear, more dear than can be told.

Wie zum Empfang sie an den Pforten weilte
Und mich von dannauf stufenweis beglückte,
Selbst nach dem letzten Kuß mich noch ereilte,
Den letztesten mir auf die Lippen drückte:
So klar beweglich bleibt das Bild der Lieben
Mit Flammenschrift ins treue Herz geschrieben.

Ins Herz, das fest, wie zinnenhohe Mauer,
Sich ihr bewahrt und sie in sich bewahret,
Für sie sich freut an seiner eignen Dauer,
Nur weiß von sich, wenn sie sich offenbaret,
Sich freier fühlt in so geliebten Schranken
Und nur noch schlägt, für alles ihr zu danken.

War Fähigkeit zu lieben, war Bedürfen
Von Gegenliebe weggelöscht, verschwunden,
Ist Hoffnungslust zu freudigen Entwürfen,
Entschlüssen, rascher Tat sogleich gefunden!
Wenn Liebe je den Liebenden begeistet,
Ward es an mir aufs lieblichste geleistet;

Und zwar durch sie! – Wie lag ein innres Bangen
Auf Geist und Körper, unwillkommner Schwere:
Von Schauerbildern rings der Blick umfangen
Im wüsten Raum beklommner Herzensleere;
Nun dämmert Hoffnung von bekannter Schwelle,
Sie selbst erscheint in milder Sonnenhelle.

Dem Frieden Gottes, welcher euch hienieden
Mehr als Vernunft beseliget – wir lesens –
Vergleich ich wohl der Liebe heitern Frieden
In Gegenwart des allgeliebten Wesens;
Da ruht das Herz, und nichts vermag zu stören
Den tiefsten Sinn, den Sinn: ihr zu gehören.

How at the gate she'd wait to welcome me,
Then step by step heighten my happiness,
Even after the last kiss so eagerly
Run back, just one more on my lips to press:
All this my darling's image, burning clear,
Wrote on my heart, to live for ever here.

For like a rampart, so my heart stands fast,
Keeps faith for her, in faithful love is hers,
For her sole sake rejoicing so to last,
Knowing itself only when she appears,
Free in beloved bonds, a heart that lives
Only to give her thanks for all she gives.

For I had lost it, all capacity
For love, even for requited love no need
Remained; but then came hope, joy breaking free
Into resolve and into instant deed!
If ever love inspired a lover, where
Is there a happier instance anywhere

Than I, and she who did it? What oppression
Weighed on my mind and body, what dull dread
And fearful images were in possession
Of my whole world, all wasted, speechless, dead!
Now hope has dawned from a familiar place:
A gentle sun rose, and I see her face.

There is that peace of God, which here below
Passes all understanding (so we read),
And to it I compare love's peace, for so
It is, when one we truly love indeed
Is with us: the heart rests, our faith is strong,
Faith that to the beloved we belong.

In unsers Busens Reine wogt ein Streben,
Sich einem Höhern, Reinern, Unbekannten
Aus Dankbarkeit freiwillig hinzugeben,
Enträtselnd sich den ewig Ungenannten;
Wir heißens: fromm sein! – Solcher seligen Höhe
Fühl ich mich teilhaft, wenn ich vor ihr stehe.

Vor ihrem Blick, wie vor der Sonne Walten,
Vor ihrem Atem, wie vor Frühlingslüften,
Zerschmilzt, so längst sich eisig starr gehalten,
Der Selbstsinn tief in winterlichen Grüften;
Kein Eigennutz, kein Eigenwille dauert,
Vor ihrem Kommen sind sie weggeschauert.

Es ist, als wenn sie sagte: 'Stund um Stunde
Wird uns das Leben freundlich dargeboten.
Das Gestrige ließ uns geringe Kunde,
Das Morgende – zu wissen ists verboten;
Und wenn ich je mich vor dem Abend scheute,
Die Sonne sank und sah noch, was mich freute.

Drum tu wie ich und schaue, froh verständig,
Dem Augenblick ins Auge! Kein Verschieben!
Begegn ihm schnell, wohlwollend wie lebendig,
Im Handeln seis, zur Freude seis dem Lieben.
Nur wo du bist, sei alles, immer kindlich,
So bist du alles, bist unüberwindlich.'

Du hast gut reden, dacht ich: zum Geleite
Gab dir ein Gott die Gunst des Augenblickes,
Und jeder fühlt an deiner holden Seite
Sich augenblicks den Günstling des Geschickes;
Mich schreckt der Wink, von dir mich zu entfernen –
Was hilft es mir, so hohe Weisheit lernen!

In our clear souls an instinct stirs, deep down,
To yield ourselves in willing thankfulness
To something higher, purer, never known
Or named, unriddling the Eternal Guess:
We call it piety. And when I stand
Before her, that great joy I understand.

Before her eyes, as when sun rules the day,
Before her breath, as at mild airs of spring,
The ice of all self-seeking melts away
In the deep chasms of its cold wintering;
Self-interest, self-will, none can abide
Her coming, none dare linger at her side.

She seems to say: 'How kindly, hour by hour,
Life gives itself to us! Our yesterdays
Leave little trace behind, and time's stern power
Hides our tomorrows. In the sun's last rays
With troubled thoughts I have watched night fall, and yet
That sun still looked on beauty as it set.

So do as I do: understand, confront
The moment, look it gladly in the face;
Use it at once, with good, with keen intent,
For action or for pleasure. Let your place
And time be always in the present; be
As children are, and so be whole and free!'

You may well talk, I thought; some god on you
Conferred the favour of the Moment; so
Your presence makes us for that moment too
The favourites of Fate. But now I know
That I must leave you: what for this great fear
Can it avail, such lofty words to hear?

Nun bin ich fern! Der jetzigen Minute,
Was ziemt denn der? Ich wüßt es nicht zu sagen;
Sie bietet mir zum Schönen manches Gute,
Das lastet nur, ich muß mich ihm entschlagen.
Mich treibt umher ein unbezwinglich Sehnen,
Da bleibt kein Rat als grenzenlose Tränen.

So quellt denn fort! und fließet unaufhaltsam;
Doch nie gelängs, die innre Glut zu dämpfen!
Schon rasts und reißt in meiner Brust gewaltsam,
Wo Tod und Leben grausend sich bekämpfen.
Wohl Kräuter gäbs, des Körpers Qual zu stillen;
Allein dem Geist fehlts am Entschluß und Willen,

Fehlts am Begriff: wie sollt er sie vermissen?
Er wiederholt ihr Bild zu tausendmalen.
Das zaudert bald, bald wird es weggerissen,
Undeutlich jetzt und jetzt im reinsten Strahlen;
Wie könnte dies geringstem Troste frommen
Die Ebb und Flut, das Gehen wie das Kommen?

—

Verlaßt mich hier, getreue Weggenossen!
Laßt mich allein am Fels, in Moor und Moos;
Nur immer zu! euch ist die Welt erschlossen,
Die Erde weit, der Himmel hehr und groß;
Betrachtet, forscht, die Einzelnheiten sammelt
Naturgeheimnis werde nachgestammelt.

Mir ist das All, ich bin mir selbst verloren,
Der ich noch erst den Göttern Liebling war;
Sie prüften mich, verliehen mir Pandoren,
So reich an Gütern, reicher an Gefahr;
Sie drängten mich zum gabeseligen Munde,
Sie trennen mich, und richten mich zugrunde.

Now I am far off; for the present minute
What proper use remains I cannot say.
Though there is beauty still and goodness in it,
Both now are burdens I must cast away.
A ceaseless passion drives me to and fro;
For its relief, what endless tears must flow!

Flow on then, tears that nevermore shall dry
But still can never quench this burning strife
That tears my soul apart, that flames so high,
This hideous struggle between death and life!
The body's agony some herb may heal,
But in my mind no strength is left, no will,

No concept of her loss, of how to bear
Her absence. Now a thousand thoughts invite
Her image back to me: it lingers here
And then is snatched away; now dim, now bright
As purest gold. What comfort can this bring,
This ebb and flow, this idle wandering?

—

Leave me, my loyal comrades, leave me here
Alone with rocks and wilderness; but do
Not cease your journey. See, the mighty sphere
Of earth and heaven is open wide for you:
Explore, collect, examine evidence,
Probe Nature's wonders, lisp her secret sense.

All this is lost, my self is lost to me,
Beloved of the gods though once I was.
They tempted me, Pandora's mystery
They taught me, rich yet still more perilous.
To the all-bounteous lips they raised me high,
They part me from them now, and now I die.

Aussöhnung

Die Leidenschaft bringt Leiden! – Wer beschwichtigt,
Beklommnes Herz, dich, das zu viel verloren?
Wo sind die Stunden, überschnell verflüchtigt?
Vergebens war das Schönste dir erkoren!
Trüb ist der Geist, verworren das Beginnen;
Die hehre Welt, wie schwindet sie den Sinnen!

Da schwebt hervor Musik mit Engelsschwingen,
Verflicht zu Millionen Tön um Töne,
Des Menschen Wesen durch und durch zu dringen
Zu überfüllen ihn mit ewger Schöne:
Das Auge netzt sich, fühlt im höhern Sehnen
Den Götter-Wert der Töne wie der Tränen.

Und so das Herz erleichtert merkt behende,
Daß es noch lebt und schlägt und möchte schlagen,
Zum reinsten Dank der überreichen Spende
Sich selbst erwidernd willig darzutragen.
Da fühlte sich – o daß es ewig bliebe!
Das Doppel-Glück der Töne wie der Liebe.

Reconcilement

Passion brings suffering. Who can console
The grief-choked heart? Too much you have lost: how vain
Fate's precious gift, the fleeting hours that stole
Away so fast! What now is left? The brain
Dulled and confused, bereft of clear intent.
Oh splendid world, all faded and all spent!

But music soars forth on angelic wings
Tone upon tone a millionfold to weave:
Oh how it penetrates the soul, and brings
Eternal beauty to us as we grieve!
The eye grows moist, the heart's longing feels and hears
The heaven-sent gift of music and of tears.

Then in relief the heart knows suddenly
That it still lives, in purest gratitude
Still beats for this great generosity,
Still gives itself in answer as it would:
I felt – oh stay, for ever let me have
This double joy of music and of love!

DER BRÄUTIGAM

Um Mitternacht, ich schlief, im Busen wachte
Das liebevolle Herz als wär es Tag;
Der Tag erschien, mir war, als ob es nachte,
Was ist es mir, so viel er bringen mag?

Sie fehlte ja! mein emsig Tun und Streben
Für sie allein ertrug ichs durch die Glut
Der heißen Stunde; welch erquicktes Leben
Am kühlen Abend! lohnend wars und gut.

Die Sonne sank, und Hand in Hand verpflichtet
Begrüßten wir den letzten Segensblick,
Und Auge sprach, ins Auge klar gerichtet:
Von Osten, hoffe nur, sie kommt zurück.

Um Mitternacht, der Sterne Glanz geleitet
Im holden Traum zur Schwelle, wo sie ruht.
O sei auch mir dort auszuruhn bereitet!
Wie es auch sei, das Leben, es ist gut.

THE BRIDEGROOM

At midnight, as I slept, love in my heart
Lay wide awake, as if the sun shone still;
The morning came, it was like nightfall – what
Is day to me, bring me what joys it will?

She was not there! How I would work and strive,
And all for her alone, bearing the hard
And burning hours; and how I would revive
When the cool evening brought its good reward!

The sun went down, and hand in hand its last
Blessing of light we watched and greeted, then
Her eyes would speak a promise clear and fast:
Look east, and hope: there it will rise again!

At midnight, by the starlight, by the grace
Of dreams, to where she lies I find my way.
Oh grant me too at last that resting-place!
How good is life, let it be what it may!

1824

89

[BEI BETRACHTUNG VON SCHILLERS SCHÄDEL]

Im ernsten Beinhaus wars, wo ich beschaute,
 Wie Schädel Schädeln angeordnet paßten;
 Die alte Zeit gedacht ich, die ergraute.
Sie stehn in Reih geklemmt, die sonst sich haßten,
 Und derbe Knochen, die sich tödlich schlugen,
 Sie liegen kreuzweis, zahm allhier zu rasten.
Entrenkte Schulterblätter! was sie trugen,
 Fragt niemand mehr, und zierlich tätge Glieder,
 Die Hand, der Fuß, zerstreut aus Lebensfugen.
Ihr Müden also lagt vergebens nieder,
 Nicht Ruh im Grabe ließ man euch, vertrieben
 Seid ihr herauf zum lichten Tage wieder,
Und niemand kann die dürre Schale lieben,
 Welch herrlich edlen Kern sie auch bewahrte.
 Doch mir Adepten war die Schrift geschrieben,
Die heilgen Sinn nicht jedem offenbarte,
 Als ich inmitten solcher starren Menge
 Unschätzbar herrlich ein Gebild gewahrte,
Daß in des Raumes Moderkält und Enge
 Ich frei und wärmefühlend mich erquickte,
 Als ob ein Lebensquell dem Tod entspränge.
Wie mich geheimnisvoll die Form entzückte!
 Die gottgedachte Spur, die sich erhalten!
 Ein Blick, der mich an jenes Meer entrückte,
Das flutend strömt gesteigerte Gestalten.
 Geheim Gefäß! Orakelsprüche spendend,
 Wie bin ich wert, dich in der Hand zu halten?

[ON CONTEMPLATING SCHILLER'S SKULL]

Skull upon skull arranged in fit array
 In solemn vault of burial I beheld
 And thought of bygone years and times turned grey.
Near neighbours now, in rows they stand tight-held:
 Rough bones that clashed in deadly strife before
 Lie crosswise here, their rage to quiet quelled.
Unjointed shoulderblades! what once they bore
 None now will ask; and limbs once full of grace,
 Hands, feet, lie scattered and will move no more.
So all in vain you sought this resting-place,
 Poor weary ones! they would not let you lie,
 Whom daywards from your shadowy grave they chase,
And none cares now for husks that have gone dry
 Though glorious kernels they did once contain.
 Yet here was written what my adept's eye,
Though few would guess its sacred sense, read plain:
 Amid the rigid throng one shape I saw
 Of rare nobility – and at once again
In this cold mouldering chamber's narrow maw
 I felt refreshed and warmed, alive and free:
 What welling life-spring here outleapt death's law?
O outline traced by God, still clear to see!
 O lineaments enchanting to my eyes,
 Transporting me to that mysterious sea
Whence transformed forms perpetually rise!
 Strange vessel, fountainhead of sapience,
 How dares my hand to hold you? Precious prize

Dich höchsten Schatz aus Moder fromm entwendend
Und in die freie Luft, zu freiem Sinnen,
Zum Sonnenlicht andächtig hin mich wendend.
Was kann der Mensch im Leben mehr gewinnen,
Als daß sich Gott-Natur ihm offenbare?
Wie sie das Feste läßt zu Geist verrinnen,
Wie sie das Geisterzeugte fest bewahre.

90

Dämmrung senkte sich von oben,
Schon ist alle Nähe fern;
Doch zuerst emporgehoben
Holden Lichts der Abendstern!
Alles schwankt ins Ungewisse
Nebel schleichen in die Höh;
Schwarzvertiefte Finsternisse
Widerspiegelnd ruht der See.

Nun im östlichen Bereiche
Ahn ich Mondenglanz und -glut,
Schlanker Weiden Haargezweige
Scherzen auf der nächsten Flut.
Durch bewegter Schatten Spiele
Zittert Lunas Zauberschein,
Und durchs Auge schleicht die Kühle
Sänftigend ins Herz hinein.

Which from decay I snatch with reverence
 And into free air, freely there to muse,
 Out into sunlight, piously bear hence.
To what more noble end our life we use
 Than knowing God and Nature, which are one?
 Firm matter melts which she as Mind renews,
 And she makes firm what fertile Mind has done.

90

Dusk has fallen, and already
All that's near grows faint and far;
But the first to rise has risen,
High it shines, the evening star!
All is in uncertain motion,
Creeping mists enshroud the sky;
Gulfs of night as deep as ocean
Mirrored on the dark lake lie.

Now I sense the gleam and glowing
Of the moonlight's eastering day;
Slender willow-tresses flowing
With the nearby waters play.
Through the flickering shadows lunar
Magic dances, coolness seems
To have touched my eyes and soothes me,
Steals into my inmost dreams.

DEM AUFGEHENDEN VOLLMONDE

Willst du mich sogleich verlassen?
Warst im Augenblick so nah!
Dich umfinstern Wolkenmassen,
Und nun bist du gar nicht da.

Doch du fühlst, wie ich betrübt bin,
Blickt dein Rand herauf als Stern!
Zeugest mir, daß ich geliebt bin,
Sei das Liebchen noch so fern.

So hinan denn! hell und heller,
Reiner Bahn, in voller Pracht!
Schlägt mein Herz auch schmerzlich schneller,
Überselig ist die Nacht.

92

[VERMÄCHTNIS]

Vor die Augen meiner Lieben,
Zu den Fingern, die's geschrieben –
Einst, mit heißestem Verlangen
So erwartet, wie empfangen –
Zu der Brust, der sie entquollen,
Diese Blätter wandern sollen;
Immer liebevoll bereit,
Zeugen allerschönster Zeit.

TO THE RISING FULL MOON

Must you leave me, must I lose you?
For a moment you were near,
Now thick darkling clouds enclose you,
Now you fade and disappear.

But your gleaming rim consoles me,
Beacons like a rising star,
Brings the words my darling tells me:
I am loved, though she is far.

Shine on then in brightest ardour,
Soar in pure triumphant flight!
Though my lonely heart beats harder,
Still this splendour fills the night.

<div align="center">92</div>

[A LEGACY]

Now let her dear eyes behold them
Now again her dear hand hold them –
How I longed to read their burning
Words of love, my love returning –
To the heart they poured from, may
These her letters find their way,
Ever fondly to recall
Still that loveliest time of all.

CHOR DER ELFEN Wenn sich lau die Lüfte füllen
Um den grünumschränkten Plan,
Süße Düfte, Nebelhüllen
Senkt die Dämmerung heran,
Lispelt leise süßen Frieden,
Wiegt das Herz in Kindesruh,
Und den Augen dieses Müden
Schließt des Tages Pforte zu.

Nacht ist schon hereingesunken,
Schließt sich heilig Stern an Stern,
Große Lichter, kleine Funken
Glitzern nah und glänzen fern,
Glitzern hier im See sich spiegelnd,
Glänzen droben klarer Nacht;
Tiefsten Ruhens Glück besiegelnd,
Herrscht des Mondes volle Pracht.

Schon verloschen sind die Stunden,
Hingeschwunden Schmerz und Glück;
Fühl es vor: du wirst gesunden!
Traue neuem Tagesblick!
Täler grünen, Hügel schwellen,
Buschen sich zu Schattenruh,
Und in schwanken Silberwellen
Wogt die Saat der Ernte zu.

Wunsch um Wünsche zu erlangen,
Schaue nach dem Glanze dort!
Leise bist du nur umfangen,
Schlaf ist Schale, wirf sie fort!

CHORUS OF ELVES When a fragrance has descended
All about the green-girt plain,
Richer air with mist-clouds blended,
Evening dusk comes down again;
Lulls to infant-sweet reposing,
Rocks the heart with whispering sighs,
And this wanderer feels it closing
On his daylight-weary eyes.

Now to night the world surrenders,
Sacred love joins star to star;
Little sparkles, greater splendours,
Glitter near and gleam from far,
Glitter in the lake reflecting,
Gleam against the clear night sky;
Deepest seals of rest protecting
Glows the full moon strong and high.

Soon the hours have slipped away,
Pain and happiness are past;
Trust the light of the new day,
Feel your sickness will not last!
Green the valleys, hillsides swelling,
Bushing thick to restful shade,
And the fields, their wealth foretelling,
Rippling ripe and silver-swayed!

Have you wishes without number?
Watch the promise of the dawn!
Lightly you are wrapped in slumber:
Shed this husk and be reborn!

from FAUST *Part Two*, 1800–31

Säume nicht, dich zu erdreisten,
Wenn die Menge zaudernd schweift!
Alles kann der Edle leisten,
Der versteht und rasch ergreift.

94

FAUST Des Lebens Pulse schlagen frisch-lebendig,
Ätherische Dämmerung milde zu begrüßen;
Du, Erde, warst auch diese Nacht beständig
Und atmest neu erquickt zu meinen Füßen,
Beginnest schon mit Lust mich zu umgeben,
Du regst und rührst ein kräftiges Beschließen,
Zum höchsten Dasein immer fortzustreben. –
In Dämmerschein liegt schon die Welt erschlossen,
Der Wald ertönt von tausendstimmigem Leben;
Talaus, talein ist Nebelstreif ergossen,
Doch senkt sich Himmelsklarheit in die Tiefen,
Und Zweig und Äste, frisch erquickt, entsprossen
Dem duftgen Abgrund, wo versenkt sie schliefen;
Auch Farb an Farbe klärt sich los vom Grunde,
Wo Blum und Blatt von Zitterperle triefen:
Ein Paradies wird um mich her die Runde.

Hinaufgeschaut! – Der Berge Gipfelriesen
Verkünden schon die feierlichste Stunde;
Sie dürfen früh des ewigen Lichts genießen,
Das später sich zu uns herniederwendet.
Jetzt zu der Alpe grüngesenkten Wiesen
Wird neuer Glanz und Deutlichkeit gespendet,
Und stufenweis herab ist es gelungen –
Sie tritt hervor! – und leider schon geblendet,
Kehr ich mich weg, vom Augenschmerz durchdrungen.

Venture boldly; hesitation
Is for lesser men – when deeds
Are a noble mind's creation,
All his enterprise succeeds.

94

FAUST How strong and pure the pulse of life is beating!
Dear earth, this night has left you still unshaken,
And at my feet you breathe refreshed; my greeting
To you, ethereal dawn! New joys awaken
All round me at your bidding: beckoning distance,
New-stirring strength, new resolution taken
To strive on still towards supreme existence. –
A gloaming-shine reveals the reborn world,
The forest sings with myriad-voiced insistence,
Through vale and dale the morning mists have curled,
But heaven's radiance pierces them, descending,
And branch and bough appear, revived, unfurled
From the vaporous chasm, their slumber ending;
Now deep-down colours grow distinct, as flower
And leaf gleam moistly, tremulous pearls suspending.
Oh paradise again, oh encircling power!

Let me look up! – Each giant summit-height
Proclaims already this most solemn hour:
They are the first to taste the eternal light,
As we shall, when its downward course is ended.
Now the green-slanting meadow-slopes are bright
Again, each detail new and clear and splendid,
And day spreads stepwise with the dark's downsinking:
See, the sun rises! – But my eyes offended
Turn away dazzled, from this great sight shrinking.

So ist es also, wenn ein sehnend Hoffen
Dem höchsten Wunsch sich traulich zugerungen,
Erfüllungspforten findet flügeloffen;
Nun aber bricht aus jenen ewigen Gründen
Ein Flammenübermaß, wir stehn betroffen:
Des Lebens Fackel wollten wir entzünden,
Ein Feuermeer umschlingt uns, welch ein Feuer!
Ists Lieb? ists Haß? die glühend uns umwinden,
Mit Schmerz- und Freuden wechselnd ungeheuer,
So daß wir wieder nach der Erde blicken,
Zu bergen uns in jugendlichstem Schleier.

So bleibe denn die Sonne mir im Rücken!
Der Wassersturz, das Felsenriff durchbrausend,
Ihn schau ich an mit wachsendem Entzücken.
Von Sturz zu Sturzen wälzt er jetzt in tausend,
Dann abertausend Strömen sich ergießend,
Hoch in die Lüfte Schaum an Schäume sausend.
Allein wie herrlich, diesem Sturm ersprießend,
Wölbt sich des bunten Bogens Wechseldauer,
Bald rein gezeichnet, bald in Luft zerfließend,
Umher verbreitend duftig-kühle Schauer!
Der spiegelt ab das menschliche Bestreben.
Ihm sinne nach, und du begreifst genauer:
Am farbigen Abglanz haben wir das Leben.

And thus, when with our heart's whole hope for guide
Towards our goal we have struggled on unthinking,
And find fulfilment's portals open wide –
From those unfathomed depths a sudden mass
Of fire bursts forth, we stand amazed: we tried
To set the torch of life alight – alas,
A sea of flame engulfs us, ah what flame
Of love or hate, burning, consuming us
With pain and joy, which strangely seem the same!
We look back earthwards, hiding from this blaze
Behind a youthful veil of awestruck shame.

So be it! I will turn from the sun's rays.
At that rock-riving torrent, with increasing
Ecstasy at that waterfall I gaze:
From cliff to cliff it pours down never-ceasing,
It foams and streams a thousand thousandfold,
Spray upon spray high in the air releasing.
But from this tumult, marvellous to behold,
The rainbow blooms, changing yet ever still;
Now vanishing and now drawn clear and bold.
How cool the moisture of its scattering spill!
I watch a mirror here of man's whole story,
And plain it speaks, ponder it as you will:
Our life's a spectrum-sheen of borrowed glory.

from FAUST *Part Two*, 1800–31

HELENA Bewundert viel und viel gescholten, Helena,
Vom Strande komm ich, wo wir erst gelandet sind,
Noch immer trunken von des Gewoges regsamen
Geschaukel, das vom phrygischen Blachgefild uns her
Auf sträubig-hohem Rücken durch Poseidons Gunst
Und Euros' Kraft in vaterländische Buchten trug.
Dortunten freuet nun der König Menelas
Der Rückkehr samt den tapfersten seiner Krieger sich.
Du aber heiße mich willkommen, hohes Haus,
Das Tyndareos, mein Vater, nah dem Hange sich
Von Pallas Hügel wiederkehrend aufgebaut
Und, als ich hier mit Klytämnestren schwesterlich,
Mit Castor auch und Pollux fröhlich spielend wuchs,
Vor allen Häusern Spartas herrlich ausgeschmückt.
Gegrüßet seid mir, der ehrnen Pforte Flügel ihr!
Durch euer gastlich ladendes Weit-Eröffnen einst
Geschahs, daß mir, erwählt aus vielen, Menelas
In Bräutigamsgestalt entgegenleuchtete.
Eröffnet mir sie wieder, daß ich ein Eilgebot
Des Königs treu erfülle, wie der Gattin ziemt!
Laßt mich hinein! und alles bleibe hinter mir,
Was mich umstürmte bis hieher, verhängnisvoll!
Denn seit ich diese Schwelle sorgenlos verließ,
Cytherens Tempel besuchend, heiliger Pflicht gemäß,
Mich aber dort ein Räuber griff, der phrygische,
Ist viel geschehen, was die Menschen weit und breit
So gern erzählen, aber der nicht gerne hört,
Von dem die Sage wachsend sich zum Märchen spann.

HELEN So much admired and so much censured, Helena,
Now from the sea I come; we are not long ashore,
And drunken still with rocking upon the lively waves
Which on their high-uptossing backs, from Troy's wide plain,
By great Poseidon's favour and by the east wind's force
Brought us once more to harbours of our fatherland.
Down there the king, my husband Menelaus, now
With his most valiant fighters feasts his homecoming.
But you must bid your queen here welcome, noble house
Built by my father Tyndareus on his return,
Nearby the slopes of Pallas Athene's lofty hill:
Here with my sister Clytemnestra and the twins
Castor and Pollux happily playing I grew up,
While he adorned it like no other in the land.
All hail to you now, mighty doors of bronze! You once
Stood open wide in hospitable welcome, when
It came about that Menelaus, the elect
Of many wooers, shiningly appeared to me.
Let them once more be opened! for as a loyal wife
I must fulfil an urgent bidding of the king.
So let me enter, and let all the storms of fate
That have been raging round me now be left behind.
For since I crossed this threshold last, as duty bade,
All unsuspecting, visiting Cythera's shrine,
And there was ravished by an adventurer from Troy,
Much has befallen: far and wide men tell the tale
And take their pleasure in it. But no tale can please
One round whose name long legend spins its false report.

FAUST Und duldet auch auf seiner Berge Rücken
Das Zackenhaupt der Sonne kalten Pfeil,
Läßt nun der Fels sich angegrünt erblicken,
Die Ziege nimmt genäschig kargen Teil.

Die Quelle springt, vereinigt stürzen Bache,
Und schon sind Schluchten, Hänge, Matten grün.
Auf hundert Hügeln unterbrochner Fläche
Siehst Wollenherden ausgebreitet ziehn.

Verteilt, vorsichtig-abgemessen schreitet
Gehörntes Rind hinan zum jähen Rand;
Doch Obdach ist den sämtlichen bereitet:
Zu hundert Höhlen wölbt sich Felsenwand.

Pan schützt sie dort, und Lebensnymphen wohnen
In buschiger Klüfte feucht-erfrischtem Raum,
Und, sehnsuchtsvoll nach höhern Regionen,
Erhebt sich zweighaft Baum gedrängt an Baum.

Altwälder sinds! Die Eiche starret mächtig,
Und eigensinnig zackt sich Ast an Ast;
Der Ahorn, mild, von süßem Safte trächtig,
Steigt rein empor und spielt mit seiner Last.

Und mütterlich im stillen Schattenkreise
Quillt laue Milch bereit für Kind und Lamm;
Obst ist nicht weit, der Ebnen reife Speise,
Und Honig trieft vom ausgehöhlten Stamm.

Hier ist das Wohlbehagen erblich,
Die Wange heitert wie der Mund,
Ein jeder ist an seinem Platz unsterblich:
Sie sind zufrieden und gesund.

FAUST The jagged summits on its mountain ridge
Suffer the sun's cold arrows sharp and clear;
But rocks blush green with scanty pasturage
And nibbling goats can seek their nurture here.

The springs leap up, down gush the mingling rills,
Ravines and slopes are verdant now, the grass
Covers in turn a hundred fields and hills
Where the wide-wandering fleecy flocks may pass.

Horned grazing cattle, scattered, warily
Pacing, approach the brink of the sheer fall;
But darkly arching in the cliffside, see!
A hundred caves are shelter for them all.

There Pan protects them, there they lie at ease
In the moist wooded clefts where life-nymphs dwell.
With upthrust branches the close-crowding trees
Aspire to higher regions. Mark them well,

These ancient forests! Mighty oaks extrude
Their stubborn and anfractuous limbs; here too
The maple, heavy with sweet liquid food,
Plays with its burden, soaring straight and true.

Here in the quiet shade a lamb, a child,
Sucks warm maternal milk with eager lips;
Here in the plains the fruit grows ripe and wild,
And from the hollow tree-trunk honey drips.

Contentment is a birthright here,
A smiling mouth, a cheek that glows;
Each is immortal in his sphere,
No sickness, no disquietude he knows;

from FAUST *Part Two*, 1800–31 237

Und so entwickelt sich am reinen Tage
Zu Vaterkraft das holde Kind.
Wir staunen drob; noch immer bleibt die Frage:
Obs Götter, ob es Menschen sind!

So war Apoll den Hirten zugestaltet,
Daß ihm der schönsten einer glich;
Denn wo Natur im reinen Kreise waltet,
Ergreifen alle Welten sich.

97

EIN TEIL DES CHORS

Wir in dieser tausend Äste Flüsterzittern, Säuselschweben
Reizen tändelnd, locken leise wurzelauf des Lebens Quellen
Nach den Zweigen; bald mit Blättern, bald mit Blüten über-
 schwenglich
Zieren wir die Flatterhaare frei zu luftigem Gedeihn.
Fällt die Frucht, sogleich versammeln lebenslustig Volk und Herden
Sich zum Greifen, sich zum Naschen, eilig kommend, emsig
 drängend,
Und wie vor den ersten Göttern bückt sich alles um uns her.

EIN ANDERER TEIL

Wir, an dieser Felsenwände weithinleuchtend-glattem Spiegel
Schmiegen wir, in sanften Wellen uns bewegend, schmeichelnd an;
Horchen, lauschen jedem Laute, Vogelsängen, Röhrigflöten,
Sei es Pans furchtbarer Stimme: Antwort ist sogleich bereit.
Säuselts, säuseln wir erwidernd, donnerts, rollen unsre Donner
In erschütterndem Verdoppeln dreifach, zehnfach hintennach.

EIN DRITTER TEIL

Schwestern, wir, bewegtern Sinnes, eilen mit den Bächen weiter;
Denn es reizen jener Ferne reichgeschmückte Hügelzüge.

And thus the children grow in this pure day
To fatherhood. We ask again
As in astonishment we gaze: are they
Not gods indeed, or are they men?

Apollo lived with shepherds so, and passed
For one, and all were beautiful:
For where the laws of purest Nature rule,
All separate worlds unite at last.

97

PART OF THE CHORUS

We shall dwell amid this tremor of a thousand whispering branches,
Tease their roots to woo the life-sap softly up into the rustling
Tree-tops; there these floating tresses we shall deck with leaves and
 blossoms,
In extravagant abundance, free to thrive at airy heights.
When the ripe fruit falls, the people with their flocks will crowd here, eager
Hands will gather, mouths will nibble; thus they'll throng to snatch a
 harvest,
And they'll all bow down around us, as before the earliest gods.

ANOTHER PART

We shall linger by these cliffs with mirror-smooth far-shining faces,
Cling like gentle waves about them, flatter them in close caress;
So to every sound we'll listen, songs of birds, the reed-pipes playing,
And though Pan's dread voice assail us, we shall instantly reply.
Even murmuring wind we'll answer, thunder we shall double-thunder,
Utter shattering iteration, mutter threefold, tenfold roll.

A THIRD PART

Sisters, we prefer more movement, we shall hasten with the streaming
Waters, lured by those well-wooded hills, those ranges in the distance.

Immer abwärts, immer tiefer wässern wir, mäandrisch wallend,
Jetzt die Wiese, dann die Matten, gleich den Garten um das Haus.
Dort bezeichnens der Zypressen schlanke Wipfel, über Landschaft,
Uferzug und Wellenspiegel nach dem Äther steigende.

EIN VIERTER TEIL

Wallt ihr andern, wos beliebet: wir umzingeln, wir umrauschen
Den durchaus bepflanzten Hügel, wo am Stab die Rebe grünt;
Dort zu aller Tage Stunden läßt die Leidenschaft des Winzers
Uns des liebevollsten Fleißes zweifelhaft Gelingen sehn.
Bald mit Hacke, bald mit Spaten, bald mit Häufeln, Schneiden,
 Binden
Betet er zu allen Göttern, fördersamst zum Sonnengott.
Bacchus kümmert sich, der Weichling, wenig um den treuen Diener,
Ruht in Lauben, lehnt in Höhlen, faselnd mit dem jüngsten Faun.
Was zu seiner Träumereien halbem Rausch er je bedurfte,
Immer bleibt es ihm in Schläuchen, ihm in Krügen und Gefäßen,
Rechts und links der kühlen Grüfte, ewige Zeiten aufbewahrt.
Haben aber alle Götter, hat nun Helios vor allen,
Lüftend, feuchtend, wärmend, glutend, Beerenfüllhorn aufgehäuft,
Wo der stille Winzer wirkte, dort auf einmal wirds lebendig,
Und es rauscht in jedem Laube, raschelt um von Stock zu Stock.
Körbe knarren, Eimer klappern, Tragebutten ächzen hin,
Alles nach der großen Kufe zu der Keltrer kräftgem Tanz.
Und so wird die heilige Fülle reingeborner, saftiger Beeren
Frech zertreten: schäumend, sprühend mischt sichs, widerlich
 zerquetscht.
Und nun gellt ins Ohr der Zimbeln mit der Becken Erzgetöne;
Denn es hat sich Dionysos aus Mysterien enthüllt,
Kommt hervor mit Ziegenfüßlern, schwenkend Ziegenfüßlerinnen,
Und dazwischen schreit unbändig grell Silenus' öhrig Tier.
Nichts geschont! Gespaltne Klauen treten alle Sitte nieder,
Alle Sinne wirbeln taumlig, gräßlich übertäubt das Ohr.

Ever deeper down shall wander our meandering refreshment:
Now the pastures, then the meadows, soon the garden round the house.
There slim cypresses will mark us, tapering proud above the landscape,
By our banks and mirroring waters rising headup to the sky.

A FOURTH PART

Wander where you like, the rest of you: our murmuring shall encircle
The close-cultivated hillside, where staked vines are growing green,
Tended daily, tended hourly by the vintager, whose toiling
Passion and devoted labour earn their ever-doubtful prize.
We shall see him hoeing, digging, heaping soil up, pruning, tying,
Praying to the gods to aid him, to the sun-god most of all.
The voluptuary Bacchus, careless of his faithful servant,
Rests in caves and lolls in arbours, flirting with the youngest faun.
All his dreaming, his half-drunken reveries have ever needed
Stands supplied for him in wineskins, stands in jars and hollow vessels,
Right and left in cooling caverns, stored from immemorial time.
But when all the gods, and Helios first among them, giving breezes,
Giving moisture, warmth and fire, have heaped the grapes to horns of
 plenty:
Then at last, where quiet growers worked, all springs to life and motion,
All the leafy arbours rustle, all's astir from vine to vine.
Baskets creak and buckets clatter, groaning hods are fully loaded;
All to the great vat are carried, to the treader's lusty dance.
So by those rude feet the sacred bounty of the ripe unblemished
Grape is trodden, spurting grape-flesh crushed and mixed to foaming
 messes.
Now the ear is penetrated by the cymbals' brazen clangour:
For the unveiled Dionysus from his mysteries comes forth,
Leaping with goat-footed satyrs, with goat-footed satyresses,
And among them wildly braying comes Silenus' long-eared beast.
No constraints now! Cloven hooves will trample down all decent custom,
All our senses reel, our ears are deafened with the hideous din.

Nach der Schale tappen Trunkne, überfüllt sind Kopf und Wänste;
Sorglich ist noch ein- und andrer, doch vermehrt er die Tumulte:
Denn um neuen Most zu bergen, leert man rasch den alten Schlauch!

98

LYNKEUS DER TÜRMER

Zum Sehen geboren,
Zum Schauen bestellt,
Dem Turme geschworen,
Gefällt mir die Welt.
Ich blick in die Ferne,
Ich seh in der Näh,
Den Mond und die Sterne,
Den Wald und das Reh.
So seh ich in allen
Die ewige Zier,
Und wie mirs gefallen,
Gefall ich auch mir.
Ihr glücklichen Augen,
Was je ihr gesehn,
Es sei, wie es wolle,
Es war doch so schön!

Drunken revellers grope for liquor, heads and bellies overflowing;
Some still call for moderation, but can only swell the tumult;
For old wineskins soon are empty which the grape's new juice must
 fill!

98

LYNCEUS THE WATCHMAN

> A watchman by calling,
> Far-sighted by birth,
> From this tower, my dwelling,
> I gaze at the earth:
> At the earth near and far,
> At the world far and near,
> At the moon and the stars,
> At the woods and the deer.
> A beauty eternal
> In all things I see,
> And the world and myself
> Are both pleasing to me.
> Oh blest are these eyes
> All they've seen and can tell:
> Let it be as it may –
> They have loved it so well!

CHOR UND ECHO

Waldung, sie schwankt heran,
Felsen, sie lasten dran,
Wurzeln, sie klammern an,
Stamm dicht am Stamm hinan.
Woge nach Woge spritzt,
Höhle, die tiefste, schützt.
Löwen, sie schleichen stumm-
Freundlich um uns herum,
Ehren geweihten Ort,
Heiligen Liebeshort.

PATER ECSTATICUS *auf- und abschweifend*

Ewiger Wonnebrand,
Glühendes Liebeband,
Siedender Schmerz der Brust,
Schäumende Gotteslust!
Pfeile, durchdringet mich,
Lanzen, bezwinget mich,
Keulen, zerschmettert mich,
Blitze, durchwettert mich!
Daß ja das Nichtige
Alles verflüchtige,
Glänze der Dauerstern,
Ewiger Liebe Kern!

PATER PROFUNDUS. *Tiefe Region*

Wie Felsenabgrund mir zu Füßen
Auf tieferm Abgrund lastend ruht,
Wie tausend Bäche strahlend fließen
Zum grausen Sturz des Schaums der Flut,
Wie strack, mit eignem kräftigen Triebe,

CHORUS AND ECHO

Woods, hitherwavering,
Rocks, cliffs, downburdening,
Roots close to roots they cling,
Trunk to trunk neighbouring.
The rushing waters leap,
The sheltering caves are deep.
Lions prowl round us, dumb,
Gentle and shy to come
Into this holy place,
Sacred to love and grace.

PATER ECSTATICUS *hovering up and down*

Joy of immortal fire
Lovebond of hot desire,
Heart's seething agony,
Godspring of ecstasy!
Arrows, pierce through me now,
Spearpoints, subdue me now,
Clubs, strike and break me now;
Lightnings, unmake me now!
All that is vain and void
Let it be all destroyed:
Shine, star, for evermore,
Love's everlasting core!

PATER PROFUNDUS *in a lower region*

The rocky precipice below
Weighs on a chasm still more deep;
A thousand streamlets shine and flow
Down to the foaming flood's dread leap;
By its own energy ascending

from FAUST *Part Two*, 1800–31

Der Stamm sich in die Lüfte trägt:
So ist es die allmächtige Liebe,
Die alles bildet, alles hegt.

Ist um mich her ein wildes Brausen,
Als wogte Wald und Felsengrund,
Und doch stürzt, liebevoll im Sausen,
Die Wasserfülle sich zum Schlund,
Berufen, gleich das Tal zu wässern;
Der Blitz, der flammend niederschlug,
Die Atmosphäre zu verbessern,
Die Gift und Dunst im Busen trug:

Sind Liebesboten! sie verkünden,
Was ewig schaffend uns umwallt.
Mein Innres mög es auch entzünden,
Wo sich der Geist, verworren-kalt,
Verquält in stumpfer Sinneschranken
Scharfangeschloßnem Kettenschmerz!
O Gott, beschwichtige die Gedanken,
Erleuchte mein bedürftig Herz!

100

CHORUS MYSTICUS

Alles Vergängliche
Ist nur ein Gleichnis;
Das Unzulängliche,
Hier wirds Ereignis;
Das Unbeschreibliche,
Hier ists getan;
Das Ewigweibliche
Zieht uns hinan.

The tree thrusts skywards straight and tall:
All these show forth the love unending
That shapes all things and shields them all.

How wild a roar is this, as if
The forest shook, the abyss were stirred!
Yet the great torrent from the cliff
Pours down like love, its sound half-heard,
To the valley's thirst, and by and by
Lightning has struck, its flame makes clean
The poisoned air, the sultry sky
Where swollen thunder-clouds have been;

These are love's messengers! They tell
Of power all-making, all-surrounding.
Oh let it burn in me as well!
Bonds of dull sense, my mind confounding,
Torment and chill me: oh release
Me from these chains that bind so tight!
Oh God, between my thoughts make peace
And to my needy heart give light!

100

CHORUS MYSTICUS

All that must disappear
Is but a parable;
What lay beyond us, here
All is made visible;
Here deeds have understood
Words they were darkened by;
Eternal Womanhood
Draws us on high.

from FAUST *Part Two*, 1800–31

Notes

1. May Song

First published in a periodical in 1775, but probably written in 1771 at the time of the 21-year-old Goethe's emotional attachment to Friederike Brion, the parson's daughter in Sesenheim (see Introduction). The original title 'May Festival' ('Maifest') may refer to the Whitsun festival of that year which he attended. The strongly emphasised word 'Natur' in the first sentence (literally 'How splendidly nature shines about me') is lost in translation.

2. Welcome and Parting

An early version of the first ten lines was found among Friederike's papers, suggesting that the poem was addressed to her and at least partly written during the Sesenheim period, 1770–1. Like 'May Song' it first appeared in the periodical *Iris* in 1775; Goethe then slightly revised it for the 1789 edition of his works. The revised (canonical) version suggests that a night has been spent with the beloved, but this is poetic stylization rather than autobiography. In the second stanza I have taken the liberty of conflating the two versions (the earlier text read 'sah schläfrig aus dem Duft hervor') and translating the line accordingly.

3. Ganymede

Published in the 1789 collection, but the date of composition is quite uncertain. Traditionally seen as paralleling a famous passage in *The Sufferings of Young Werther* (1774) in which the hero lies in the grass and communes with the May morning; thus 1774 has been suggested as a date for this poem, as have 1772, 1773 and 1777 on various other grounds. The Ganymede of the title is the beautiful young Trojan prince whom Zeus, in the form of an eagle, literally picked up, though the specifics of the myth are barely recognizable in the poem itself. The celestial lover descends to the poet as the spring, or nature generally, in whose glowing embrace he is mysteriously carried upwards. Goethe probably knew that whereas in medieval times the Ganymede story was seen as yet another example of unnatural vice in the pagan world (the word 'catamite' was derived from the Latin form of his name), the Renaissance tended to interpret it as symbolizing the soul's union with God. This comes nearer to Goethe's conception, in which however God is pantheistically identified with nature rather than a transcendent absolute. The poem also seems to suggest an analogy or fusion between erotic and mystical experience.

4. Prometheus

In Greek myth, the Titan or demiurge Prometheus, one of the ancient gods of the generation before Zeus, was thought of as the heroic champion of mankind against the hostility of Zeus and the other Olympians. In some versions of the story he himself had created men, shaping them out of clay; he taught and gave them many things, notably the divine secret of fire which he stole from Zeus. His punishment was to be chained to a rock where an eagle daily devoured his liver, letting it grow again overnight. Goethe freely adapts and selects from this material – he gives no hint, for instance, of the final tragic defeat of Prometheus by Zeus. He emphasizes two themes above all: (1) the suffering of the human race and Zeus's indifference to it, (2) the hero's rebellion against 'Zeus' for this reason, his espousal of human suffering and his refusal in spite of it to deny the value of human life or adopt an attitude of ascetic humility. Goethe's train of thought, thinly disguised in the pre-Christian mythology, seems closely to approach the crucial problem of 'theodicy' which has pervaded Western religious thought: why does God create us and then merely allow us to suffer? Has he fallen asleep, or does he seek merely to gratify his whims and cow the human spirit into submission? The closing passage about the creation of men by Prometheus, with its clear biblical echo in 'nach meinem Bilde', seems to be a symbolic allusion to the poet's own creativity, in which his 'heart of sacred fire' takes pride. The poem probably dates from 1774, when Goethe had also been writing a fragmentary Prometheus drama; the ode however is not an extract from this other text but appears to be an independent dramatic monologue, complete in itself.

5–10. 'Urfaust' extracts

Goethe's early *Faust* fragment is discussed in the Introduction; for further commentary on both the 'Urfaust' and the canonical *Faust* Part One, see *Faust* OUP1, introduction and notes. The 'Urfaust' texts are printed here not in their original (unpublished, posthumous) version but as Goethe revised them for the 1808 edition, with slight emendations and standardization of spelling.

5. Faust's disillusioned reflections on conventional learning were the traditional opening for a Faust drama since Marlowe's *Tragical History of Doctor Faustus*, which began in a similar way. The vivid near-doggerel of this first speech is a popular sixteenth-century metre, the so-called 'Knittelvers', which the young Goethe revived in his search for an authentically German style.

6. Faust has conjured up the 'Earth Spirit', which appears in fire as a terrifying vision, and according to the original stage-direction in a 'repulsive' (widerlich) shape. Its last two lines seem to define its function as that of a demiurge creating the phenomena of terrestrial nature.

7. 'Thule' (pronounced as two syllables) was the name given by ancient Greek explorers and geographers to a land far to the north of Britain, thought to lie

within the Arctic circle but variously and uncertainly identified as Iceland, Shetland or Norway.

8. This is strictly speaking a dramatic soliloquy spoken by Gretchen, not (like 'The King of Thule') a ballad which she sings, though it has of course often been set to music as 'Gretchen at the spinning-wheel', most famously by Schubert.

9. The remorseful Faust's comparison of himself to a rushing torrent, an *homme fatal* doomed to destroy whatever lies in his path, anticipates by more than one generation a whole category of such figures in German, English, French and Russian Romantic literature.

10. What Gretchen sings is her crazed personal variant of the song from *The Tale of the Juniper-Tree*, one of the folk-tales later collected and published by the brothers Grimm (1812). In the early 1770s Goethe evidently knew this story, or at least the song, from some unidentified source. In the story, a little boy is murdered by his stepmother and served up as a stew for his father to eat; after his sister has buried his bones under a juniper-tree, he comes back to life as a bird which sings the song and eventually recovers his human shape. Gretchen adapts the words as if they were those of her baby which she has killed.

11. On the Lake
The biographical context of this poem was the year 1775 during which Goethe decided to break off his engagement to Lili Schönemann (see Introduction) and to accept the patronage of the Duke of Weimar. In a state of indecision, he let his father persuade him to set off on a journey to Italy but got no further than Switzerland. The immediate occasion of the poem was a boat trip on Lake Zurich with some friends; in the central trochaic quatrain his thoughts seem to return to the Lili problem. For publication in the 1789 *Works* he modified the original opening lines in which he felt himself to be sucking Nature's nourishment through his umbilical cord ('Ich saug an meiner Nabelschnur nun Nahrung aus der Welt').

12. Restless Love
Since it is supposed to be characteristic of Goethe's poems, as he himself professed, that they were usually suggested to him by specific external occasions ('Gelegenheiten'), the documented composition-date in this case (6 May 1776, in Ilmenau) has been questioned on account of the reference to wintry weather in the opening lines. Later research, however, has shown that there was in fact a prolonged snowfall in Ilmenau at the time in question.

13. 'Why was deep insight given to us'
Also known as 'To Charlotte von Stein', this intimate psychological meditation was sent as a letter to Charlotte (see Introduction) which is still extant and dated 14 April 1776. Goethe never included it in any edition of his poems, so that it first became known when his letters to Charlotte were published in 1848–51. A few days before sending her the poem, he had written to his friend Wieland that her

significance for him, the power she had over his emotions, could only be explained in terms of the theory of transmigrant souls. 'Yes,' he adds, 'we were once man and wife! Now we know about each other – but it is a veiled knowledge, a mist of the spirit.' That Goethe seriously believed in metempsychosis is doubtful, but the somewhat obscure and tortuous thought of the poem is evidently influenced by Platonic or Neoplatonic ideas. The central passage beginning at line 29 ('Did you not know...') is usually quoted out of context as if it were a later reminiscence of his actual relationship with Charlotte in those years. In fact it describes an imaginary pre-existence, a former life ('abgelebte Zeit'), and may be read as the evocation of an ideal relationship with a quasi maternal or sisterly beloved: the word 'sister' in line 28 which stirs up this 'memory' or oedipal dream is at least as important as 'wife'. The ideal state is contrasted with the present reality: the 'new situation', the obstacles (her marriage, the prevailing social conventions, etc.) that come between the poet and Frau von Stein. As its other central theme, the poem explores a further contrast: that between the intellectual lover who can ponder the discrepancy between his vision ('the old truth') and his present pain, and the naive lover who can live more spontaneously in his feelings, in an enviable bliss of illusion; in this second category Goethe perhaps includes himself in his more youthful emotional adventures. A new note is struck in this relatively early poem, consonant with its more solemn and 'classical' iambic verse: that polarization of reflectiveness and immediacy which was to become a theme so deeply embedded in European literature and thought from Goethe's time to our own.

14. A Wanderer's Night Song I
Goethe sent this poem to Charlotte as well, dating it 14 February 1776. Her mother wrote on the back of the manuscript the words of Jesus 'Peace I leave with you, my peace I give unto you...' (John 14.27). In 1780 the poem was published in a Swiss periodical called *Christliches Magazin*, under the title 'For peace', for which Goethe was perhaps not responsible, but which suggests quite wrongly that it is to be read as a prayer to God for peace (a suggestion already contained in the biblical, devotional style of the opening words). In fact, of course, the words are addressed not to God but to 'peace' itself, the 'du' of line 1, the peace which the 'wanderer' cannot find.

15. A Wanderer's Night Song II
The title, reverting again to the poet's persona as 'wanderer', suits this as well as the preceding poem but would also be appropriate enough for, say, 'To the Moon' and some others. Goethe scribbled the lines on the wall of a little mountain hut near Ilmenau, dating them September 1780. In August 1831, only seven months before his death, he revisited the hut and shed tears as he reread his own words. In the nineteenth century a forester is said to have discovered a literary English tourist attempting to saw the poem out of the wooden wall, and this led

to a photographic record being made. The hut was burnt down in 1870, and later exactly restored; Goethe's lines are there again, engraved on a brass plate. After two unauthorized periodical publications, in 1801 and 1803, the poem found its way into the 1815 edition of Goethe's works, with the original 'Gefilden' (fields) altered or corrected to 'Gipfeln' (hill-tops), and 'Vögel' to 'Vögelein'; it is this canonical version of the text that has become perhaps the most famous poem in the German language.

16. To the Moon

The less well-known, but more straightforward first version in six stanzas was probably written in the summer of 1777, though its dating is much disputed. Charlotte's son Fritz was the first to make the often repeated suggestion that Goethe was inspired to write it by the suicide of Christiane von Lassberg, a young lady who drowned herself in the river Ilm outside his house in January 1778 with a copy of *Werther* in her pocket. But even apart from the chronological objection to this theory, there is no real evidence for it in the text itself. The poem makes adequate sense as a meditation by Goethe on the moonlit valley of the Ilm (in which he sometimes bathed at night) and as the elaboration of a comparison (line 7) between the moon and his beloved (presumably Charlotte). The third quatrain, with its alternation of single and plural pronouns (lines 9, 11), seems to be addressed to both Charlotte and the moon: between them they hold him spellbound, like a ghost doomed to linger in a loved place. When Goethe later rewrote the poem, giving it the nine-stanza form in which it would appear in the 1789 *Works*, he deleted this quatrain and added four new ones which modulate to a different theme, that of the unhappy lover. It is not known when this revision was carried out, and the question is further complicated by the fact that Charlotte herself, again at some uncertain date between 1777 and 1789, wrote what she called 'An den Mond nach meiner Manier' ('To the Moon, *à ma façon*'), a reworking or parody of Goethe's poem, rather bitterly and clumsily expressing her sorrow at the poet's absence. As her model for this exercise she probably knew only the 1777 version, but her added quatrains intermittently resemble Goethe's final text. It has been suggested that she may have sent her reproachful parody to Goethe while he was travelling in Italy in 1786–8, and that what he eventually published was in effect a third variant of 'To the Moon', a subtle conflation of Charlotte's words and his own, tacitly accepting her reproaches and smoothing out her verbal infelicities, but leaving an insoluble problem for all those who seek to ascertain exact authorship and composition-dates.

Charlotte's intervention may partly explain why the 1789 version gives the impression, not only by the revision of 'der Liebsten Auge' to 'des Freundes Auge' in line 7, that in this later conception the speaker is a woman. Only one detail in the 1777 text has the same effect: the phrase 'einen Mann' (man? husband?) in line 19, whereas at least three of the stanzas added later (3 to 5) do seem to suggest

an absent faithless male lover by whom the speaker has been deserted. Neverthe-less the earlier and later material has been sufficiently skilfully integrated for the final and canonical poem to work well as an expression of the feelings of Charlotte or of Goethe, or of any other lover, and to be beautiful and moving whichever way we take it. The last three stanzas (1789, 7 to 9) are essentially the same in both versions; the last two, though they remain enigmatic, might be read as an evoca-tion of that solitude *à deux* in which both Goethe and Charlotte longed to explore the heart's mysteries together.

17. The Fisherman
A letter from Goethe to Charlotte (19 January 1778) alludes to the suicide of Christiane von Lassberg (see previous note) and comments on the 'dangerous attractiveness' of water, but we need see no more than a very tenuous link between this and the ballad, which was probably written in 1777 or 1778. Its compelling poetic force lies in its evocation of ancient mythical themes: nature-demons (sirens, mermaids, nixies, etc.) associated with lakes and rivers, the rejuvenating cyclic journey of the sun and moon through the depths of the sea (third stanza), the story of Narcissus (lines 23f.). Nor need we take very seriously Goethe's remark to Eckermann, about fifty years later, that the poem 'merely expresses a feeling for water (das Gefühl des Wassers), its charm which entices us to bathe in summer' (3 November 1823). Herder, with his sensitivity to the prim-itive power of myth, was nearer the mark when he included it as 'The Song of the Fisherman' in the collection of 'folksongs' which he published in 1779. In 1804 Goethe received a visit from his enthusiastic French admirer Madame de Staël, who read him her translation of 'The Fisherman'. He objected to her rendering of 'Todesglut' as 'l'air brûlant', explaining that what he had had in mind here was not the fish dying in the noon-day heat but the fish being grilled on the kitchen stove. Like the remark to Eckermann, this was probably no more than a pro-vocative demystifying tease. It is more illuminating to see 'Der Fischer' as a companion-piece to 'Erlkönig'.

18. The Elf King (1781)
The fascinating coinages 'Erlkönig' and 'Erlenkönig', which strictly should mean 'king of the alder-trees', are Herder's inspired mistranslations of the Danish word 'ellerkonge' or 'elverkonge'; the 'king of the elves' thus becomes a forest sprite associated with trees. In his folksong collection, Herder had published his version of an anonymous Danish ballad in which a knight, riding through the forest, is ensnared by an elvish *belle dame sans merci* who introduces herself as 'the elf king's daughter'. Goethe adopted Herder's evocative hybrid forms, of which 'Erlking' (as the ballad is sometimes called in English) is a defensible alternative rendering. His story features a more unconventional eroticism than that of the knight and his seductress, and is strongly realistic and dramatic. The male child paedophil-

ically desired and 'taken' by a male goblin has precedents and parallels from antiquity onwards, including Ganymede and the 'little Indian boy' craved by Shakespeare's Oberon; but Goethe's distinctive presentation balances the myth on the edge of a possible reality, which the father represents. Only the sick child hears the elvish voice and sees the sinister presences: in a three-way dialogue, the father and the elf king compete for his attention, the father as the voice of reason reassuring him that he is feverish, that it is only the wind, that there is nothing there. Yet the father himself, as he rides on, half succumbs to the surrounding bewitchment which reaches its climax in the boy's death.

19. [The Song of the Fates]
The first version of Goethe's classicistic drama *Iphigenia in Tauris* was in prose and written in 1779, but included this poem; the play was revised into iambic blank verse in 1786. 'The Song of the Fates' is thus strictly speaking an extract from *Iphigenia*, but has a certain autonomy as an old traditional song which at a moment of crisis the heroine remembers having heard in her childhood. It expresses a grim and tragic view of the world, resembling the older Greek conception of the gods as cruel and morally indifferent in their dealings with mankind. Specifically, as the dramatic context tells us, Iphigenia is caught in a tragic dilemma, forced to do evil whatever she decides: either to deceive her host and benefactor Thoas or to betray and kill her brother Orestes. In despair she remembers the words of the song, which laments the inescapable suffering and disharmony of human life, recalling in particular the curse that seems to lie on Iphigenia's own family, the descendants of Tantalus whom the gods have punished from generation to generation. In the upshot her humane spirit rebels against this view of things, and the dilemma is unexpectedly resolved by her purity and nobility of heart. Even out of the context of this story, however, the 'song of the Fates' may stand on its own as a meditation not very different from 'Human Limitations' and 'Divinity' in style and theme. The 'Fates' (Latin *Parcae*, Greek *Moirai*) were the three goddesses of destiny, or perhaps of birth, who spun the threads of human life; they were also thought of as present on great occasions and offering comment in song.

20. Human Limitations (1781 or before)
An older MS variant, which may represent Goethe's original intention, reads 'reihen *sie* dauernd' in the antepenultimate line, but this does not essentially affect the sense, which in fact depends more on whether '*ihres* Daseins' is to be taken as referring to the gods' existence or to that of men. The rhetoric of the poem as a whole suggests an antithesis between gods and men – in this closing passage, between the infinity of divine life and the brevity of ours – though strictly speaking, it is not in accordance with ancient mythology to speak of endless divine 'generations', as the generational succession was not thought of as going back

beyond the father and grandfather of Zeus (respectively Cronus and Uranus) or as continuing beyond those of Zeus's children who were also divine. This may be less important, however, than the maintenance of the antithetical sense, in particular its continuation from the previous strophe.

21. Divinity

This further meditation on mankind and 'the gods' (1783) strikes a more positive, humanistic note. Man is not, as in 'Ganymede', drawn into mystic union with nature, which here appears as a stark deterministic nexus without emotional or moral significance, but he is superior to all other animals (the 'beings we know') by virtue of his capacity for moral choice and for artistic creation (lines 41f.). We 'know' of no supernatural beings more noble than man, though intuition tells us that such beings may exist. Yet Goethe no sooner makes this tentative concession to objective theism than he withdraws it: the 'gods' are merely ideal projections of man's own best qualities. Those qualities should encourage us to believe in their reality (it is implied that there are no other grounds for belief); he must so to speak bring them into existence by setting a good example which they (*sic*) can take as 'a model'. The sense of the poem's title would not be very different if instead of 'Divinity' or 'The divine' it were 'Humanity', 'Human divinity', or perhaps 'Divine humanity'. It is interesting that the tenth line of the poem ('Let man resemble them') directly contradicts the penultimate line ('Let him be a model. . .'), which may be the reason why line 10 was dropped from the original manuscript in all the printed editions until the historical-critical Weimar Edition, rightly or wrongly, restored it. Another solution has been to suggest that 'Vorbild' means not 'model' but something like 'provisional image'.

22, 23. 'Oh do you know the land' (1783), 'Only the lonely heart' (1785)

Both these poems are excerpted from *Wilhelm Meister's Theatrical Mission* (*Wilhelm Meisters theatralische Sendung*), the first version of the novel Goethe later published in revised and enlarged form as *Wilhelm Meister's Apprenticeship* (*Wilhelm Meisters Lehrjahre*). The 'Sendung' was begun as early as 1773, and Goethe was working on it between 1782 and 1785. These two famous lyrics are among those associated with a mysterious character whom Wilhelm encounters in Book 3 of the novel, a child of indeterminate sex and Italian origin known only as Mignon, who appears to be haunted by a tragic destiny. Wilhelm supposedly translates her songs from Italian into German. Apart from this fictional context, the first song in particular clearly also expresses Goethe's longing to travel to Italy, as he was to do a few years later. To the translator, the second song ('Nur wer die Sehnsucht kennt') is particularly elusive. I can only guess at the meaning of lines 5f. Lines 9f., with characteristic vivid immediacy, literally read 'I am dizzy, my guts are burning'.

24. 'Who never wept to eat his bread' (*c.* 1783)

Goethe fictionally attributes these lines to another of the characters in his novel *Wilhelm Meister*, the 'Harfner' (harp-player), a half-crazed wandering minstrel who in the end is revealed to have been the father of Mignon by an incestuous union with his sister. The poem expresses much the same feeling of unavoidable tragedy as Iphigenia's 'Song of the Fates', no. 19. The verb 'laßt' is used here in the sense not so much of allowing (the gods let us incur guilt) as of compelling (they cause us to incur guilt); the deserved or undeserved punishment is an automatic consequence.

25. Anacreon's Grave

Written probably in 1785, the year before his Italian journey, this is one of Goethe's first experiments in the elegiac metre adapted from classical Latin and Greek verse, a style which he was to develop very successfully from the *Roman Elegies* onwards. 'Anacreon's Grave' follows the conventions of ancient elegiac epigrams (memorial inscriptions) in honour of dead poets. The name of the Greek lyric poet Anacreon (b. *c.* 570 BC) became associated in the German literary tradition of the eighteenth century with a certain formal and lighthearted style of poetry praising life's material pleasures. By allusion to this tradition and on a deeper level (reached again later in Hugo Wolf's exquisite setting) Goethe seems here to celebrate the poetry of death as part of the poetry of life. The first of the 'Venetian Epigrams' (no. 34) is in a similar vein.

26–33. *Roman Elegies*

For the biographical background and composition-date of this cycle of poems, see Introduction. Further detailed commentary, including discussion of the metre, may be found in *Erotic Poems*. The numbering of the elegies in *Erotic Poems* is retained for the present representative selection, in which the poems largely speak for themselves, though the following specific points should be noted:

27 ('More than I ever had hoped' – elegy III) and 30 ('You were two perilous serpents' – elegy XVII): Schiller, who first published the *Elegies* in 1795 in his new literary periodical *Die Horen* (The Hours), felt that these two poems were somewhat indecent and was unhappy about printing them. Goethe withdrew them from the cycle, and consequently, innocuous though they now seem, they never appeared in the canonical editions of his works. *A fortiori*, he never even attempted to publish the prologue and epilogue (elegies I and XXIV, of which the latter is here included, see no. 33 below): these indeed were more than indecent, they were, in the German locution, 'drastisch'. In this way, what was probably first envisaged as a cycle of twenty-four poems was reduced to twenty, and has traditionally remained at that number.

28 ('Now on classical soil' – elegy VII): Even this elegy was in earlier days considered slightly *risqué*, though in fact it holds in perfect balance the twin themes of

sexual gratification and intellectual or artistic achievement. The 'three poets of Love' were Goethe's acknowledged Latin models, Catullus, Tibullus and Propertius.

29 ('Eros was ever a rogue' – elegy xv): As in vii, where the two central themes of the cycle, love and art, are brought together by the poet's caressing and creative fingers, so they are united here (lines 39f.) in the potent bodily 'memorial' of his love-making – a morning memorial which stands in the centre of his description of the still sleeping beloved. The obvious phallic meaning of 'Denkmal' and of this distich generally, obscured by editorial interference with Goethe's original punctuation, has been overlooked or ignored by almost all previous commentators (see *Erotic Poems*, pp. 128ff.).

30 ('You were two perilous serpents' – elegy xvii): This was one of the self-censored elegies (see above) on account of its frank discussion of the perils of syphilis. Goethe's argument that lovers in ancient Rome are to be envied because venereal diseases were then unknown in Europe rests on a still controversial historical assumption. The poem's many conventional allusions to mythological motifs are in imitation of the Propertian style; they culminate in the developed reference to Hermes (Mercury) at the end, which ironically puts all the others in their place (Hermes the divine messenger = Mercury = quicksilver = the supposed cure for syphilis still used in Goethe's day).

31 ('Caesar would hardly have got me' – elegy xviii): The taverns of Rome were praised in an epigram by the poet Florus, who declared that he would prefer their pleasures to the emperor Hadrian's arduous military expeditions; Hadrian wrote a mocking reply. Setting the scene of this elegy in a tavern, Goethe again combines two central themes: the glories of ancient Rome and the happiness of his clandestine affair with 'Faustina'. The motif of amorous messages scribbled in spilt wine appears in the Latin poets. The assignation is made for the fourth hour after nightfall, by the old system of time-keeping still used in Italy when Goethe was there.

32 ('Strength, and a bold and liberal nature' – elegy xxiii): From Ovid's *Metamorphoses* (11, 174ff.) Goethe takes the story of Midas, king of Phrygia, who for presuming to criticize Apollo's musicianship had his ears turned into those of a donkey, an embarrassment which he managed to hide from everyone except his barber. This legend and its folkloristic development, with the barber longing but not daring to reveal the secret, seems oddly remote from the modern lover's excited longing to tell the whole world about his beloved mistress, but the poem integrates the two themes with great charm and humour. In its last ten lines especially, xxiii reads very much like a poem concluding the *Elegies* as a whole, and in the absence of xxiv has always been traditionally so read.

33 ('Once in the garden's far corner' – elegy xxiv): Elegies i and xxiv have not until very recently (see *Erotic Poems*) been recognized as part of the cycle, having

always been excluded from publication with it. But they belong to it at least as its prologue and epilogue, enclosing in a different and larger frame of reference the personal story of the eighteenth-century poet's discovery of Rome and of Faustina/Christiane (II–XXIII). Goethe's intention seems to have been to reinstate the once popular, primitive phallic fertility-god Priapus as an appropriate living element in modern erotic poetry. This was not merely a literary exercise, as it paralleled his reinstatement in 1788 of sexual activity at the centre of his own life. As well as Catullus, Tibullus and Propertius, Goethe had at this time been studying the anonymous *Carmina Priapea*, a first-century Latin collection of very bawdy poems in honour of the phallic god. He adopts Priapean motifs, such as the enormous erect penis which was the god's conventional trademark, and the common use of his effigy as a kind of garden scarecrow to keep intruders at bay. In this case the 'garden' is the 'Erotica Romana', the poems themselves, the 'golden fruit of the life-tree' as Goethe calls them in the first elegy. He places, or would wish to place, Priapus at the beginning and the end of the cycle, to watch over it so to speak, and as if to indicate that as well as being his own love-story, the *Elegies* are related by their bold eroticism to a more ancient, impersonal and wholesomely earthy folk-tradition from which the modern poet should learn. Goethe is aware that he is here creating a kind of love-poetry which is both new and old, and in the unpublished epilogue (XXIV) he imagines Priapus himself appreciating and praising it. In gratitude to the poet for rehabilitating him and restoring his neglected image, the god gives him his own particular blessing, a prediction of untiring sexual prowess. (Philaenis, mentioned in the last line, was an ancient Greek courtesan to whom the authorship of a well-known erotic manual was attributed.) Goethe, two centuries ago, knew that neither of these Priapean elegies could be printed; he may have looked ahead to a later age of more liberal values and more faithful editions.

34–41. *Venetian Epigrams*

These were written during Goethe's second and shorter visit to Italy in the spring of 1790, when he was in Venice on court business (see Introduction). They are not so much a cycle of poems like the *Roman Elegies* as a collection of miscellaneous observations. Many are polemical and more or less indecent (Goethe published about a hundred which have become canonical, and withheld about fifty more). Others have considerable charm and wit (the descriptions for example of a group of street acrobats and their star performer, a young girl whom Goethe calls Bettina). The numbering of the small sample here included follows that of the larger selection in *Erotic Poems*.

42–46. Miscellaneous classical epigrams

In addition to the 'Venetian Epigrams' Goethe wrote a large number of others either in the same elegiac form or in modern rhymed forms such as 'Knittelvers'. Many were written in collaboration with Schiller, and they were usually collected

under some general title such as 'The Four Seasons', 'Xenia' (=parting gifts, i.e. for the persons satirized) etc. A few examples of the elegiac type are included here.

47, 48. *Hermann and Dorothea*

This small-scale epic poem in nine cantos was written in 1796 at the height of Goethe's 'classical' period, and published in the following year. He had found the subject-matter in an old German chronicle from the period of religious persecutions in the seventeenth and early eighteenth centuries. He transferred the story to his own time and set it against the background of the French Revolution and its consequences as they affected Germany. In a sense, this was Goethe's poetic answer to the Revolution which he abhorred and dreaded. It takes place in and around an unnamed and peaceable small market town, where the young Hermann's father is a prosperous innkeeper, and the family and community in general typify stable middle-class values, contrasted with the current disorder in France which threatens to spread into the German territories. Dorothea is one of a number of refugees from the revolutionary war who are making their way past the town in a straggling crowd. The encounter and mutual love of the two young people is a symbolic conjunction of contrasting worlds, and an obstacle has been placed between them by Hermann's socially ambitious father who angrily opposes his only son's choice of, as he supposes, a mere beggar and vagrant as a wife. The story's anecdotal central point is the behaviour of the young lover when he meets the girl: like his counterpart in Goethe's source, he is too shy to declare himself and propose marriage, but instead offers her a position as maidservant with his parents, and she comes home with him on this basis. The embarrassing misapprehensions that arise from his stratagem are quickly resolved, and the betrothal takes place to everyone's satisfaction. Goethe, by writing his version of this unmomentous and charming tale in the German equivalent of Homeric epic hexameters, gives it a faintly ironical monumentality, and the whole poem takes on an idyllic patina from his slight idealization of the principal characters and constant use of the *epitheton ornans* (the splendid horses, the well-timbered barns, the well-laden boughs). This is not simply an antiquarian stylistic exercise but an 'idyll' in the more modern, profounder sense: a celebration of happiness, of stability, of normality. As such it is more effective by being set against a dark and threatening background, and just enough of an element of opposition and tension is fed into the otherwise purely idyllic-epic narrative to give it a subtly dramatic nuance. *Hermann and Dorothea*, on its publication, deservedly became one of Goethe's most popular and acclaimed works, second only to *The Sufferings of Young Werther*, and remained so during the nineteenth century; it has found less favour in the present embittered and cynical age. The two extracts here selected may serve to illustrate some of these points. In the fourth canto Hermann's mother goes in search of her son to comfort him, a deliberate echo of the passage

in the *Iliad* where Thetis comes to comfort Achilles as he weeps on the sea-shore; on her way she passes through her garden, orchard and cornfields, and rejoices that everything in them is as it should be. In the highly evocative eighth, penultimate canto, Hermann is bringing Dorothea back to his family, retracing his steps from the great pear-tree on the boundary of their land where his mother found him weeping that morning. In what must be one of the subtlest and most delicate love-scenes in German literature, he has not yet spoken to her of his true feelings and intentions, despite the clear hints of her willingness (the change from 'Ihr' to 'du' in line 50, the scarcely accidental stumble, etc.).

49–52. *Faust* Part One
Goethe decided in 1797 to divide *Faust*, which had been left as '*Faust*: a fragment' in the *Works* of 1789–90, into two parts, and substantially completed 'Part One' between 1797 and 1801, though it was not published until 1808. The first of the selected extracts (strictly an introductory poem to the whole of *Faust*) expresses the nostalgia for the mysterious world of the 'Urfaust', and for his youth generally, which Goethe felt in 1797 when resuming work on his early masterpiece. The second extract is the opening of the 'Prologue in Heaven' (also conceived as an introduction to the *Faust* drama as a whole) in which the Devil (Mephistopheles) appears before God and the angels, as Satan does in the Book of Job, and offers God a wager on the destiny of Faust. The third is the opening passage of a scene in which Faust takes a walk outside the town, temporarily relieved of his despairing mood by the Easter celebrations and the spring weather. The fourth is from Faust's meditations after he has returned to his study. Mephistopheles, in the form of a black dog, has followed him into the room, and reveals himself by frenzied barking as he hears Faust translating the opening words of St John's gospel. The predominantly positive, optimistic and here and there humorous mood of all these speeches from the 1808 version of 'Part One' is noteworthy by its contrast with the tragic character of most of the 'Urfaust' passages. More detailed commentary may be found in the introduction and notes to *Faust* OUP 1.

53. The God and the Dancing-girl
Goethe wrote this poem in 1797, and it is possible (in the light of one of the suppressed Venetian Epigrams which alludes provocatively to the tradition that Jesus liked to keep company with prostitutes) that he would have preferred the divine visitor to be the incarnate Christian god, but chose a Hindu legend instead for the sake of publishability. The story was one that he may have found in Pierre Sonnerat's *Voyage to East India and China* (original French edition 1782) which tells how the Hindu demigod Devendren visited a prostitute and tested her fidelity by feigning death. The theme of sexual relations between gods and mortal women is of course ancient and widespread; the sentimental motif of the court-esan whose heart is touched by redeeming love is also recognizable as one that

would become dear to the nineteenth century. A moving variant of the theme occurs in Flaubert's *Légende de St Julien l'Hospitalier* (1877). The term 'bayadère' (Portuguese 'bailadeira', from 'bailar', to dance) was applied especially to the temple courtesans of southern India, known as 'divadasis' (slave-girls of the gods), the Hindu counterpart of the 'hierodoulai' or temple slaves associated with the shrine of Aphrodite in Corinth. Goethe's version replaces Devendren by the incarnate Shiva, one of the supreme deities ('Mahadiva', great god).

54. Permanence in Change
In 1803 the neurologist Johann Christoff Reil sent Goethe his book *Rhapsodic Reflections on the Application of Psychological Therapy to Mental Disorders*. Goethe replied on 15 August, thanking Reil and enclosing 'my bold attempt to express in verse what you have so well expounded on pp. 58ff. of your treatise'. Goethe does not specify the title of the poem, but there can be no doubt that it was 'Permanence in Change'. The passage in Reil that interested him concerns the personal sense of identity which, as he points out, paradoxically persists through the successive total metamorphoses of our physical existence: 'our organism transitorily and progressively changes its material composition; it perpetually destroys and recreates what it has destroyed.' Lines 15f. of the poem quote the well-known saying with which Heraclitus emphasized his doctrine of the perpetual flux of all things.

55. Nature and Art
In 1802, when a new theatre was opened in Bad Lauchstädt, Goethe inserted this sonnet (probably written two years earlier) into a kind of allegorical prospectus in dramatic form which he was hastily putting together to mark the occasion, under the title 'Was wir bringen' ('What we have to offer'). He never reprinted the sonnet in the collected editions of his poems, possibly because he regarded it as an integral part of this relatively trivial theatrical piece. In modern editions, however, 'Natur und Kunst' has often been included as a poem in its own right. The thought, quite characteristic of both Goethe and Schiller at this time, seems to be that if a poet is to achieve the classical mastery of a mature style, two apparently antithetical elements or processes must come together in balance and synthesis: the inspirational, emotional impulse ('nature') and the intellectual, formal discipline here called 'art' in the sense of craft or artifice. The poem appropriately uses the difficult stylized form of the Petrarchan sonnet, with which Goethe was to experiment further a few years later.

56. Nocturne
First printed in 1804 and probably written in that year. Goethe modelled it on an Italian folksong which had a similar, technically interesting verse-form, with the refrain 'Dormi, che vuoi di piu?'

57. *The Diary* (see also Introduction)

Goethe finished writing *The Diary*, which along with the *Roman Elegies* is cert-ainly the most important of his erotic poems, in April 1810, though it is probable that he conceived it some years earlier and that he also had it in mind in 1808–9 when he was working on his novel *Elective Affinities*, with which *The Diary* shares, though more openly, the central theme of the role of fantasy in sexual perform-ance. Although he rightly regarded it as a serious poem with a positive moral tendency, he never attempted to publish it in his lifetime, so that it is only in the present century that it has appeared in unexpurgated form, and even now not in all editions. The narrative's realistic setting in the middle-class society of the middle-aged Goethe's own day made it an even bolder experiment than the Roman cycle, in which the erotic immediacy had been mitigated by the classical elegiac metre, even in the conventionally Priapic elegies I and XXIV (see above). In *The Diary* the phallus is unveiled in a wholly personal and realistic way, though ironically we read here of its failure as well as of its earlier triumphs. The Latin pronoun *iste*, elegantly selected to designate the recalcitrant organ, means approx-imately 'that (thing) of mine', in a sense somewhere between *hic* (this here) and *ille* (that there). The passage (135f.) in which Goethe deliberately rhymes it with the vocative *Christe*, thus provocatively confronting so to speak the central sym-bol of paganism with that of Christianity, has always been found particularly offensive by editors and printers, and its correct wording, buried obscurely in the depths of the historical–critical Weimar edition of Goethe's works, was not re-vealed until more than a hundred years after he had written it. The paradoxical 'moral' of the poem, namely the observation that the penis itself may come to the aid of loving fidelity, cannot be faulted even from a Christian point of view. For a more detailed discussion of *The Diary* see *Erotic Poems* (introduction and notes).

58–77. *West-Eastern Divan*

This last major cycle of Goethe's lyric poems, published in 1819, was written mainly in 1814–5 in circumstances which are discussed above in the Introduc-tion. The inspiration was both literary (the fourteenth-century Persian poet Ḥāfiz) and personal (Goethe's love for the young wife of Johann Jakob von Willemer, a family friend whom he was visiting in Frankfurt). Marianne von Willemer was poetically gifted, and contributed several poems to the *Divan* herself, which Goethe adopted as his own. He broke off the relationship with her in 1816. The *Divan* (assembly, collection) is divided, like that of Ḥāfiz, into twelve sections or 'books'.

58. Hegira (from 'The Book of the Singer')

December 1814. Goethe thought of his visit in the summer of 1814 to the Main and Rhine area (see Introduction), and of his visit to Italy in 1786, as journeys of liberation taking him back to a simpler and more youthful world, and thus as

turning-points in his life. He explicitly compared both of them to the 'Hegira' (departure, escape) of the Prophet Muhammad from Mecca to Medina in AD 622, the chief event in Islamic religious history. The same word is used as the title for this poem, which was one of the first of the *Divan* poems to be written. The opening lines allude to the wars and upheavals of the Napoleonic period. Khiser (line 6) was the guardian, in Islamic legend, of the fountain of life, who in a vision brought to Hāfiz the cup of eternal youth and immortal fame.

59. Singing and Shaping (from 'The Book of the Singer')
Date uncertain, perhaps 1816 but possibly 1814. The poem symbolically celebrates Goethe's post-classical transition to the more 'fluid' lyrical style of the *Divan*. The closing lines recall the Indian legend of the pure in heart who are able to draw water from the Ganges in the form of solid crystal spheres. Goethe was to take up this motif again in 1823 in the dramatic narrative of 'The Pariah' (see below, no. 86). In the context of the *Divan*, the emphasis is not so much on the classical perfection of the spherical form, as on the refreshment of the soul by water and the pure singing which the free element transforms into art.

60. A Phenomenon (from 'The Book of the Singer')
Written on 25 July 1814, a week or two before Goethe's first meeting with Marianne. The rainbow whitened by the mist seems to have been an actual observation, which Goethe took as a favourable omen.

61. A Past within the Present (from 'The Book of the Singer')
The castle is the twelfth-century Wartburg near Eisenach; Goethe could see it from the town as he wrote this poem there in the early morning of 26 July 1814. The scene recalls to him his early days at Weimar, the hunting expeditions in the Thuringian forests with Karl August and his courtiers, the time of his first love for Charlotte von Stein. The third stanza celebrates the faculty of recollection in later years (the poem was first conceived with the title 'Erinnerung') which enables him to identify his own experience sympathetically with that of others at their various stages of life. Youth mirrors itself in age, and as he remembers Hāfiz's poetry the east is mirrored in the west.

62. Talismans (from 'The Book of the Singer')
May 1815 or earlier. The fifth epigram, on the theology of breathing, is derived from a passage which Goethe read in a seventeenth-century German translation of another Persian poet, Muslih ud din Abdullah Sa'di (1215–?1292).

63. Unbounded (from 'The Book of Hāfiz')
November 1814. The poem was originally called 'Hāfiz', to whom it pays homage. The 'song' is Goethe's own: 'younger' because more recent, 'older' because historically later.

64. Suleika Speaks (from 'The Book of Reflections')
May 1815 or earlier. The theme is reminiscent of one of the classical epigrams (no. 42 above). The motif of the Eternal Moment is also central to Goethe, occurring notably in *Faust* and elsewhere in his poetry.

65. The Secret (from 'The Book of Love')
c. August 1814.

66. Engulfed (from 'The Book of Love')
May 1815 or earlier. (Line 11) 'liebevoll' is varied to 'liebeviel', a remarkable and untranslatable coinage.

67. 'Love for love and hour for hour. . .' (from 'The Book of Suleika')
25 September 1815, written in Heidelberg on the day before Goethe's final parting from Marianne. 'Joseph' (line 8) is the young Joseph of the Biblical narrative (Genesis 39), whose legendary beauty inspired a passionate infatuation in the wife of Potiphar, his Egyptian benefactor. In the Koranic version of the story her name was Suleika, and she achieved a mystical sublimation of her passion which led her to embrace the true faith of Islam.

68. 'Beloved, let me show you. . .' (from 'The Book of Suleika')
This too was written during the productive last few days of September 1815 in Heidelberg with Marianne. The central simile may have been suggested to Goethe by ripe chestnut-trees in the Heidelberg castle park.

69a, 69b. 'As I sailed on the Euphrates. . .', 'This I'm happy to interpret. . .' (from 'The Book of Suleika')
17 September 1815. These may be read as two parts of one and the same poem, a dialogue between 'Suleika' and 'Hatem'. Hatem's answer alludes to the Venetian custom by which, on Ascension Day, the Doge was ceremonially rowed out in the great state gondola, the 'Bucintoro', and cast a golden ring into the water, to symbolize the marriage of Venice with the sea. The Venetian lagoon is here both the Euphrates and the Main, 'marrying' Goethe and Marianne.

70. Ginkgo biloba (from 'The Book of Suleika')
Heidelberg, September 1815. The ginkgo tree (*ginkgo biloba*) originates in the Far East, but has grown in European botanical gardens since about 1800. Its fan-shaped leaf has a deep central indentation which gives it the appearance of two leaves that have grown into one.

71. The Night of the Full Moon (from 'The Book of Suleika')
October 1815. Suleika's refrain is a line quoted verbatim from Hāfiz in Hammer-Purgstall's translation. Line 12: 'Karfunkel' strictly means a glowing red stone such as a ruby, but seems to be used here in a wider sense (? a sparkling point of light).

72. Suleika: 'West wind, how I envy. . .' (from 'The Book of Suleika')
This is one of the poems written by Marianne and adopted by Goethe with slight
emendations. Her poem to the west wind (another addresses the east wind in
similar vein) was probably written in September 1815 on her way back from
Heidelberg to Frankfurt.

73. 'King Behramgur, they say. . .' (from 'The Book of Suleika')
In May 1818 Goethe read Hammer-Purgstall's account of how, according to an
old Persian tradition, the Sassanid king Behramgur (d. AD 440) spoke in verse
to his favourite slave-girl Dilaram, and how she expressed her love for him
by answering in the same rhythm, her lines ending in harmoniously repeated
sounds; between them they had thus invented the art of rhyme. This legend
seemed to Goethe to reflect his own experience with Marianne, who had not only
returned his love, but also been moved by some sensitive instinct of imitation to
respond to his poetic courtship with poems of her own but written in Goethe's
style. His poem about King Behramgur commemorates this, and was inserted in
the *Divan* when the book was already being printed. Goethe returned to the same
theme in the remarkable central scene of *Faust* Part Two (Act III 9365–84) in
which Faust teaches Helen to speak in rhymed verse, a convention unknown in
ancient Greek poetry, so that her adoption of it symbolizes her union with Faust
and the marriage of the two cultures they represent.

74a. Summer Night (from 'The Book of the Cupbearer')
June–December 1814. In Hāfiz there is no 'Suleika' and very little heterosexuality
in general, whereas the theme of adolescent male beauty runs all through his work.
Goethe, although for him, on the whole, matters stood otherwise, thought it
appropriate to give some minimal representation to this theme in his own *Divan*.
It went hand in hand with the celebration of wine and drunkenness: Hāfiz had
been fortunate enough to live in a tolerant epoch during most of his career; later,
when the Islamic prohibition of alcohol was applied more strictly, it could be said
that the wine was merely allegorical, and if necessary the same could be said of the
boys. The two motifs (and that of wine, at least, was very congenial to Goethe
personally) could be conveniently combined in a 'Book of the Cupbearer' in
which a young wine-waiter plays the role of Ganymede. 'Summer Night' is the
most important and beautiful poem in this section. The relationship is less that of
master and servant than of wise teacher and favourite pupil: affectionate, delicate-
ly paederastic. Their discussion here is largely astronomical, and ambiguously
located: the 'golden shimmer' of twilight lingers as in northern Europe, and the
nightingale, 'Bulbul', sings as in a Persian grove. The cupbearer expects the night
to become completely dark, making the stars fully visible. The poet points out that
at this time of high summer the night is so short that daybreak is visible in the
north-east before the afterglow of sunset has quite disappeared in the north-west;

in mythological terms, the dawn-goddess is pursuing the evening star Hesperus as he follows the setting sun. (In her marriage to the immortal but ever-ageing Tithonus, Aurora is 'forsaken', and lusts after any young man she sees.) The phrase 'des Nordgestirnes Zwillingswendung' remains obscure: the Pole Star (if a single star is meant by 'Nordgestirn') does not move or turn, and the Great and Little Bear to which commentators often refer are not 'twin' constellations; in any case the boy is invoking not a continual circumpolar movement but a moment, a significant division in time which must not be missed (the onset of deep night being one of the prescribed times of prayer for pious Muslims). He also seems to identify it with midnight, the centre of the night as the 'north star' is the centre of the sky, and midnight might be said to have the 'twin' halves of the diurnal period on either side of it; its 'Wendung' is then perhaps the passage of time from one half to the other. But this reading, too, seems less than satisfactory. The poem contains many examples of the grammatical condensations and other linguistic liberties characteristic of the *Divan* and of Goethe's late style generally, and these somehow give a touchingly naive and *volkstümlich* colouring to the boy's speech in which they chiefly occur: 'niedergangen' for 'niedergegangen', 'außer' for 'außerhalb', 'meiner Stelle' for 'an meiner Stelle', the strange collective 'aller Vogel' for 'alle Vögel', 'Eule' for 'wie eine Eule', 'kauzen' as a verb coined from 'Kauz' (another kind of owl), the ellipsis of 'du' in line 36, 'Blumenfelds Gelänge' for 'das lange Blumenfeld', etc.

74b. 'Well, so at last I've learnt. . .' (from 'The Book of the Cupbearer')
Written in July 1818 but inserted at this point in the final edition of 1827, where it reads like a continuation or coda of 'Summer Night'.

75. Privileged Animals (from 'The Book of Paradise')
February 1815. The old Christian and Islamic legend of the Seven Sleepers told how seven brothers, fleeing from persecution by the emperor Decius (d. AD 215) took refuge in a cave near Ephesus. The emperor had the cave walled up, but by angelic protection they slept on unharmed for three hundred years, with a shepherd's dog for company. Abuherrira (line 17) was a friend of the Prophet Muhammad.

76. Higher and Highest Matters (from 'The Book of Paradise')
September 1818. The first five stanzas ironically develop the naively anthropomorphic and earthly conception of Paradise found in the Koran. The remaining stanzas, with subtle transition, return to a serious sense of the mystery of what lies beyond human life, human speech and the human senses. The mystical note of the closing lines is one that Goethe was not to strike again until the closing scene of *Faust* Part Two.

77. Ecstatic Longing (from 'The Book of the Singer')

Although this enigmatic and compelling poem was one of the first *Divan* poems to be written (in July 1814), its importance makes it a fitting conclusion to the present selection. It was originally called 'Selbstopfer' ('Self-Immolation'), later 'Vollendung' ('Perfection'), and finally, if untranslatably, 'Selige Sehnsucht'. These changes betoken a certain complexity in the development of its train of thought, and it is possible that the last, rhythmically different stanza may have been a later addition to the first four. It has also been suggested that there are two distinct themes in the poem which are not clearly or consistently related to each other: that of self-immolation (stanza 4) and that of metamorphosis (stanza 5). Stanzas 2 and 3 are addressed to the human lover who, having gratified his earthly desire, begins to long for a stranger and 'higher' union with the fire of the divine life, an image no doubt suggested by the candle-flame of line 8. The 'du' of stanza 4 is likewise the lover, now rhetorically identified with the moth whose passion draws him into the consuming flame. This allegory of the soul's ecstatic absorption into God can be traced back to Neoplatonic, Christian and Sufic mysticism; the image of the burnt moth or other insect is constantly found in Hāfiz, Sa'di, and other Arabic and Persian poets. The second and concluding theme of the poem is an injunction: the poet bids the reader learn to 'die and become', to die into becoming, to accept the self-metamorphoses that are involved in the natural development of earthly life; if he learns this, it is his life on earth that will be enhanced. This exhortation seems more closely related to Goethe's own essentially naturalistic thought than to any transcendental mysticism, still less to a romantic cult of death as such. In the allegory, the moth is destroyed: in fact, however, the end of the matter is not self-destruction but self-transformation. At the end of *Faust*, similarly, we are left with a hero not disappearing into the Absolute, but reaching out into further stages of change and growth in a realm beyond knowledge. The seeming discrepancy between the immolation-theme and the metamorphosis-theme may be resolved if we understand that the enhancement and enrichment of life suggested *per contrarium* by the poem's closing lines depends on being ready to die, on learning the concept of 'dying into becoming', rather than on actual death.

78–83.

These rhymed-verse epigrams and short poems, which are self-explanatory, all belong to the late period (after about 1810).

84. At Midnight (February 1818)

Goethe stated in his diary, and again in a later essay, that this mysterious poem was one of which he was particularly fond, all the more so because, on the bright moonlit night of 13 February, it had come into his mind unexpectedly and with-

out explanation. His state of mind at the time, he writes, had been 'wundersam', and he would be at a loss to explain the origin or the purport of the poem ('woher es kam und wohin es wollte'). It seems however to be an evocation of three successive stages of life and thus to be what Goethe calls a 'song of life (Lebenslied)'. It may also be significant, as has been suggested, that all three stanzas are linked by an imagery of light, of brightness increasing from that of the stars to that of the full moon. Goethe's description of his father in line 3 as 'der Pfarrer' has never been explained.

85. Primal Words. Orphic (1817)

In the confused history of ancient Greek religions, the terms 'Orphic' and 'Orphism' have sometimes been applied to mystery-cults associated with the legendary figure of Orpheus and poetry attributed to him. Such cults, mentioned by Plato and others, concerned secret rites, initiation, purification, the fate of the soul after death, etc, and have no discernible connection with the thoughts expressed in Goethe's poem. On 9 October 1817 he wrote to his friend Knebel that he had been studying certain learned works on Greek mythology and even 'the Orphic obscurities', which seem to have left him none the wiser: it was, he wrote, 'a strange world, which unfortunately even the efforts of such excellent scholars do not fully clarify, for when anything is illuminated by one of them it is obfuscated again by another'. His intention in the poem seems to have been, as he puts it in another letter, 'to summarize certain very ancient, succinct pronouncements on human destiny', but reference to what little we know of the 'Orphic' mysteries in fact adds nothing to our understanding of what he is saying here. In the published poem he headed each stanza with a Greek word and his translation of it; variants of some of these translations appear in a manuscript discovered in 1914. We also have the commentary he added in 1820 after the poem had been published, though this too is not a model of lucid exegesis. The word δαίμων in classical Greek meant a man's appointed lot, fortune, destiny or fate (hence also εὐδαίμων, fortunate, and δυσδαίμων, unfortunate, ill-fated) as well as the god or other supernatural being who imposed it on him. In his manuscript version Goethe loosely renders δαίμων as 'Individualität, Charakter', which he explains in the 1820 essay as the sum total of innate, unalterable, unique individual characteristics by which one's 'fate' is largely determined; 'Schicksal' is thus obliquely suggested as the meaning of 'δαίμων'. In the published poem he reverted to the more ambiguous German equivalent '*Dämon*'. By 'chance (τύχη, das Zufällige)' in the second stanza he appears to mean the random factors in one's origin or early environment by which one is also influenced, and which to some extent conflict with the persistent pressure of the individual δαίμων. 'ἀνάγκη' (Nötigung, i.e. strictly 'necessity' or 'compulsion') is interpreted in the manuscript version as 'Beschränkung (limitation)' or 'Pflicht (duty)'. The remaining two 'primal words' (stanzas 3 and 5) are self-explanatory. The word 'Urwort' (akin to Goethe's earlier coinages 'Urpflanze'

and 'Urphänomen') suggests not simply 'ancient' or 'original', but somehow 'timeless', as of a fundamental unchanging element of human life.

86. The Pariah

Goethe began writing this narrative trilogy in 1821 and finished it in 1823. The Indian legend which is its centrepiece was one with which Goethe had long been familiar, possibly from Pierre Sonnerat's book about his travels in the Far East (see above, note on no. 53). The essential mythical motif is that of a possessor of magical powers, miraculous strength, etc., who forfeits them by becoming impure: this of course is found from ancient times, as in the Biblical story of Samson (Judges 13–16), and recurs in Schiller's tragedy *The Maid of Orleans* (1801), where the warrior–heroine is weakened by losing her inner virginity when she falls in love with an enemy instead of killing him. The specific variant in the Indian story is that the divine Mariatale (she later became the goddess who could cure chickenpox) has control over the elements, and can lift a solid sphere of water out of the river with her bare hands, until love strikes her and impure thoughts enter her heart. The theme of the unclean outcast, the pariah, appears in Goethe's source-story when the heroine's head is mistakenly rejoined to the body of a criminal pariah woman: in the poem Goethe gives this much more subtlety and scope by framing the whole Mariatale action between 'the Pariah's prayer' and his thanksgiving. The gods are merciful not only to Mariatale, but also to the whole race of 'untouchables', who are now given their own divine yet human mediator, pure yet involved in their experience. The three parts of the poem become together, as it were, a timeless religious rite celebrating the mercy of the Creator even to the lowest of men. Goethe also knew two modern literary treatments of the subject of the pariah caste, which was a matter of interest in Europe at this time: a one-act play by Michael Beer (*Der Paria*) and a tragedy (*Le Paria*) by Casimir Delavigne, both published in 1821. In a review written shortly after the appearance of his own poem, Goethe comments on the tragic, despairing character of these two minor works, commending his own very different, more balanced and conciliatory treatment. Stylistically, the central 'legend', in blank trochaics, is remarkable for its idiosyncratic syntax (ellipsis and displacement of pronouns, etc.) which I have not attempted to reproduce in the translation.

87. A Trilogy of Passion

The component poems of this three-part cycle, unlike those of 'The Pariah', were conceived quite separately and written at different times; for their biographical background see Introduction. The first, 'To Werther', was written last, in March 1824 as a prologue or preface to a fiftieth anniversary reprint of the novel. The 'Elegy', recording Goethe's painful renunciation of Ulrike von Levetzow, was written in September 1823 and at first not meant for publication. The poem eventually called 'Reconcilement' had already originated in August 1823 as an occasional

tribute to the pianist Maria Szymanowska. Goethe later decided to integrate the three poems, in reverse order, as a trilogy with the tragic 'Marienbad Elegy' as its centrepiece. The epigraph he added to it is a quotation from *Torquato Tasso*, his classical drama (1790) about the tragic psychology of the creative artist; I have here used Michael Hamburger's translation (Goethe's *Collected Works*, Suhrkamp, 1987, vol. viii). The two lines are also echoed at the end of 'To Werther'.

88. The Bridegroom

It is now thought probable that this poem, which Goethe never mentions in any letter or conversation, was written in 1824. Its only publication in his lifetime was in a small weekly periodical called *Chaos*, privately printed by his daughter-in-law Ottilie for the Weimar literary circle. 'Der Bräutigam' (the word can mean either 'bridegroom' or 'betrothed') appeared here in September 1829, and was then virtually ignored for about a century, but has been much discussed in more recent times. Its problems include the usual search for identification: is the 'bridegroom' or 'betrothed' merely a role, a persona, a 'lyric ego', or is the beloved here a specific woman in the historical Goethe's experience? Is she now alive or dead? ('die Schwelle, wo sie ruht', literally 'the threshold where she lies', may be understood as 'the place where she lies', but may or may not be her grave). The first three stanzas are in the past tense, the fourth in the present; does this suggest that the lover, in old age and perhaps in dreams (line 14), is remembering a past love or loves? Is 'sie fehlte' in line 5 past indicative ('she was not there') or subjunctive ('she would not be there')? Candidates for identification with the beloved of this poem include Marianne, Charlotte, Christiane whom Goethe did actually marry, and Lili Schönemann to whom he was for a time conventionally engaged (see Introduction, and note on no. 11). It has been pointed out that in 1824, when he is thought to have written' The Bridegroom', he may also have been working on the section of his autobiography (*Fiction and Truth*, Book 17) that deals with his betrothal to Lili, and that some passages there seem to echo the poem or to be echoed by it: the first two lines, for instance, have been compared to Goethe's description of his state of mind after spending the evening in her company: '. . . Es war ein Zustand, von welchem geschrieben steht: "Ich schlafe, aber mein Herz wacht." Die hellen wie die dunkeln Stunden waren einander gleich; das Licht des Tages konnte das Licht der Liebe nicht überscheinen, und die Nacht wurde durch den Glanz der Neigung zum hellsten Tage' ('It was a condition in which, as it is written, "I sleep, but my heart wakes". The bright and the dark hours were one and the same; the light of day could not outshine the light of love, and night was turned into broad daylight by the radiance of affection').

'The Bridegroom', in our century, has of course also attracted attention by its lapidary closing statement (line 16), which tends to be quoted as Goethe's final judgement on human existence as a whole, though contextually it is closer to the deep emotion of the preceding line.

89. [On Contemplating Schiller's Skull] (September 1826)
On his death in 1805, Schiller had been given a relatively modest burial in the old communal cemetery in Weimar. By 1826 this had long become overcrowded and fallen into disuse, and the civic authorities decided to clear it out; Schiller's family planned to re-bury his remains in the new cemetery which had replaced it. Much trouble was taken to pick out his skull and other bones, though their identification is still doubtful. For a short time they were lodged in the Weimar State Library, which also served as a museum; the skull was ceremonially incorporated in a bust of Schiller by a contemporary artist. In September it was removed for proper examination and cleaning, and kept for some time in Goethe's house. Wilhelm von Humboldt, one of the very few whom Goethe allowed to see it, reported in a letter to his wife that Goethe had now had a burial-vault prepared for himself, in the hope that Schiller's bones would be buried there beside him. About a year later however, in December 1827, they were transferred to their final resting-place in the tomb of the Grand Ducal family. It is generally assumed that Goethe wrote the poem while he had the remains in his possession, and although the text nowhere explicitly identifies the skull as Schiller's, and the title was a posthumous editorial addition by Goethe's literary executors Eckermann and Riemer, it is reasonable to read the poem as Goethe's meditation on the mortal remains of a great man and as a celebration of the intellectual genius of a friend whom he admired more than any of his contemporaries. A note of special solemnity is struck by the metre, the *terza rima* form invented by Dante for his *Divine Comedy*, a continuous chain of thrice-repeated linked rhymes. Goethe used this difficult rhyme-scheme on only one other occasion: for the great speech by Faust (no. 94 below) when he wakes at the beginning of Part Two. In both these cases the poet's thought moves from particular observations (the noble shape of the skull and head, the sunrise among high mountains, the rainbow in the spray of the waterfall) to a profound or striking generality ('that mysterious sea whence transformed forms perpetually rise', and the 'many-coloured reflection' which is all that mortal sight can perceive of the eternal fire of life).

90. 'Dusk has fallen...'
Goethe spent much of the summer of 1827 in his secluded 'garden house' on the outskirts of Weimar. He had been reading some examples of Chinese prose and verse, which prompted him to write a cycle of short and simple lyric poems and to call them 'Chinesisch-deutsche Tages- und Jahreszeiten' ('Chinese-German Hours and Seasons'). They cannot be said to be modelled on Chinese poetry in any but a quite superficial sense; nevertheless, as in the case of the *Divan*, Goethe had found the indirect impact of a remote and exotic culture creatively stimulating, even when mediated by inadequate French and English translations. This poem, with its vision of a twilit and moonlit landscape, is perhaps the outstanding piece in the cycle. It is interestingly similar in metre and theme to

part of the chorus of elves at the beginning of *Faust* Part Two (lines 4642–9; see no. 93 below) which Goethe was also writing at about this time.

91. To the Rising Full Moon
Goethe in his later years would often retreat into the country to Dornburg, a small group of hunting lodges belonging to the Grand Duke, one of which Karl August had placed at his disposal. They were not very far from Weimar, picturesquely situated at the edge of the Thuringian hills and overlooking the river Saale. In June 1828, to Goethe's great sorrow, Karl August died; Charlotte von Stein had died in the previous year. Goethe withdrew to Dornburg in August, isolated but still productive. 'To the Rising Full Moon' is one of a group of short lyric poems written there at that time. In the *Divan*, 'The Night of the Full Moon' (no. 71) had alluded to a romantic agreement between Goethe and Marianne in 1815: that at every full moon they would think of each other. The Dornburg poem seems to refer back to this theme.

92. [A Legacy]
About three weeks before his death, Goethe returned Marianne von Willemer's letters to her, enclosing this poem (see Introduction).

93–100. *Faust* Part Two (see also Introduction)
Goethe conceived, and at least fragmentarily sketched, certain scenes for Part Two as early as about 1800, while he was still creatively engaged on Part One, and some of his ideas for it are thought to go back to a much earlier date. He did not, however, seriously revise and complete his material for the 'second Part of the Tragedy' until the last few years of his life, beginning in 1825 and finishing it in 1831. Like the composition of Part One, that of this second Part may therefore be said to have occupied him intermittently for at least three decades; the vague dating '1800–1831' will have to serve here as a summary indication of this complex chronology. Further information and detailed comment are available in the introduction and notes to *Faust* OUP2.

93, 94. Both these passages are from the opening scene of Part Two, which is effectively a prologue to the whole of it. A chorus of elvish nature-spirits sings to Faust as he lies between sleeping and waking in the bosom of nature. This healing sleep purges him of all memory of the terrible events of Part One. For purposes of the quite different style and milieu of the second Part, in which Faust is to be launched on a new career, Goethe could not have a hero haunted by remorse, nor one who simply dismissed from his mind the destruction of Gretchen and her family and his responsibility for this. As a transition, Faust is therefore lulled into a sleep of forgetfulness, a 'death-like' trance (as Goethe described it to Eckermann) in which the natural healing powers, external and internal, can take effect. Faust wakes to a kind of resurrection of his spirit, expressed in the second passage.

The words of the first evoke the passing hours of the night, and Faust, on waking, hails the sunrise and morning light in the high mountains. His speech is in the rare and difficult *terza rima* metre invented by Dante (see note to the poem on Schiller's skull, no. 89). The remarkable description of the landscape is partly based on Goethe's memories of Switzerland, especially of the Rhine waterfall at Schaffhausen, where he was fascinated by the phenomenon of the rainbow appearing in the rising spray. The symbolism of this passage in Faust's speech is disputed (see note in *Faust*OUP2, p. 268) but seems to suggest a turning away from the Absolute, or from extremes of experience, in a spirit of renunciation or mature acceptance of human limitations.

95. Traditionally, in the Faustus legend, Faust uses the help of Mephistopheles to conjure up from the dead the half-divine Helen of Troy, the world's most famous beauty. In Goethe's adaptation of this theme, he travels to a magical or 'virtual' ancient Greece, and after a long quest finally encounters Helen. At the symbolic level their union represents a synthesis of classical Greek and modern German culture. This extract is the opening speech of Helen at the beginning of Act III, when she appears by magic outside her husband Menelaus's palace in Sparta. In her speeches Goethe deliberately uses the iambic trimeter line to recreate the style of a classical Greek tragedy. The metres are of special importance in this Act, since the union of Faust and Helen will presently be symbolized by her learning from him to speak in modern rhymed verse (see note to no. 73, and *Faust*OUP2 pp. xliiif.).

96. Faust concludes his wooing of Helen by inviting her to take refuge with him in Arcadia; his description of the paradisal realm of pure nature, from which this extract is taken, is probably the most beautiful piece of pastoral poetry in German.

97. The Arcadian idyll ends with the death of Euphorion (who falls from the sky like Icarus) and the immediately following return of Helen to the underworld. In the conventional manner of Greek drama, she has been attended by a chorus of women, who now also vanish, not returning to the underworld but reverting, as elemental nature-spirits, to various manifestations of nature itself (trees, mountains, rivers and vineyards).

98. After the loss of Helen, Faust has achieved power and wealth and is now a hundred years old. The sentinel on the watchtower of his palace is Lynceus, formerly one of the mythical Argonaut heroes, called 'lynx-eyed' because he is gifted with far-sight. These words are sung by him, but the poem is generally quoted out of its context as a comment on life in general by Goethe in his old age, comparable to the last line of 'The Bridegroom' (no. 88). If we do take account of the context (although in *Faust* it is not always historically correct to do so) it may be said that

there is some irony in the fact that the very next thing Lynceus observes from his vantage-point is the brutal murder of two innocent old people by Faust and his demonic henchmen.

99. After his death, Faust is snatched from the clutches of Mephistopheles and carried to heaven by angels for reasons which commentators have been trying to clarify ever since Part Two was published. The final scene takes place in a wild, mysterious region on the fringes of heaven. The imagery is partly based on the fourteenth-century frescoes of the cathedral cemetery in Pisa, which portray early Christian hermits meditating in a rocky desert near Egyptian Thebes. The first ten lines in particular, with their strange, elliptical grammar and redundant pronouns, are an extraordinary example of Goethe's late style; see also no. 74 ('Sommernacht') and no. 86 ('Paria'). The scene is unified by the prevailing theme of divine love in its various manifestations.

100. Goethe's *Faust* ends with the enigmatic 'Chorus Mysticus', which he originally called 'Chorus in Excelsis'. The sense of the third line is disputed. 'Unzulänglich' has usually been taken to mean 'insufficient' or 'inadequate' as in modern German, but Goethe occasionally also used it in the sense, current in the seventeenth century and earlier, of 'inaccessible' (modern German 'unzugänglich'). The latter perhaps makes better sense if we read 'Ereignis' in the next line as not simply 'event', but in the older sense of 'Eräugnis', a manifest or visible thing revealed to the eye (Auge). The famous concluding statement of Goethe's personal myth of 'eternal womanhood' (literally 'the eternal-feminine'), may be read as an echo of Dante's *Paradiso*: the spiritual traveller is 'drawn on' or 'drawn aloft' by his beloved, in Dante's case Beatrice, in Faust's case Gretchen, who reappears in this last scene. She prays for her lover to the Mater Gloriosa, the Virgin Mother of God (God the Father and Christ are here conspicuously absent) who tells her to rise to higher spheres, drawing Faust after her. Goethe insisted that he was using Catholic imagery for purely aesthetic reasons, thereby authorizing us to read the passage in a more earthly sense as well. Helen, as the supreme paragon of physical beauty and sensuality, may be understood as a 'pagan' counterpart to the Mater Gloriosa, and both Helen and Gretchen as further manifestations of the Eternal Feminine, the ultimate principle of heterosexual and maternal Eros.

Index of German titles and first lines

GOETHE: SELECTED POETRY

INDEX OF TITLES AND FIRST LINES

Index of English titles and first lines

GOETHE: SELECTED POETRY

FAUST, PART I

Goethe

'Any scrap of paper will do very well. You sign your name
with a little drop of blood'

Goethe's *Faust* reworks the late medieval myth of Dr Faust, a
brilliant scholar who makes a wager with Mephistopheles. The
devil will do all he asks on Earth and grant him a moment in life
so glorious that he will wish it to last for ever. But if Faust bids
the moment stay, he falls to Mephisto and must serve him eternally.
In this first part of Goethe's great work the embittered thinker
and Mephistopheles enter into their agreement, and soon Faust
is living a glorious life and winning the love of the charming
Gretchen. But he inexorably heads towards destruction, in a
compelling tragedy of arrogance and self-delusion.

Translated with an Introduction by David Constantine
With a preface by A. S. Byatt

ISBN: 978 0 14 044 901 3

FAUST, PART II

Johann Wolfgang von Goethe

'The corpse is prone and when the spirit flies I show her my
entitlement, blood-signed'

After the sorrowful loss of his beloved Gretchen, Faust is tempted
by the demon, Mephistopheles, with the grandest distractions of
politics and power. Eager for new sensations, Faust calls for a
vision of the unsurpassed beauty of Helen of Troy, and then,
overwhelmed, for her to be brought back from the underworld
and delivered to him bodily. But even this does not bring
contentment, or satisfy his appetite for fresh experience. Completed
a few months before Goethe's death, the concluding part of his
masterpiece is a rich and allusive work, weaving together a wealth
of diverse philosophical ideas and influences, reworking the
medieval myth of Dr Faustus, and specualting upon the search
for truth in the Age of Enlightenment.

Translated with an introduction and notes by
David Constantine
and with a preface by A. S. Byatt

ISBN: 978 0 14 044 902 0

TALES OF HOFFMAN

E. T. A. Hoffman

'Soft, uncertain footsteps approached the apartment ...
Spellbound, without strength to move, she waited for the worst'

This selection of Hoffmann's finest short stories vividly demonstrates his intense imagination and preoccupation with the supernatural, placing him at the forefront of both surrealism and the modern horror genre. Suspense dominates tales such as *Mademoiselle de Scudery*, in which an apprentice goldsmith and a female novelist find themselves caught up in a series of jewel thefts and murders. In the sinister *The Sandman*, a young man's sanity is tormented by fears about a mysterious chemist, while in *The Choosing of a Bride* a greedy father preys on the weaknesses of his daughter's suitors. Master of the bizarre, Hoffman creates a sinister and unsettling world combining love and madness, black humour and bewildering illusion.

Selected and translated with an
Introduction by R. J. Hollingdale

ISBN: 978 0 14 044 392 9

SELECTED TALES

Brothers Grimm

'Two of her tears dropped on his eyes, and the light was restored
to them and he could see again'

The folktales collected by Jacob and Wilhelm Grimm are among
the most memorable stories in European culture – conjuring up
a world of spells and bewitchment, outwitted villains and cruel
stepmothers, animal bridegrooms and enchanted princesses. Tales
such as *Hansel and Gretel*, *Little Redcape* and *The Robber Bride-
groom* depict the dangers lurking in dark forests, and others,
including *Briar-Rose* and *Snowwhite*, show young beauties
punished by unforgiving sorceresses. Other tales include
Thickasathumb, which portrays a childless couple whose wish for
a baby is granted in an unexpected way, while *The Frog King* tells
of a rash promise made by a haughty princess to share her bed
with a frog and a fortune is won in *The Blue Lamp*, when a soldier
gains a kingdom with the help of a magic lamp.

Translated with an introduction and notes by David Luke

ISBN: 978 0 14 044 401 8

NOVELS, TALES, JOURNEYS

Alexander Pushkin

'At that moment it seemed to him that the queen of spades
winked and grinned. The extraordinary likeness struck him ...
"The old woman!" he cried in horror'

Universally acknowledged as his nation's greatest poet, Pushkin
was also a master of prose, whose works expanded the boundaries
of Russian storytelling. This collection of his prose writing ranges
from satires to comedies, travel narratives to imaginative historical
fiction, and includes his greatest stories: the haunting dreamworld
of 'The Queen of Spades', the five short *Tales of the Late Ivan
Petrovich Belkin* and the novella *The Captain's Daughter*, which
has been called the most perfect book in Russian literature.

Translated by Richard Pevear and Larissa Volokhonsky

ISBN: 978 0 24 129 037 8

ONE HUNDRED POETS,
ONE POEM EACH

'How the night deepens.
A ribbon of frost
is stretched across
the bridge of magpie wings
the lovers will cross.'

The best-loved and most widely read of all Japanese poetry collections, the Ogura Hyakunin Isshu contains 100 short poems on nature, the seasons, travel, and, above all, love. Dating back to the seventh century, these elegant, precisely observed waka poems (the precursor of haiku) express deep emotion through visual images based on a penetrating observation of the natural world. Peter MacMillan's new translation of his prize-winning original conveys even more effectively the beauty and subtlety of this magical collection.

Translated with an Introduction and commentary
by Peter MacMillan

ISBN: 978 0 14 139 593 7

THE PENGUIN BOOK OF
SCOTTISH VERSE

'The kind of definitive, caring and intelligent collection that
Scottish poetry has been waiting for' A. L. Kennedy

The Penguin Book of Scottish Verse is the first anthology ever to
offer a view over the entire history of Scottish history,
extending from the 6th century to the end of the 20th, and
representing each of its stylistic currents with clarity and verve.

Acknowledged masters such as Robert Burns and Don Paterson
are well represented, their work augmented by that of neglected
and unknown writers. Throughout the volume, poetry in Gaelic,
Latin and other languages is given in parallel text; poems in Scots
are fully glossed. With its comprehensive, lively Introduction, this
unique anthology – mingling Highland and Lowland, the religious
and the profane, poems by kings and crofters – is the definitive
guide to the whole poetry of Scotland.

Edited with an Introduction by Robert Crawford
and Mick Imlah

ISBN: 978 0 140 424 66 9